MAN OR CITIZEN

KAREN PAGANI

MAN OR CITIZEN

Anger, Forgiveness, and Authenticity in Rousseau

The Pennsylvania State University Press
University Park, Pennsylvania

Library of Congress Cataloging-in-Publication Data

Pagani, Karen, 1980- author.
Man or citizen : anger, forgiveness, and authenticity
in Rousseau / Karen Pagani.
pages   cm
Summary: "Examines the role of anger and forgiveness
in the autobiographical, literary, and philosophical works
of Jean-Jacques Rousseau. Argues that for Rousseau,
anger is an inevitable outcome of social intercourse,
and that forgiveness is central to his understanding of
subjectivity and hence of moral and political action"
—Provided by publisher.
Includes bibliographical references and index.
ISBN 978-0-271-06590-8 (cloth : alk. paper)
ISBN 978-0-271-06591-5 (pbk. : alk. paper)
1. Rousseau, Jean-Jacques, 1712–1778—Criticism
and interpretation.
2. Anger—Philosophy.
3. Forgiveness—Philosophy.
I. Title.

B2137.P34 2015
194—dc23
2014044322

The Pennsylvania State University Press is a member of
the Association of American University Presses.

It is the policy of The Pennsylvania State University Press
to use acid-free paper. Publications on uncoated stock
satisfy the minimum requirements of American National
Standard for Information Sciences—Permanence of Paper
for Printed Library Material, ANSI z39.48–1992.

Frontispiece: detail of Sir Edward Burne-Jones,
The Tree of Forgiveness, c. 1881/82, oil on canvas.
Located at the Lady Lever Art Gallery,
Port Sunlight, United Kingdom.

Contents

Acknowledgments

This work would simply not have been possible without the guidance and critical insights offered along the way by a host of colleagues and friends who continually offered their time and support. I am forever indebted to Patrick Coleman for his assistance in navigating the enormous and often overwhelming amount of critical literature devoted to Rousseau, as well as his explications of the intricacies and contradictions inherent to Rousseau's treatment of anger. Doug Biow and Richard Ratzlaff read numerous incarnations of this work, and their stylistic suggestions, as well as their mentoring, were integral to making this book publishable. Françoise Meltzer, David Wellbery, and Larry Norman were and remain essential to my development as a scholar, and their guidance in this project's earliest stages led me to pose the questions that this book (more or less successfully) attempts to answer. Lisa Moore's support and input at crucial moments along the way was invaluable to bringing this work to fruition. I am grateful for the attention to detail of the anonymous readers who have read this work, as their numerous suggestions—at the level of both style and content—were first rate. Above all, I am thankful for the love, patience, and support of the father of my children, and my best friend, Olivier Boudou.

INTRODUCTION

From Achilles's rage and the banishment of Prometheus, anger has long been more than simply a private emotion. Western philosophy has a far-reaching tradition of considering the social meanings of anger and its various resolutions, be they in the form of forgiveness, punishment, or some sort of retribution. Yet it is only recently that we have begun to see scholarly studies that contrast these sentiments and actions from antiquity and early Christianity with those from more contemporary debates. These studies illustrate just how dramatically the concepts of forgiveness, punishment, and retribution have evolved over time.

The contributions of Donald W. Shriver Jr. and David Konstan are exemplary.[1] Though addressing two very different literary and cultural traditions (Shriver's focus is early Christianity while Konstan's is ancient Greece and Rome), both authors convincingly illuminate the connection that existed between forgiveness, pragmatism, and politics throughout antiquity. They point to the lack of concern for the emotions of the agents involved in these early discussions of conciliatory action. This observation leads both to conclude that the meaning of forgiveness and, we may presume, of anger has undergone drastic revision. Konstan, for example, posits that a more emotive variety of forgiveness probably emerged in the late eighteenth or early nineteenth century, though he makes only the barest of assertions as to how or why this may have been the case.[2] If Konstan is correct, then we are left to ponder, first, when the modern idea of forgiveness appeared and, second, how and why it came into existence.

There is, to be sure, no shortage of theological studies addressing the evolution of the meaning and significance of forgiveness within various religious traditions. Much work has already been done by philosophers and political theorists discussing the question as to what forgiveness can and should mean within secular ethics and what role (if any) it should have in politics. Yet there are still few scholarly studies that focus on how the secular meanings of anger and its various antidotes have evolved throughout modernity.

The following study is intended as a contribution to filling this void. In the philosophy of Jean-Jacques Rousseau we see anger portrayed—for the first time by a major philosophical figure—not only as an inevitable outcome of social intercourse but also as a definitive aspect of his own identity. Moreover, Rousseau situated the problem of anger and its various resolutions at the very heart of modern subjectivity, a characteristic of his approach to ethics that sets it apart from those of his contemporaries. Rousseau is important therefore for anyone who wishes to better understand how modern conceptions of conciliatory action came to be, especially when one considers how central he was to establishing both sincerity and authenticity as moral values.

What follows is a reconstruction and critical analysis of the meaning and significance of anger and its most potent corrective, forgiveness, within Rousseau's philosophical system. My aim is, first, to situate the different types of conciliatory action and sentiment portrayed in Rousseau's corpus within the multifaceted network of sentiments that have, in his view, both moral and political relevance. Second, I elucidate how different varieties of anger (indignation, rage, cool disdain, etc.) and the varied modes according to which they may be resolved figure in his project for social reform and his moral philosophy more generally, particularly where civic virtue is concerned. Finally, I explore the degree to which an individual's encounter with conflict may contribute to, ratify, or complicate an individual's experience of subjective identity. To do so, I examine how the way in which an individual processes, expresses, and, most important, eventually resolves feelings of anger constitutes a decision about the moral categories one invokes when deliberating the way one responds toward the perpetrator of a wrong. Rousseau's ideas about various forms of anger, resentment, indignation, complaint, and cool disdain and their correctives serve to further underscore the distinction between public and private in the figure of the republican subject within his thought. By this I mean that these responses to slight reveal the extent to which an individual chooses either to act (and feel) in accordance with civic virtue or, alternately, to adhere to individualized moral imperatives that are rooted more firmly in sentiment, personal predilections, and the demands of conscience, as Rousseau understood it.

I stress at the outset that it is not my objective to sketch a transhistorical, secular account of forgiveness. Further, I do not mean to suggest that Rousseau's views on the subject could fulfill such a role. However, Rousseau's thoughts can help us to articulate both the problems and potential inherent in defining forgiveness as a modern moral secular ideal, particularly given the centrality of anger to both his person and philosophical system. For this reason Rousseau is an important transitional figure in the ways that forgiveness and anger have come to be understood in the modern period.

Much of the impetus behind this work stems from the observation that Rousseau's thoughts on both anger and forgiveness were deeply influenced by the very important distinction between man and citizen that underpins his political philosophy and the radically different ethical imperatives regarding how one could and should respond to conflict that resulted on account of it. My task here is to outline what precisely these ethical imperatives consisted in for Rousseau and, in turn, to interrogate the philosophical suppositions on which they were based. I hope thereby to shed new light on Rousseau's conceptions of sociability and personal identity.

This particular study challenges the view that anger and misguided amour propre are always inextricably linked within Rousseau's system. Allan Bloom has observed, "Anger is allied with and has its origin in *amour-propre*. Once it is activated, it finds intention and responsibility everywhere. . . . It moralizes the universe in the service of *amour-propre*."[3] Whereas there are numerous examples in Rousseau where this is indeed so, there are just as many instances where anger is portrayed as a self-sacrificial and even quasi-divine quality of which only the most righteous are capable. This becomes clearer when one considers the distinctions that Rousseau makes between emotions and actions, such as anger, rage, indignation, hatred, complaint, and cool disdain, in the stories and scenarios he recounts.

One of the challenges in dealing with Rousseau's treatment of these concepts is that he often ascribes the French word *colère*, as well as *mépris*, *dédain*, or *haine*, to *all* these experiences, even as he goes to great lengths to distinguish among them both conceptually and qualitatively. Part of my task, therefore, must be to distinguish among the various instantiations of anger we find throughout his work and the motivations behind them. In this study, "anger" shall simply denote the feelings of displeasure or pain that one experiences in response to either real or imagined malfeasance.

One of my goals is to use terms that are more precise and readily comprehensible for the emotions that Rousseau describes, such as "indignation," "resentment," "rage," and the like. This will make it possible to analyze more precisely the moral attributes and flaws they designate.

Rousseau's tendency to privilege certain varieties and articulations of anger over others makes his approach to conciliatory action particularly novel compared with the discussions of his contemporaries and immediate intellectual predecessors, particularly Francis Bacon, Thomas Hobbes, Joseph Butler, and Denis Diderot. For Rousseau, anger in response to slight was not necessarily something that always needed to be kept in check out of fear and the desire for peace. Rather, when properly reflected on and calibrated, anger was a potentially enlightening experience that could provoke further reflection as to how one viewed oneself in relation to the moral law and to civic virtue. Accordingly, the experience of anger reveals the extent to which one's allegiance to the law and what passes for civic virtue is revealed to be merely performative or wholly sincere. As my discussion of the Christian in chapter 3 illustrates, those who are incapable—for whatever reason—of experiencing principled anger are not considered moral subjects under the rubric of Rousseau's system and cannot be considered either virtuous citizens or ethical individuals.

The analysis that follows is intended to be a development of two recent investigations of the meaning of both anger and forgiveness within Rousseau's philosophy, those of Jeremiah Alberg and Patrick Coleman.[4] I also consider Rousseau's views on anger and reconciliation in relation to a second line of inquiry that addresses his thoughts on subjectivity and the radically dissimilar psychological experiences of the individual-acting-as-such and that of the citizen qua citizen that underpin his philosophical system. At least since Judith Shklar's seminal work, *Men and Citizens: A Study of Rousseau's Social Theory* (1969), these experiences have been central to analyses of Rousseau's ethical system.

Rousseau is popularly and correctly seen as an avatar of inner authenticity, and this directed his views on how forgiveness could be exchanged within the intimate realm. As I suggest in my conclusion, it is for this reason that he can largely be credited with having established the framework within which many contemporary accounts of private, interpersonal forgiveness operate. Yet we also find within his corpus many discussions of how conciliatory action can and must display itself as a public good. My analysis is therefore complementary to the efforts of scholars such as Konstan and Shriver, who have attempted to chart the origins of the modern ideal of forgiveness within the political and the private, interpersonal realms and, in the case of Shriver, within both religious and secular contexts. Like them, I too believe that the secular ideal of forgiveness is a product of history and that it cannot be interpreted independently of this history. Whereas much scholarly attention has already been devoted to the concept's development within a religious and specifically Christian context, there is still much to be done to uncover the attempts made in the early modern period to construct a wholly secular model of forgiveness. One of my aims in this study is to demonstrate how seminal Rousseau's contributions were to the construction of the secular understandings of forgiveness that dominate today in both political and philosophical discourse. In particular, I want to elucidate the degree to which he paved the way for the now-popular conception that there are indeed two fundamentally distinct varieties of forgiveness: namely, an emotive variety applicable within private, interpersonal relationships and a fundamentally political one that seeks its ratification within the public realm.

Rousseau was, if not the first, certainly the most vocal advocate of the view that those deliberating the appropriateness of anger in the face of conflict and the possibility of forgiveness must in certain contexts take into account their emotional orientation vis-à-vis their malefactor and in other cases must bracket such emotional attachments. He therefore set the stage for what is now a prevailing tendency among those who have attempted to define forgiveness to distinguish between private, interpersonal forgiveness and political reconciliation. On account of his political and moral theory, Rousseau began a new approach to conciliatory action: how individuals experience, process, express, and eventually resolve the pain they suffer in response to malfeasance is regarded as highly dependent on, first, the relationship that individuals have with their malefactor prior to the misdeed and, second, on whether or not they conceive of the misdeed as threatening their identity and, more specifically, their status as an autonomous individual or as a virtuous citizen. I deal with both of these models in their turn, contextualizing them within the historical and philosophical situations from which they emerged.

Forgiveness, Anger, and the Ethic of Authenticity

That Rousseau would be integral to an evolution in modern, secular approaches to forgiveness is not entirely surprising, perhaps particularly to those who have explored private, interpersonal forgiveness and who propound the more emotive variety. A common attribute of many contemporary accounts of forgiveness is that there is typically a large (and, depending on one's theoretical allegiances, inordinate) amount of attention paid to the agent's experience of the action when deciding whether or not a specific instance of forgiveness may be considered genuine, authentic, or, to use Charles L. Griswold's term, "paradigmatic."[5] The consensus has often been that for forgiveness to be considered genuine in the private, interpersonal sphere, it must be produced by the autonomous subject and with consideration for the individuated distinctness of the individual on whom it is bestowed. It must not simply be performed by the agent but must also in some sense be felt. Vladimir Jankélévitch's *Le pardon* is a prime example of this. Derrida's account of forgiveness in "Le siècle et le pardon" is yet another. Griswold's *Forgiveness: A Philosophical Exploration* is a case in point, as is the exchange between Jeffrie G. Murphy and Jean Hampton in *Forgiveness and Mercy*. With certain qualifications, the same could be said of Hannah Arendt's understanding of the concept in *The Human Condition*.

What these otherwise disparate accounts all share is that they cast forgiveness as an "eminently personal experience," to use Arendt's words, and in so doing insist that forgiveness must entail a reorientation of agents vis-à-vis their malefactor at the emotive level.[6] All these accounts are thus deeply concerned with what could arguably be considered the aesthetic attributes of the action (i.e., how it is perceived, narrated, and esteemed by the agent), more so than with the actual effects it may have in the world. These accounts of forgiveness all rely, to a surprising extent, on the ethic of authenticity that pervades our age, one that instructs us that we are not obliged to locate our true self (or, for that matter, our most self-revelatory actions) at the point where action and principles fully coincide. Proof of this is the fact that all the aforementioned thinkers describe forgiveness in terms hostile to impersonality, reason, calculation, and, in many cases, even duty.[7] And although many of these thinkers tend to consciously resist resorting to moral subjectivism in their descriptions of moral impulses more generally, their accounts of forgiveness would nevertheless be incomprehensible without a subject-centered value system that has more or less been generalized within the Western tradition, one that accords a great deal of credence to the predilections and emotional states of the individual. Their great methodological and ideological differences notwithstanding, in constructing their accounts of forgiveness all these thinkers rely heavily on the belief that the wholly psychological I-ness of personality and the emotional state of the agent possess a certain amount of social, cultural, and ethical currency.

But such an ethic of authenticity did not begin to pass into common parlance until the end of the eighteenth century. This was in large part due to Rousseau. He was, if not the first, certainly the most vehement advocate of the view that moral salvation consists in recuperating authentic moral contact with oneself by means of interrogating one's desires, emotions, and moral failings with excruciating candor.[8] Charles Taylor aptly describes Rousseau's contribution to the experience of modern identity as follows: "Rousseau is at the origin point of a great deal of contemporary culture, of the philosophies of self-exploration, as well as of the creeds which make self-determining freedom the key to virtue. He is the starting point of a transformation in modern culture towards a deeper inwardness and a radical autonomy."[9]

Though it has often been overlooked by those who have interrogated the history of forgiveness as a secular ideal, the rigorous assessment of an agent's own feelings—of anger, fear, and rancor and of residual love and affection—toward the perpetrator of a misdeed as a means of determining both if forgiveness should be granted and when bestowals of it are felicitous is inconceivable apart from such a development.[10] Accordingly, if we wish to chart the development of the concept of forgiveness in the history of ideas, Rousseau's contributions cannot be ignored. After all, he was the most notorious early modern intellectual to champion the now widespread belief that, in determining the significance of private, interpersonal relationships, one must adopt a nonrepressive attitude toward one's emotions and inner nature. This obliged Rousseau to espouse the position that the continuation of such relationships in the wake of misdeeds must not be regarded as a duty imposed by exterior demands of authority, tradition, pragmatism, utility, and bienséance if these relationships are to be considered both sincere and authentic. For this reason alone we do well to seek out a precursor to contemporary accounts of forgiveness of the private, interpersonal variety in Rousseau's works.

But Rousseau's significance for more recent discussions concerning the meaning and value of forgiveness does not end there. His social and political theory, as well as his literary and autobiographical works, reveal that he was also deeply concerned with how anger functioned, how it could be resolved, and, when properly calibrated, what its productive capacities could be within political contexts. He lay the groundwork for contemporary studies addressing the limits and possibilities of forgiveness and the effects, both positive and negative, that resentment might have within the political realm.[11] In particular, he recognized the threat to subjective identity that anger and resentment potentially entail. He in turn sketched a model of political forgiveness that, far from being rooted in wholly pragmatic concerns and thus primarily actional, attended to the need for both victims and persecutors to be reintegrated into the community in a manner that acknowledges the suffering of the victim, while simultaneously attending to the alienation that culpability necessarily engenders. He thereby broke rank with many of his contemporaries, the vast majority of whom tended to regard the essential value of and thus the primary motivating force behind forgiveness as its capacity to preserve peace, contribute to self-preservation, and, quite often, construct a moral hierarchy observable to third parties. Rousseau moved beyond such an approach and thus anticipated many contemporary discourses that stress the importance of constructing shared perspectives and historical narratives to the processes of reconciliation.

Rousseau's Anger Versus Rousseauvean Anger

In the history of ideas, Rousseau stands as perhaps *the* philosopher who was the most unabashed about his own anger and indignation—toward society on the one hand but also toward individuals from whom he felt he had not received the consideration and respect that was due to him. Anger and its variants were not just emotions that Rousseau expressed with relative frequency. They were central to his very existence and thus a primary motivating force behind his work. As Shklar rightly puts it, "in his tone of undeviating contempt for all he saw around him, [Rousseau] was singularly consistent."[12] The expressed aim of the *Confessions* (first six books published in 1782) and, for that matter, of the *Reveries of a Solitary Walker* (1782) is to depict the real Jean-Jacques, with all his weaknesses, perversions, failings, sentiments, and regrets. Yet one does not get very far in either text before one realizes that the texts were also composed with a rather ardent and only very thinly veiled desire to settle some scores—against his fellow philosophes, his former friends and confidants, and a world that had always misunderstood him. Rousseau was not ashamed of his anger but rather built a monument to it through the written word.

In his political theory Rousseau was no less indignant, for in his view society was a corrupting force, shot through with amour propre, dissimulation, and false virtue. Society "nourishes itself only with betrayal and hatred" (se nourrit que des trahisons et de haine) and was therefore the enemy of human dignity and of freedom.[13] Society would eventually prove unworthy of the tireless and altruistic efforts that he had taken to reform it, leaving him to wallow alone in his misery and indignation. Society's indifference and, at times, hostility toward his contributions is something that Rousseau would never forgive. Given the prevalence of anger in Rousseau's personal psychology, we do well to examine in detail the significance of anger within his thought; Patrick Coleman has already done so with admirable clarity and detail.[14]

But the decision to focus on the sentiment of the anger is not rooted solely in the citizen from Geneva's seemingly boundless reserves of the sentiment. Rather, what I want to explore here is the degree to which anger functions within Rousseau's corpus as a central component of the construction and affirmation of the subjective identities of both the individual qua individual and the citizen-acting-as-such. Some of the primary questions that we consider are these: In Rousseau's philosophical system, is righteous indignation simply another manifestation of false pride and amour propre, or is it a necessary attribute of all moral beings? Are ideal citizens supposed to be immune to anger and shun its appearance in the world, or are they bound by the social contract to internalize the anger of others in some circumstances, make it their own, and act on it? Under what circumstances (if any) is anger compatible with the general will? And, from a sociological perspective, what role can disdain and indignation toward outsiders play in group formation within the political sphere?

One of Patrick Coleman's key observations is that the inherited standards for acceptable behavior in the wake of both slight and favor became problematic in eighteenth-century France on account of shifting social, political, and intellectual tides. There were major changes in the way anger and gratitude were expressed in literary works of the period. Anger became increasingly democratized, a development that was itself an outgrowth of the increasingly widespread belief that merit was its own legitimization. No longer the exclusive privilege of individuals of high rank, anger was claimed by the philosophes for themselves in the belief that "their intelligence and sensibility entitled them to social recognition above and beyond what was warranted by their birth." Coleman notes that Rousseau was an "outstanding case" of this change; a hallmark of both his life and work was the conviction with which he expressed "his angry response to perceived slight, even on the part of those who offered to be his patrons and friends, and even more, his claim to determine for himself what *counted* as a slight."[15]

Coleman makes clear that, when read in the larger context of the eighteenth century, Rousseau's vehement claims to anger represented less a radical break with his age than an intensification and acceleration of changes that had been under way for quite some time. For Rousseau and so many other Enlightenment writers, expressing one's displeasure at perceived malfeasance had long ceased to be a privilege reserved solely for those of higher social rank. Such a democratization of anger became more pronounced as the eighteenth century progressed, particularly among intellectuals. In Enlightenment writing there was, says Coleman, a "growing tendency to give significant moral weight to the anger expressed by people of inferior status: to commoners, to women, even to children."[16] Rousseau was central to this development, as he seized on anger not only to further his own project of self-justification but also to bolster both his political and moral theory. The *Discourse on Inequality* (1755) is a prime example: Rousseau maintains that one has a moral duty to feel anger and indignation at the suffering and degradation of others. He thus challenges his fellow philosophers for their apathy toward the suffering they witness. Of Rousseau's own experience of anger, Coleman observes, "Rousseau's anger is not a symptom of a disease but a healthy form of protest against complacency. Indignation is a sign of moral vigor, of commitment to truth."[17]

Much of Coleman's focus is on the increasing need in the eighteenth century for anger to be acknowledged and expressed by individuals who had previously been prevented from doing so by social constraints and etiquette. Rousseau was exemplary, as he vehemently rejected the notion that the right to express anger was the domain of a select and meritorious few. Yet, as I argue in part 1, Rousseau went even further in his commendations of anger than many of his contemporaries. In his political theory and in particular his *Social Contract* (1762), he presents the ability to experience anger—when appropriately depersonalized and sufficiently generalized in its object—not only as a right but as a *duty* of the virtuous citizen. What is more, anger is presented as having pedagogical attributes, insofar as the experience of being both its object and its agent is presented as a necessary step to becoming a good citizen. Individuals who are incapable of experiencing and expressing what we describe today as righteous indignation when faced with violations of civic law are essentially relegated to the margins of the ideal state that Rousseau imagines. This is an important component of Rousseau's discussion of the Christian, which I analyze in chapter 3.

But the obligation to experience and express righteous indignation is not necessarily indispensable within the private sphere, in which there are no generalized codes of conduct and where one may therefore follow one's subjective predilections, individualized taste, and the dictates of one's heart when responding to slight. Rousseau suggests that there are at least two different sets of ethical imperatives for the expression, acknowledgment, and resolution of conflict, namely, one for the citizen acting in a public context and one for the individual acting in the more intimate realm. These two different systems entail two very different varieties of forgiveness, which I shall undertake to outline in parts 1 and 2.

Forgiveness is largely beyond the scope of Coleman's study. But his analysis of Rousseau and the latter's commendation of anger does raise a few very important questions. First, did Rousseau believe that there needed to be limits, temporal or otherwise, on indignation and anger, even when these emotions were justified? If so, did he offer any criteria by which one could determine when those limits had been breached and thus guidance as to when and under what conditions a remedy to anger should be applied? Does the kind of forgiveness that he considered paradigmatic—if indeed such a concept can be extracted from his thought—act as a remedy for such anger? Does such forgiveness occur with any degree of frequency? Does it resemble the accounts of forgiveness that were offered by Rousseau's contemporaries? The answers to all these questions are "yes," "no," and "in part," depending on whether Rousseau is speaking of the citizen or the individual. Rousseau presents at least two different models of reconciliation in his corpus: one for individuals relating to one another as citizens and another for individuals relating to one another in private, interpersonal relationships. Rousseau was, according to my reading, the first major thinker to systematically distinguish between private, interpersonal forgiveness and its more public and politicized counterpart.

Men or Citizens

At least since the publication of Judith Shklar's *Men and Citizens: A Study of Rousseau's Social Theory* and Jean Starobinski's seminal work, *Jean-Jacques Rousseau: La transparence et l'obstacle*, Rousseau's philosophical system has been regarded by both political philosophers and literary critics as being primarily concerned with the alienation that results within the social milieu on account of the irreconcilable nature of socially imposed duties and obligations on the one hand and the demands of both emotion and natural freedom on the other.[18] Because of this metaphysical dualism, it is often the case that the whole of Rousseau's thought is viewed (correctly) as containing at its core the doleful observation that one must ultimately choose between self-realization and public acceptance; between self-fulfillment and alienation; between nature and civilization; and between authenticity and a life consumed by very calculated and insincere social intercourse. Ultimately, one must make the choice between being a wholly integrated man or a virtuous citizen. Shklar, who attributes Rousseau's "enduring originality and fascination . . . to the acute psychological insight with which he diagnosed the emotional diseases of modern civilization," describes this either/or decision in the following terms:

> His quiet village, and golden age, also held a message addressed to all men, while his Spartan city was a damning mirror held up to the élite of Paris. What is strikingly novel, moreover, is [Rousseau's] insistence that one must choose between the two models, between man and the citizen. It contains the core of Rousseau's diagnosis of mankind's psychic ills. This necessity for choice is not a call for a decision, but a criticism. All our self-created miseries stem from our mixed condition, our half natural and half social state.[19]

According to Shklar, in such works as the *First Discourse* Rousseau invoked a "deliberately contrived" model of ancient Sparta with its "perfected civic mores" as an "image of the perfectly socialized man, the citizen whose entire life is absorbed by his social role" to provide a contrast to modern corruption, alienation, and unpredictability. Overwhelmingly military in character, Sparta later served as the model for Rousseau's *Considerations on the Government of Poland* (1772) and, to a lesser extent, *The Social Contract*. In both texts Rousseau explicitly addresses the problems of social reform, political education, legislation, and civic virtue. He creates what I refer to throughout this work as the "emphatic citizen," a social being whose *moi humain* has effectively been utterly metabolized by the *moi commun* and what the agent perceives to be the general will. The emphatic citizen's adherence to the *moi commun* is so strong that he cannot even articulate or recognize the sacrifice that he has made, so complete has the sacrifice been, so integral to his own sense of self has the *moi commun* become. Such drastic alienation and the destruction of the individual-as-such are necessary because the soldier-citizen's mentality—as Rousseau understands it—cannot sustain self-expression or inner conflict. When determining one's course of action in any instance that concerns the state, the emphatic citizen cannot lend credence to any other emotion than that of the most devout patriotism and self-sacrificing love of whatever passes for civic virtue in the society in which one happens to reside.[20] The magistrate's primary concern is thus to cultivate a public and political environment that will, through education, imbue its citizens with such an attitude.[21]

The most striking contrast to the model of the emphatic citizen and the only possible alternative within Rousseau's philosophical imagination is found in natural man, as described in the *Discourse on Inequality* and invoked as Rousseau's point of departure in *Émile* (1762). The absolute freedom and goodness of natural man is only slightly diminished and minimally corrupted during the prepolitical golden age, which begins with the advent of the nuclear family. At this point, the social demands on the individual do not exceed or interfere with the pragmatic concerns of maintaining a healthy and happy home. Man at this stage possesses only enough amour propre to seek out and take pleasure in the company of those who are part of his household, without wishing to dominate or subdue them. He is not obsessed with the opinions that outside observers may have of him or of the household that he leads.

Rousseau recognized that a return to this golden age was unrealizable in modern society, though at times one has the impression that the *Reveries of a Solitary Walker* functions as Rousseau's declaration that he had himself succeeded in this endeavor. Nevertheless, his literary works, his educational treatise, *Émile*, and his autobiographical writings struggle—and eventually fail—to resolve the problem as to how the human soul and its emotional cognitions and judgments may, through inner withdrawal and the cultivation of small, intimate societies, flourish in a society that is shot through with amour propre and defined by corrupt normative conceptions of duty and social commerce. The closest Rousseau came to solving this predicament was the creation of Émile, a meticulously educated natural and self-possessed man who lives in civil society, without being a product *of* civil society.[22] In *Émile* the tutor proudly informs the reader that

> it is not the philosophers who know men best. They see them only through the prejudices of philosophy. . . . A savage has a healthier judgment of us than a philosopher does. . . . My pupil is that savage, with the difference that Émile, having reflected more, compared ideas

more, seen our errors from closer up, is more on guard against himself and judges only what he knows.

(Ce ne sont point les philosophes qui connoissent le mieux les hommes; ils ne les voyent qu'à travers les préjugés de la philosophie. . . . Un sauvage nous juge plus sainement que ne fait un philosophe. . . . Mon élève est ce sauvage, avec cette différence qu'Émile ayant plus réfléchi, plus comparé d'idées, vû nos erreurs de plus près, se tient plus en garde contre lui-même et ne juge que de ce qu'il connoit.)[23]

The tragic endings to *Émile* and its sequel *Émile and Sophie, or the Solitaries* (ca. 1768) and *Julie, or the New Heloise* (1761), coupled with the miserable denouement of Rousseau's own life, certainly leave one with the sense that Rousseau did not succeed in coming up with a solution to the problem he had diagnosed. That is, Rousseau does not pronounce definitively whether, from an eudaemonistic perspective, one should cultivate one's inner self at the expense of perfectly fulfilling one's socially recognized role or satisfy one's social and civic duties to the detriment of one's true sentiments and self.

Rousseau thought that a choice must be made regarding whether to prioritize the individual-as-such or the emphatic citizen both in education and in one's own person, but evidence suggests that Rousseau also believed that the choice could be and even needed to be reaffirmed repeatedly throughout an individual's life. My own view is that the experience of conflict constituted a prime occasion for such affirmation. The experience of displeasure or pain as a result of malfeasance and the attendant deliberations regarding how it could be resolved (be it through forgiveness, punishment, vengeance, or some other means) are integral parts of the experience of subjectivity as Rousseau understood it, both for the individual qua individual and for the emphatic citizen. This is because experiencing moral wrongs committed by others, perhaps particularly if we have a personal relationship with them, renders palpable the degree to which our personal and very strong desire to forgive or avenge is often contrary to the expectations society has of us. Conflict highlights the fact that we must constantly decide whether to identify more strongly with either our civic or personal identity. Discord, according to my reading, was thus not simply an unrelenting theme within Rousseau's own life but also an integral formative experience to the characters he invented and analyzed in both his political and literary works. Throughout his corpus it is through the experience of conflict that one's attachment to society as a whole and to the morals, laws, and beliefs that reign there is tested and, in turn, proven to be authentic or, alternately, merely performative. This comes into focus most clearly in my reading of *Rousseau, Judge of Jean-Jacques* in part 1, though my readings of *Émile and Sophie* and *Julie* also illustrate how conflict can either reaffirm or undermine civic identities depending on how it is articulated and metabolized. According to my reading, the means by which one should seek to resolve conflict through conciliatory action was certainly a pressing—if not a primary—concern for Rousseau.

Original Sin, the Natural Goodness of Man, and Rousseau's Quarrel with Forgiveness

Rousseau, it bears emphasizing, was notoriously unforgiving. Moreover, he rejected the idea that he himself needed to be forgiven for anything. Rousseau has been aptly described as "the man who saw himself as the hated and hating enemy of this age."[24] A study of Rousseau's understanding of forgiveness will therefore strike some readers as surprising, if not misguided.

Such skepticism is certainly warranted. First we must contend with the fact that Rousseau rejected original sin and was therefore indifferent to divine forgiveness. Rousseau's mantra was that man is by nature good, and society and the amour propre it is built on are what render man evil.[25] Because evil is the product of social individuals relating to one another in a social context, the individual qua individual never loses his innocence but only becomes incapable of exercising it in the sphere of exteriority. His inner core of goodness remains intact, though it is only rarely recovered and even more rarely able to manifest itself through action. As a result, the significance of the Final Judgment abates, and divine forgiveness loses its force. More important become man's appraisal of his own moral character and the extent to which that appraisal is ratified within his intimate relationships.[26] The result is that forgiveness is emptied of both its content and its motivation and can no longer hold any sway over the minds of men, at least not within a Christian context. Once man becomes capable of forgiving himself, certain long-venerated beliefs simply no longer hold: "For if ye forgive men their trespasses, your heavenly Father will also forgive you: But if ye forgive not men their trespasses, neither will your Father forgive

16

your trespasses" (Matt. 6:13–15).[27] In rejecting original sin, Rousseau could no longer condone forgiveness on the basis of any extramundane principle. Like other philosophes, he too wished to detach moral truths from revealed religion.

Nevertheless, unlike so many of his fellow philosophers, Rousseau was willing to admit that badness permeated the world; for him, however, it could not properly be called sin. Rousseau, the "apostle of primitivism," maintained that man was naturally good and kindhearted on account of his ignorance and lack of civilized refinements.[28] Sin was not the result of God's will but rather the outcome of men confronting a corrupt social order and proving too weak to maintain their natural goodness in the face of it. As Robert Roswell Palmer puts it, "It was the genius of Rousseau to state clearly and eloquently what his contemporaries were waiting to be told. He announced that man in the state of nature was not rational, but that the state of nature was nevertheless a standard by which society might be judged."[29]

But to leap from Rousseau's rejection of original sin to the notion that he must have therefore rejected forgiveness of any variety is unwarranted; this is a widespread assumption about both Rousseau's corpus and person that I am challenging in this study. Likewise, it is also incorrect to assume that all that Rousseau wrote on forgiveness was necessarily composed as a critical response to theological doctrine. Here I challenge Jeremiah Alberg's study, *A Reinterpretation of Rousseau: A Religious System.* Alberg has argued that the ordering of Rousseau's theological argument is, in fact, the reverse of that which I just outlined. Specifically, he challenges the epistemological priority that Rousseau accorded to sin in relation to salvation. In so doing, he suggests that it was Rousseau's "scandal at the forgiveness offered by God in Christ" that led him to the discovery of man's innate goodness—not the other way around.

> Removing the forgiveness of sin entails removing the light by which one sees what sin is. And so one can say that the deepest truth and unity of Rousseau's thought are not the natural goodness of man, nor conversely the rejection of the dogma of original sin. Neither of these cuts deep enough. Rather, Rousseau's scandal at the forgiveness offered by God in Christ grounds the unity of his system. Where there is no forgiveness, there is no sin, and then one is left with the theory of natural goodness, which is taken to imply that there is no need for forgiveness, and so there can be no original sin.[30]

Much of Alberg's reading rests on the supposition that Rousseau rejected any kind of forgiveness on account of his attitude toward the Christian doctrine of absolution. The problem with such a reading is that it does not adequately consider the secular models that were circulating in Rousseau's intellectual milieu and to which he was responding. It overlooks the fact that felicitous bestowals of forgiveness do indeed occur in Rousseau's novels and autobiographical works; Rousseau's hostility toward forgiveness was not absolute.

My own reading follows Palmer's more closely than Alberg's: I read Rousseau's rejection of salvation as derivative of what was, first and foremost, his rejection of original sin. As the numerous examples in what follows demonstrate, Rousseau did *not* for that reason reject forgiveness altogether. Forgiveness—when properly deliberated on and utterly secularized—was for him both a laudable and necessary ideal. Rousseau believed in the natural goodness of man, but he just as readily acknowledged that the evils that society forced men to commit against one another were inevitable. According to him, a remedy for those evils had yet to be sufficiently theorized. A wholly secularized notion of forgiveness was thus indispensable to the feasibility of his philosophical system. Rousseau was not merely—or even primarily—waging a battle against divine forgiveness per se. In his mind, that model had already been sufficiently debunked (and, in his mind, rightfully so on account of the fallacious nature of original sin). Instead, as regards conciliatory action, his project was more firmly directed toward deciding what should replace it. His views on conciliatory action were thus drafted more as a response to his philosophical interlocutors than to his theological nemeses. As I argue in the pages that follow, Rousseau's categorical rejection of the Christian principles of justification and reconciliation and of confession and absolution does not necessarily mean that forgiveness is a logical impossibility within his ethical system. There were numerous secular models that Rousseau would have had at his disposal and with which he could (and did) take issue.

Indirectly, then, I also challenge a fairly widespread belief in certain theological circles, namely, that Enlightenment philosophy was fundamentally incompatible with forgiveness, however one wishes to define it. The work of numerous nineteenth- and twentieth-century theologians, such as Albrecht Ritschl, Karl Barth, Dietrich Bonhoeffer, A. C. McGiffert, and Paul Lehmann, has been central to fostering such a low estimation of the treatment accorded to forgiveness within secular ethics during the early modern period. This is largely because these thinkers all begin with the observation that the popularization of deist thought during the British, French, and, to a lesser extent, German Enlightenments reduced religion's primary function to that of being merely an appendix to morality as dictated by the utilitarian needs of the public sphere. Since at least the publication of Ritschl's mammoth work, *A Critical History of the Christian Doctrine of Justification and Reconciliation* (1872), there has been a tendency to assume that the Enlightenment had no thoroughgoing notion of forgiveness. Enlightenment thinkers are either accused of illegitimately appropriating the Christian notion, voiding it of its contents, repackaging it, and presenting it as something new or described as having little to no interest in the concept.

It is telling that even those who have been quite critical of the more constructive aspects of Ritschl's work on forgiveness and of his positive contributions to Protestant theology more generally have enthusiastically embraced his critiques of rational humanism's treatment of the concept.[31] This is true to such an extent that some have gone so far as to conclude that the period's secular thinkers were minimally concerned with and even hostile to the very existence of forgiveness.[32] Barth, who vehemently critiqued the Enlightenment and described the rational humanism that characterized it as "absolutist" in its desire to rationally systematize the world, invoked forgiveness as that which set his thought apart from such a tradition. He did so explicitly when he claimed that he belonged to the Church "solely on the basis of forgiveness."[33] It is not surprising, then, that in the philosophy of Kant, whom Barth describes as the individual "in whom the century saw itself in its own limitations," Barth sees forgiveness and atonement as "making their appearance . . . like strange visitors from another world, upon the horizon of a philosophy of religion, without there being any attempt to disguise the mystery that is implied in them. They are greeted with a mixture of understanding and surprise, of request and a respectful shaking of heads, and they are acknowledged somehow as conceptions which are at any rate possible, as indicative of open questions."[34] For Barth, even in a system as impressive as Kant's, reason was not sufficient to ground forgiveness without a sleight of hand and a call to that other realm accessible only through Christian faith. In this regard, Kant was little different from his predecessors.[35]

As I show in chapter 1, this is not always, or even most often, the case. Indeed, quite often what we find in the seventeenth and eighteenth centuries are reappropriations and revisions of Aristotelian notions of magnanimity or references to self-preservation and utility when the problem of forgiveness is invoked. Joseph Butler's *Fifteen Sermons Preached at the Rolls Chapel* (the first was delivered in 1726), as well as Hobbes's *Leviathan* (1651) and the *Encyclopédie* article "PARDONNER," are exemplary in this regard.[36] And there are many other examples of this throughout the early modern period.

Does this mean that the Christian notions of forgiveness or of confession and absolution are never invoked in the eighteenth century? Certainly not. In French literature of the eighteenth century, there are many instances of Christian repentance and remorse that are either enacted or directed toward primary characters and that have felicitous consequences. Abbé Prévost's *Mémoires et aventures d'un homme de qualité qui s'est retiré du monde* (1728–30) is a fine example, as references to the model of confession and absolution abound throughout the text. Rousseau was familiar with such depictions and undoubtedly sensitive to them given his background in both Calvinism and Catholicism. What is significant, however, is that he did not feel the need to attack the Christian model of confession and absolution, of justification and reconciliation, in the ways that Voltaire, Holbach, and others had done.[37] Rather, he fixed his sights firmly on the *secular* models that other philosophers had embraced and in particular the magnanimous and utilitarian models that they championed. In his mind, these secular models were shot through with the most unbridled and unprincipled form of amour propre and thus pernicious. In Rousseau's circles Christian models of forgiveness had already been adequately discredited. The problem, as Rousseau understood it, was that a satisfactory replacement had yet to be articulated. Barth has observed of Rousseau that "it was precisely as a child of his century that he fought, passionately and radically, against its most typical tendencies, and consummated a completely different new movement in opposition to them."[38] According to my reading, such an appraisal becomes particularly relevant when we consider Rousseau's views on conciliatory action in relation to those of his contemporaries.

The methodological approach I am adopting with regard to the question of both forgiveness and secularization owes much to Hans Blumenberg's refutation of Karl Löwith's secularization thesis in the former's now classic text, *The Legitimacy of the Modern Age* (1966). Particularly useful is Blumenberg's argument that, in accusing the modern age of illegitimately appropriating Christian concepts, the theories of secularization proposed by Christian apologists most often seek to reduce the threat of secularization to merely a "worldly fearfulness, which is no more suitable to the trustingness implied by faith than is a failure to understand the refusal of dominion that characterizes the biblical figure of the kenosis, of the savior as servant." Blumenberg's point is that, according to such views, the fact of secularization is not refused but rather recast as having provided a service to and a vindication of the meaning and value of Christianity within the world. Blumenberg rejects such views of secularization and thereby challenges the notion that secularization is always bound by a "schema of degeneration, in which full weight and value are present only in the original instant." Instead, he prefers to conceive of what occurred during the Enlightenment and throughout modernity not as a *"transposition* of authentically theological contents" but rather as the *"reoccupation* of answer positions that had become vacant" but had not for that reason become unnecessary to the apparent stability of the world.[39]

Following Blumenberg, I do not read the secular ethicists of the modern age and Rousseau in particular as having appropriated Christian content and simply repackaged it in their treatment of forgiveness. Instead, I read them as having inherited a "mortgage of prescribed questions" and standards regarding the concept of forgiveness, ones that—justifiably or not—they felt obliged to satisfy.[40] Forgiveness thus remained a primary concern of those with whom Rousseau was in dialogue, their collective rejection of the notion of sin notwithstanding.

Blumenberg's thoughts on Rousseau's position in relation to these questions are also instructive. He suggests that Rousseau ascribed to an "eschatology without God" in which "infinity is secularized." Rousseau did so by maintaining that a "return to nature" could be the basis for much of his proposed political reforms, and he utilized this return to nature as a substitute for religious salvation. Blumenberg further observes that Rousseau's autobiographical project was not the "legitimation of autobiographical recklessness" but rather a "rhetorical reinforcement of reckless self-disclosure." This self-disclosure was, according to Blumenberg, a deliberate means of replacing divine judgment with a "final court of appeal," namely, the objectivity of his readers, which would be called forth once Rousseau's heart had been laid bare.[41]

I suggest that the promise of secular objectivity that Blumenberg observes in Rousseau's *Confessions* extends into the domain of civic virtue and, it follows, into conflict resolution in the sociopolitical realm. There is much evidence that Rousseau believed that men had to attempt to measure the failures of others with a similar variety of objectivity and in turn decide whether or not forgiveness was appropriate. In the domain of civic virtue, as Rousseau understood it, racking self-disclosure is thus replaced with thoughtful and disinterested contemplation of the general will. It is such contemplation that, when carried out in good faith, renders an individual or group of individuals both capable of being truly objective in their judgments of others and fully informed as to the consequences that will follow from them. Rousseau thus discovered a replacement for divine omniscience, which colored his ideal of civic virtue (see chapters 3 and 4).

In this sense, I see Rousseau as having done similarly with forgiveness what Jeremy L. Caradonna has argued that he was instrumental in doing with the notion of duty, namely, stripping it of its religious and therefore absolutist connotations. Caradonna convincingly argues that Rousseau, along with so many of his philosophical brothers in arms, succeeded in reconceptualizing duty in such a manner that freed it from its long association with Catholic doctrine and absolutism, thereby appropriating what had historically been a religious term but using it in a fundamentally secular manner. In Rousseau's political philosophy this was achieved by denying that duties or, for that matter, rights existed in the state of nature. The extent to which such a stance—however inadvertently—undermined the legitimacy of the ancien régime and "generally inverted the vertical hierarchies associated with monarchical absolutism, feudal inequality and Christian obedience" cannot be understated. This is because, if duties and rights are not naturally possessed, then they do not emanate from God. From this it necessarily follows that divine patriarchalism, with the rights that it imparts onto the monarch and the duties it subsequently imposes on subjects, is open to debate. As Caradonna observes, "in the same way that men could renegotiate the social contract and even abolish the government, the (generally hierarchical) duties that united the inhabitants of a state could also be abolished."[42]

Similarly, I suggest that by participating in a larger movement to wrest forgiveness from the Christian faith and distance it from monarchical and aristocratic privilege, Rousseau effectively democratized forgiveness, rendering it compatible with republican virtue, as he understood it. Specifically, Rousseau rejected the notion that forgiveness was a sacrosanct duty that individuals were required to perform in the wake of conflict out of allegiance to their Christian faith and thus to their king. He also rejected the notion that it should serve to reaffirm social and political hierarchies. Instead, Rousseau reconceptualized forgiveness in a manner that rendered it compatible with individual freedom, reason, and contemplation of the general will in the social realm and with sentiment and personal predilection in the private realm. Forgiveness was not a nonnegotiable duty for Rousseau. Rather, it was a choice (and at times a collective one) that required prolonged deliberations on the processes of justice and the extent to which those processes could and should apply to a particular situation.

Of course, even if Rousseau's views on original sin, divine omniscience, and salvation do not preclude the possibility of forgiveness, it is hard to deny that most of his interpersonal relationships ended in what one scholar appositely describes as "spectacular disasters."[43] It is often observed that the absence of forgiveness was one of the defining experiences of the life that Rousseau constructs in his autobiographical works, a reading I intend to complicate. As Rousseau recounts in the opening pages of the *Confessions*, his father could not help but mix "bitter regret" (un regret amer) with every caress he ever bestowed on the young Jean-Jacques on account of the fact that his birth had cost his mother her life. Rousseau thus came into the world as an unforgiven and, as he would later discover, essentially unforgivable individual.[44] Revealing as well is the fact that Rousseau began his career with the prophecy that forgiveness would be a rare occurrence in his life: "I foresee that I shall not readily be forgiven for having taken up the position I have adopted" (Je prévois qu'on me pardonnera difficilement le parti que j'ai osé prendre).[45] It has often been observed that Rousseau's autobiographical works and in particular his *Confessions* are profoundly hostile to the idea that he could or should be the object of forgiveness.

But does this mean that Rousseau rejected forgiveness as a real, human possibility and as a laudable moral and civic ideal? There is much evidence within Rousseau's literary, theoretical, and even autobiographical works that suggests that the answer to this question must be no. Rousseau was in fact actively trying to revise and challenge various understandings of forgiveness that were common in his day. This becomes clearer when one considers how Rousseau's idiosyncratic views on human nature, subjectivity, and politics must have influenced both his depictions and discussions of forgiveness and anger.

Methodology of the Current Work

There is a possible objection to my methodology that I must address explicitly. Many of Rousseau's most detailed discussions of forgiveness, guilt, and other rectificatory actions and sentiments are to be found in his autobiographical works. *Rousseau, Judge of Jean-Jacques* (1772), for example, is the only text in which we find a prolonged discussion about what forgiveness is and what it is not. It is, further, the only place where Rousseau explicitly engages his contemporaries in a debate regarding the meaning of forgiveness in a secular sense. We must therefore seriously consider how

Rousseau's autobiographical works relate to both his literary and theoretical contributions.

For some time scholars have grappled with not only how to read Rousseau's autobiographical works in relation to his political philosophy but also whether such analyses can be productive in explicating either. On the one hand, there are those who read the entirety of Rousseau's work as a psychological case study in which Rousseau's political philosophy cannot be understood independently of his personality and the events of his life. The internal divisions, contradictions, and delusions that defined his psychology permeate his philosophy. They may be muted in his theoretical works, but they are nonetheless there.[46]

On the other hand, some have made compelling arguments calling for a strict separation of Rousseau's autobiographical and philosophical works. Ernst Cassirer remains one of the more influential of these. He argues that, whereas Rousseau's project in the *Confessions* was limited to describing only Rousseau's internal "dissensions and divisions, his inner contradiction," this is not the case for his theoretical or literary works. He finds in Rousseau's political thought a level of consistency, cohesiveness, and clarity that his autobiographical works lack. Cassirer admits that the man and the work are so "closely interwoven that every attempt to disentangle them must do violence to both by cutting their common vital nerve." Nevertheless, he maintains that Rousseau's contribution to philosophy risks being either obscured or distorted if it is forced into harmony with the identity that Rousseau constructs in his autobiographical contributions: "Rousseau's fundamental thought, although it had its immediate origin in his nature and individuality, was neither circumscribed by nor bound to that individual personality."[47] If one reads Rousseau's political philosophy through the lens of Rousseau's personal psychology, Cassirer cautions, the "history of ideas threatens here to disappear into biography and this in turn appears as pure case history."[48]

Many of Rousseau's most detailed discussions of forgiveness, guilt, and other rectificatory actions and sentiments are found in his autobiographical works. If we maintain a distinction between Rousseau's political and autobiographical texts, we must ignore the latter when trying to clarify how precisely Rousseau regarded forgiveness as exchanged among men and whether he condoned such behavior in his political theory and literary works. In elucidating Rousseau's views on forgiveness and on other rectificatory sentiments, such as guilt, the literary scholar goes to such texts as *Julie, Émile and Sophie,* and, perhaps, Rousseau's opera, *The Village Soothsayer* (1752), while the political philosophers are left to ponder in their turn *The*

Social Contract, the two discourses, and Rousseau's *Considerations on the Government of Poland*. *Émile* and the *Letter to d'Alembert* are fair game for either camp. *Rousseau, Judge of Jean-Jacques*, on the other hand, can be used only with great caution.

Conversely, if we take a psychological approach to Rousseau's corpus, then the exculpatory nature of Rousseau's autobiographical works, in particular the *Confessions*, must be our point of departure for any interrogations into his thoughts on forgiveness. This hardly gets us very far. In *Rousseau, Judge of Jean-Jacques*, Rousseau claims that to be in need of forgiveness presupposes that one is guilty and therefore merits punishment: "The right of pardon presupposes the right to punish and, consequently, the prior conviction of the guilty party" (Le droit de faire grâce suppose celui de punir, et par consequent la préalable conviction du coupable).[49] If the hallmark of his existence was his unsullied innocence—regardless of any actions that he may have performed in the world—then Rousseau had no need of forgiveness. In this case we must assume that Rousseau's personal difficulties with the idea of his own culpability and thus his need to be forgiven necessarily influenced his discussions of forgiveness in his straightforwardly theoretical and literary works. One cannot avoid concluding that Rousseau rejected forgiveness, not only for himself but also for humanity.[50]

My own solution is to read Rousseau's autobiographical works as constantly renegotiating and problematizing the gap that separates fictions or "moral fables" from both the writing of political philosophy and the construction of a self. Following Christopher Kelly, I interpret the exemplary life that emerges from Rousseau's autobiographies as a case study that is intended to "illuminate general principles of human nature" and to bolster, expound on, and refine Rousseau's own political theory.[51] I too see the subtle political commentaries in Rousseau's autobiographical works as intended to be comprehended by the philosophers, though inspirational to the laypeople. Although Rousseau's discussions of conciliatory action and sentiment at times contradict those we find in his theoretical works and complicate the literary depictions we find in his novels, they also consciously overlap in ways that render the similarities too striking to ignore.

Wilhelm Dilthey observes that

> whatever [Rousseau] had done and suffered and whatever was corrupt in him, he saw himself—and this, after all, was the ideal of his age—as a noble, high-minded soul whose feelings were allied with humanity. . . . A nexus is sought that is not merely one of cause and

effect. To describe it we can only find such words as "value," "purpose," "sense," and "meaning." When we look more closely, we see that the interpretation consists of a distinctive interrelation of these categories reflecting his own concerns. Rousseau wanted, above all, to have the legitimacy of his individual existence recognized.[52]

Whether one accepts Rousseau's claim that his obsessional interest with his own fate stemmed less from amour propre than it did from the degree to which his life story reflected the madness of his times and the cruelty of the system that destroyed him, it is hard to deny that Rousseau took great pains to present his life story as reflective of humanity's predicament and therefore as an additional argument in favor of the political philosophy he championed. For him, to win recognition from the reading public that his personal complaints were legitimate was coextensive with this same public realizing it had fallen prey to false virtues, corrupted ideals, and misguided philosophies.

For this reason, I am especially careful to clarify how it is that Rousseau's recounting of his personal experiences illuminates his understanding(s) of how paradigmatic forgiveness should be exchanged within the social milieu. This clarifies the degree to which the presentation of both anger and forgiveness in Rousseau's autobiographical works approximates, complicates, and further develops his discussions of human moral impulse in his forthrightly theoretical works, such as *The Discourse on the Origins of Inequality* and *The Social Contract*, as well as his literary contributions.

To maintain a clear distinction between how conciliatory action and emotion can function in the political and private realms, respectively, I have divided this book into two parts, both of which are divided into four chapters devoted to specific works and events in Rousseau's life. The four chapters of part 1 deal with Rousseau's autobiographical works, *Rousseau, Judge of Jean-Jacques*, *The Social Contract*, and the *Discourse on Inequality*. Here I elucidate the political significance of anger and the demands that the social contract imposes on citizens qua citizens as to how they may (and must) respond to malfeasance. I provide a brief overview of the semantic tendencies with which Rousseau took issue. In keeping with the most general aims of his project for political reform as sketched in his political theory, Rousseau's political model of forgiveness takes into account utility, the need for peace, respect for property, and cultural norms, as did those offered by many of his contemporaries and intellectual predecessors. But Rousseau, I argue, went one important step further insofar as he also maintained that political forgiveness must be granted in accord with the demands of justice, equality, and the dictates of the general will, which are often obscured but nevertheless always sacred. For this reason he outlined the steps that must be taken to determine whether one should pursue anger in the form of punishment or resolve it through forgiveness in a manner consistent with civic virtue. Basically, for what he considered a fundamentally political problem, Rousseau sketched a wholly political solution. It is for this reason that, in *Rousseau, Judge of Jean-Jacques*, he levels an explicit critique against his contemporaries' understanding of forgiveness. I read this particular autobiographical work as very much aligned (and consciously so) with aspects of Rousseau's political theory and his ideal of civic virtue. Whereas Rousseau casts the variety of forgiveness he propounds in the text as having a palliative effect on the mechanizations of anger, it does not entail a reorientation of the agent or, for that matter, the perpetrator at the emotive level. Rather, it involves a careful consideration of the larger purpose that a particular misdeed threatens and the extent to which forgiveness could further support or damage that purpose. Moreover, and this is the primary point of chapter 3, because he insisted that the citizen's patriotism should be felt rather than merely performed, Rousseau also addressed the importance of justice tribunals, the creation of shared historical narratives, and the public acknowledgment of the legitimacy of a victim's anger to the processes of reconciliation. He thus anticipated many of the primary criteria for felicitous political forgiveness that twentieth- and twenty-first-century thinkers have offered, a point I return to in the conclusion.

Yet this political and, arguably, lower form of forgiveness had no place in love relationships or friendships, as Rousseau understood them. Because Rousseau recognized that the valorization of sentiment in the intimate sphere also called for a revised understanding of conciliatory action, he did indeed outline another form of forgiveness for private, interpersonal relationships, one that could and need be granted independently of all political considerations. For Rousseau, when authentic, this variety of forgiveness was an intimate, private, interpersonal experience that either preserved or reestablished emotional equilibrium among those involved.[53] This particular variety of forgiveness did not entail the dissolution of anger, at least not in the sense that most of his contemporaries understood the term. For Rousseau, expressing anger was a resolutely public (if not political) action that necessitated conceiving of one's relation to the malefactor as existing in a realm wherein the laws of reciprocity and of rights and duties obtain. Inextricably bound up with the competitiveness of a social system based on private property, vanity, and a sense of entitlement, expressing anger (colère) was the prerogative of social animals acting socially. What is more, as Coleman points out, it was often seen as a form of social privilege.[54] It was not the experience of individuals relating to one another as such. As Rousseau saw it, the public expression of anger always commanded recognition by a third party of the sentiment's legitimacy. Because sincere, intimate relationships and friendships consist in adopting and sharing a particular perspective that does not allow for the mediation of either a third party or social norms, anger in these relationships serves as proof that the relationship is itself corrupt and inauthentic. This is not to say that forgiveness does not exist within these relationships. It does. But rather than quelling already publicized manifestations of anger, such forgiveness—both in its request and its bestowal—consists in adopting a particular perspective on misdeeds and their perpetrators that leads spontaneously to reconciliation. I outline this perspective in part 2, first through an analysis of the *Confessions* alongside Rousseau's correspondence and, in subsequent chapters, through a discussion of Rousseau's literary contributions, such as *Julie*, *Émile; or, On Education*, and *Émile and Sophie*.

The conclusion suggests further lines of inquiry that may help in articulating how the modern ideal of forgiveness came to be. It also explores how and why Rousseau's critiques of contemporary secular accounts of forgiveness gained support toward the end of the eighteenth and the beginning of the nineteenth century. Rousseau's notion of the concept appealed to such thinkers and writers as Madame de Staël and Benjamin Constant, both of whom depended on Rousseau's social theory and notion of subjectivity in constructing their own accounts of forgiveness. There are reasons for this: both espoused Rousseau's belief that it was only through hard-won self-knowledge and excruciating candor that one could be purified of social corruption. Rousseau thus obliged his followers to maintain that forgiveness as exchanged among individuals qua individuals must originate within the innermost realms of the human heart to have both validity and force.

Absent from this study is a prolonged discussion of Rousseau's *Reveries*. This text reveals a breakdown and revision of the ethical imperatives regarding rectificatory action and sentiment that Rousseau so laboriously forged over the course of his life. It is essential to understanding Rousseau's own peculiar psychology and the overall trajectory of his views on anger and its antidotes, but I do not believe that the *Reveries* had the same influence that his other earlier works did on subsequent discussions of anger and forgiveness. Given the agonizingly introspective nature of the text, it lacks many of the prescriptive qualities we find in his novels, political treatises, and earlier autobiographical works. I have therefore published my analysis of this work elsewhere.[55]

I do not mean to suggest that the idiom of educated male philosophers represents the only possible articulation of forgiveness at the time. Indeed, it is fairly safe to assume that the underprivileged and uneducated had different views on conciliatory action than the writers discussed here. Yet, to contextualize Rousseau's view on conciliatory action, I have tried to provide a very general overview of the predominant semantic tendencies of the period *with which Rousseau took issue* to highlight just how innovative the latter's approach to rectificatory action and emotion really was. It is my intention in subsequent work to give a more holistic view as to how forgiveness was theorized in the early modern period.

As is often the case with opposing elements within Rousseau's system, the fluctuating judgments about the social, moral, and psychological significance of the manifestations of anger highlight considerable pressures in the broader cultural context of his day. I suggest that Rousseau must be regarded as a very important transitional figure between early modern and modern approaches to the problem of reconciliation.

PART 1

The Political Significance of Forgiveness and Anger in Rousseau's Thought

The Dialogues as a Case Study

A nation forgives if its interests have been damaged, but no nation forgives if its honor has been offended by a bigoted self-righteousness. Every new document that comes to light after decades revives the undignified lamentations, the hatred and scorn, instead of allowing the war at its end to be buried, at least morally.
—MAX WEBER, *Politics as Vocation*

Crois moi, sois bon par sagesse et clément par vengeance.
—ROUSSEAU, *Émile and Sophie*

Soyons justes, même avec les méchans.
—ROUSSEAU, *Rousseau, Judge of Jean-Jacques*

Rousseau, Judge of Jean-Jacques, also known as the *Dialogues*, was completed in 1776. Rousseau had initially intended to deposit a copy of the text on the altar at Notre Dame. When that plan failed, he had printed copies made, which he addressed to "to all Frenchmen who still love justice and truth" (1:251; 1:984; tout français aimant encore la justice et la vérité); he proceeded to distribute these copies in the streets to passersby.[1] As one scholar observed, "It is difficult to read Rousseau's account of the various schemes he devised for transmitting his writings, not just because of the anxiety that transpires through those pages, but also because they seem to show, beyond sensible doubt, that he had gone out of his mind."[2]

Because a large portion of the *First Dialogue* is devoted to outlining what was a meticulously orchestrated plot to silence Rousseau (and render his life miserable), it is difficult to deny that the *Dialogues* was the product of nothing less than a deep-seated psychosis. The character of the Frenchman outlines for his interlocutor (not coincidentally named Rousseau) the treatment that J.-J. receives at the hands of a certain group of Messieurs who, under the guise of friendship and benevolence, have devised an elaborate plan to control him. The Messieurs in question are, of course, the philosophes, in particular d'Alembert, Diderot, Grimm, and, to a lesser extent, Voltaire. Their elaborate plan includes dispatching spies, bribing J.-J.'s friends and acquaintances to betray him, paying the ticket takers in public gardens to refuse J.-J. entry, and providing J.-J. with disappearing ink—the only ink to which he could gain access while under the "protection" of his "friends."

Rousseau's fragile psychological state at the time he composed the text and such outlandish accusations notwithstanding, the *Dialogues* cannot simply be dismissed as the rantings of a madman that constitute a dreadful reversal and negation of his philosophical system. My own reading thus refutes those, most notably among them Jean Starobinski, who have claimed that the text is fundamentally pathological, to the extent that it constitutes a defense of his person to the detriment of his philosophical system.[3] Instead, and following Marco Di Palma, I reject the notion that the text can be imputed "solely to Rousseau's unbalanced mind" and instead view the characters of Jean-Jacques and Rousseau as genuinely "moved by a vision of the good consonant with the Rousseauian synthesis." As Di Palma, in my view correctly, observes, the text is not simply a "phenomenological document" limited to contemplating Rousseau's place in the world. Instead, it is a rather impressive feat of "self-objectification," mediated by its heuristic value and therefore "pointing beyond itself to a more fundamental source of truth on which it is necessarily reliant" with "lucid consistency."[4] Whereas Di Palma's focus is primarily on the character of Jean-Jacques and the rhetorical strategies employed to address and involve readers on their own terms in the judgment of Rousseau, my own reading is more squarely focused on how, under the character of Rousseau's guidance, the voice of Jean-Jacques causes an evolution in the character of the Frenchman and thus illustrates the trials and tribulations, the self-doubt and the sheer terror, that the path toward enlightenment presents. As is argued later, the text contains at its core a sustained and elegant defense of due process and a stinging critique of the faults in the French justice system, one that is in many ways complimentary to Rousseau's straightforwardly political writings. Moreover, in the *Dialogues* Rousseau once again challenges the philosophes for what he perceived to be their veiled attempts to replace the notoriously intolerant Jesuit clerics as the irrefutable judges of humankind.[5] It is arguably in the *Dialogues* where these critiques are most explicit. As Judith Shklar, Reinhart Koselleck, and Arthur Melzer, among others, have noted, Rousseau was not entirely off the mark in making such accusations. "The philosophers," Melzer observers, "transformed by the exigencies of their battle with the Church, had themselves become a dogmatic sect for the honoring of a universal being—the rational Truth. They, too, enforced unity in their ranks by persecuting 'heretics' (as Rousseau would experience personally)."[6] As Rousseau imagines the means employed to condemn him, he pulls no punches in highlighting the philosophes' opportunistic approach to philosophy and their incapacity to tolerate dissent. Of particular interest to me are the effects that the character of Rousseau's argumentation has on the Frenchman. I suggest that the character of Rousseau's defense of Jean-Jacques brings about a dramatic change in the character of the Frenchman, one that complicates his identity as an emphatic citizen and forces him to confront the alienation that inevitably arises when connection to what passes for civic virtue begins to be seen as merely instrumental. According to my reading, self-objectification through scientific rationality is not limited solely to Rousseau or to the character of Jean-Jacques, but also extends to and is exemplified by the character of the Frenchman, thereby raising interesting questions about the anticipated affective response on the part of the reader.[7] If, as Roger D. Masters and Christopher Kelly have observed, the *Dialogues* were written in response to what Rousseau conceived of as a failure of the *Confessions*, and therefore constitutes "a training manual for readers of the *Confessions* or indeed for any of Rousseau's other works," then it is reasonable to expect that the Frenchman's transformation is one that Rousseau had hoped his readership would (eventually) undergo.[8] The text thus complicates—and in my view consciously so—the ideal of civic virtue presented in *The Social Contract*.[9]

There is yet another, related aspect of the *Dialogues* by which Rousseau engages directly with his contemporaries that is relevant for our purposes, one we risk overlooking if we limit our analysis to the psychological state Rousseau was in when he composed them. Rousseau sketches a new model of forgiveness, one that he presents as antithetical to the hierarchical and magnanimous model that his persecutors had embraced. The *Dialogues*, in fact, contains the only prolonged discussion within Rousseau's corpus of what forgiveness should mean and how it should (and, more important, should not) be practiced. Whereas Rousseau's primary aim was to highlight the means by which forgiveness was employed by the philosophes to discredit him further not only in his own eyes but in the eyes of the public, the *Dialogues* also sketch what Rousseau considered to be paradigmatic forgiveness as exchanged among citizens. My claim is that the text marks a major

and very conscious deviation from how conciliatory action was being portrayed among his contemporaries insofar as Rousseau explores the productive capacities of righteous indignation, as well as the detrimental effects of
false and corrupted forgiveness in the sociopolitical realm. To understand
the novelty of Rousseau's views on forgiveness and, for that matter, anger,
it is necessary, first, to discuss the model he inherited and which he wished
to revise in some detail. I will then resume my analysis of the *Dialogues*.

THE MAGNANIMOUS PARDON

In the eighteenth century, there was a robust tendency among the philosophes and, in particular, within the *Encyclopédie* to describe forgiveness as a
hierarchical or top-down notion. By this I mean that there was widespread
belief that—when felicitous—forgiveness resulted in the subjugation of
the forgiven individual and in the *public* affirmation of superiority of the
one who forgave. The recognition and legitimization by third-party observers were therefore central to its bestowal, as was the ability to manipulate
public opinion. It is this model—the origins, pervasiveness, and function
of which I shall attempt to outline here—with which Rousseau took issue.

Understanding forgiveness as a mode of subjugation did not emerge in
the eighteenth century, as we find similar portrayals in the seventeenth century as well and even earlier. This is not entirely surprising given that in
seventeenth-century France the key occasion for political forgiveness (or its
refusal) was the offense of rebellion, particularly in the Fronde. Because, in
a monarchy, rebellion had both personal and political implications, so did
the response it elicited. Pierre Corneille's tragedies—in particular, his *Cinna*
(first performed in 1639)—are fine examples, as they demonstrate the degree
to which forgiveness could be employed not only to reconcile opposing parties but, further, to reaffirm the power of the monarch or ruling party. It
is only after Auguste is freed from the bounds of necessity and recognizes
himself victorious that he becomes capable of clemency.

I am master of myself, as I am of the universe;
I am and I want to be. Oh posterity, oh memory
Conserve forever my last victory!
Let us be friends, Cinna, it is I who invites you:
As to my enemy, I have given you life,
And despite the furor of your cowardly destiny,
As my assassin, you shall receive it again.
Let us begin a combat that shall prove at the end
Which one of us better gives and receives.
You have betrayed my goodwill, but I shall redouble it
I had bestowed great gifts upon you, and I want you to feel guilty
   for them.

(Je suis maître de moi comme de l'univers;
Je le suis, je veux l'être. O siècles, ô mémoire,
Conservez à jamais ma dernière victoire!
Soyons amis, Cinna, c'est moi qui t'en convie:
Comme à mon ennemi je t'ai donné la vie,
Et malgré la fureur de ton lâche destin,
Je te la donne encore comme à mon assassin.
Commençons un combat qui montre par l'issue
Qui l'aura mieux de nous ou donnée ou reçue.
Tu trahis mes bienfaits, je les veux redoubler;
Je t'en avais comblé, je t'en veux accabler).[1]

Once Auguste recognizes himself to be above all others and impervious to their attacks, he undergoes a conversion that enables him to pardon his adversaries. Auguste's ability both to rule and to pardon is correlative to his ability to subjugate and convert those who have offended him.

Larry F. Norman has analyzed the extent to which the desire for self-affirmation drives the depictions of reconciliation throughout Corneille's oeuvre. He shows that Corneille consistently depicts forgiveness as inspired by a desire to demonstrate the superiority of the hero, who is always of noble birth.[2] This is true not only of *Cinna* but also of *Polyeucte* (1643), *Nicomède* (1651), and *Surena* (1674). What all these plays share is the belief that the act of pardoning is, ultimately, a means of self-affirmation and, in turn, the subjugation of the offending party. It is a decidedly aristocratic virtue. As Norman points out, "To say, 'I am my own master,' is to say, 'I am your master.' This ironic magnanimity has the dramatic value of sweet revenge" (183–84; Dire 'je suis maître de moi,' c'est dire 'je suis maître de vous.' La magnanimité ironique prend la valeur dramatique d'une douce vengeance).

René Descartes's notion of generosity in *Passions de l'âme* (1649) entails a similar approach to conciliatory action, although he placed more emphasis on its pedagogical potential than did Corneille. The possibility of subjugating the forgiven individual is downplayed, but it is nevertheless present. Like Corneille, Descartes posited that the pardoning of wrongs could serve as proof that one possessed great virtue and thus that one was superior to one's malefactor. One of the primary markers of the generous individual, the absence of contempt is founded not only on the generous individual's imperviousness to external attacks on his sense of self but is also grounded in his faith that generous actions can inspire the generous individuals to moral rehabilitation.[3] Contempt is forestalled because the generous individual believes that anyone—if properly guided—can achieve a comparable level of moral refinement to that of the generous individual (art. 154). Those of noble birth are admittedly more predisposed to the sentiment (art. 161).

In Descartes's system, compassion, pity, and mercy are all the products of generosity, and the function and nature of these sentiments share numerous similarities. In article 187, for example, Descartes collapses the boundary between compassion and pity, as both are directed toward correcting the weakness of an individual who suffers. In *Passions de l'âme*, Descartes devotes more time and space to pity than to any other conciliatory action (such as mercy or forgiveness), and it is only to pity that he devotes entire articles. Other conciliatory actions and emotions are mentioned only in passing and are subsumed under discussions of other passions, most often pity. To elucidate the significance of forgiveness within his thought, we must therefore turn to his discussions of pity, particularly in articles 152, 153, and 154, in which he describes pity as a compliment of generosity. He affirms the educative and restorative powers of pity and shifts his focus away from the innocence (or guilt) of the person, thus trumping the assertion he makes in article 185 that it is bestowed on someone who is suffering undeservedly. After all, how could pity possibly function as a means of correcting moral faults and, at the same time, be bestowed on someone innocent? Descartes's discussions of repentance (article 191) and of remorse (article 177) also reaffirm the overall pedagogical thrust underlying conciliatory actions when performed by the generous individual. This is because both recommend capitalizing on the pain that an individual is experiencing to convince him to reform his ways (or, alternately, in the case of nonjustified remorse, to remove any doubts as to the moral value of a past action that said individual may be experiencing). Ultimately, the Cartesian view emphasizes the dialectical relationship with the other as being one in which the generous individual takes on a role analogous to that of a mentor or teacher.[4] Forgiveness in this context is thus shot through with knowledge of one's superior strength and wisdom.

François de La Rochefoucauld, with his Jansenist sympathies and his disdain for the court, also highlighted the power of the pardon to subjugate its object. In maxim 311 he snidely comments, "We often forgive those who bore us, but we cannot forgive those whom we bore" (Nous pardonnons souvent à ceux qui nous ennuient, mais nous ne pouvons pardonner à ceux que nous ennuyons).[5] We see that, according to La Rochefoucauld, in polite society we typically cannot forgive those who fail to recognize the worth we attribute to ourselves. The boring individual, however, can be forgiven, precisely because he lacks the social graces that might otherwise put us to shame. We thus pardon on account of pride in our own superiority—of wit, beauty, intelligence, wealth—over those who offend us.[6] Of course, being selfish and deluded creatures, our pretensions to superiority are, more often than not, fundamentally misguided: "That which makes us so easily believe that others have flaws is the facility with which one believes what one wishes" (posthumous maxim 513; Ce qui nous fait croire si facilement que les autres ont des défauts, c'est la facilité que l'on a de croire ce qu'on souhaite). Yet, for La Rochefoucauld, these pretensions—the result of amour propre—are precisely what enable us to forgive our trespassers when confronted with personal slight.

Many of the articles in the *Encyclopédie* addressing forgiveness represent less of a break with this particular tradition than a desire to compose variations on the criteria by which the old theme of the hierarchical model of forgiveness could be employed and subsequently validated by a spectatorial third party. Although these articles had yet to be published when Rousseau composed the *Dialogues*, I suggest that his goal is to forestall the philosophes' plans to abase him through the mechanizations of forgiveness, largely by refuting a semantic tradition that they would themselves publicly espouse soon after. It is therefore necessary to examine their treatment of the concept in some detail if we wish to understand Rousseau's complaints against prevailing notions of forgiveness in his day.

There are numerous entries dealing with forgiveness, its derivatives, and related concepts within the *Encyclopédie*, and not all of them are consistent with one another. Part of this has to do with the fact that they were written by different authors. Further, many of the entries that address conciliatory action address the meaning of forgiveness within the history of Christian theology, Judaism, law, and politics. As a result, these particular articles do not pretend to provide a definition that could or should have transhistorical relevance. The actual definition as to what forgiveness should mean within the secular realm and thus that which the *Encyclopédie* as a whole appears to have endorsed is expressed in only a handful of these articles: "PARDON, EXCUSE {synonyme} {grammaire}," "PARDONNER {morale}," "EXCUSE {grammaire}," and "PARDONNABLE {grammaire}." When taken together, these entries reveal that—for whatever reason—a fair amount of confusion existed among the Encyclopedists as to the respective roles of reason and sentiment in the act of forgiveness. What is more, some of the entries betray that—even if forgiveness can and must exist outside of a religious context—something akin to religious sentiment oftentimes (though, not always) remains at its core.

For example, one entry for forgiveness reads as follows:

> FORGIVENESS, EXCUSE (*Synon.*) One excuses an apparent misdeed; one asks for forgiveness for a real misdeed; one is intended to justify and is based on politeness; the other aims at stopping vengeance or forestalling punishment and designates a movement of repentance; a strong mind easily finds excuses; a good heart promptly forgives.

> (PARDON, EXCUSE, *Synon.*) on fait *excuse* d'une faute apparente; on demande *pardon* d'une faute réelle; l'un est pour se justifier & part d'un fond de politesse; l'autre est pour arrêter la vengeance, ou pour empêcher la punition, & désigne un mouvement de repentir; le bon esprit fait *excuse* facilement; le bon coeur fait *pardonner* promptement.[7]

A strict distinction is drawn here between the excuse and forgiveness. The former is presented as arising on account of a desire to explain away a misdeed, presumably on account of a rational weighing of extenuating circumstances. It is an act of justification described as having been codified within politesse. Forgiveness, however, is presented as being something decidedly other, as it is firmly rooted in sentiment. Its locus is in the heart. Forgiveness and the excuse are thus presented as being two fundamentally different concepts, at least within this article. God is nowhere invoked but, again, what inspires the heart to so promptly forgive remains unstated. It is likely that the (anonymous) author is relying on the secularization of certain aspects of Christian doctrine, though we could also attribute this to the period's more positive appraisal of the role that emotion can play in the practice of virtue. Although throughout much of the seventeenth century it was seen as bad taste to cast aside social or legal norms and due process in the name of love, by the dawn of the eighteenth century the condemnation of such behavior was much less categorical.[8] Whatever the case, the reader is left to ponder whether this sudden "movement of the heart" involves amour propre or not, since there is no clarification provided in the entry.

This careful distinction between forgiveness and the excuse remained intact within the *Encyclopédie*'s nonattributed article titled "EXCUSE," as did the resultant emotive overtones with regard to forgiveness. In this article the excuse is defined as a reason or a pretext that one gives to he who has been offended to weaken in the latter's eyes the gravity of the fault that has been committed, thereby reaffirming the idea that the excuse references reason and that forgiveness always refers to sentiment.[9] As such, the excuse can result only from protracted deliberation on a particular chain of events that has led up to a misdeed. Within the article, the excuse is thus presented as being fundamentally distinct from forgiveness.

Even so, it appears as though the question as to whether forgiveness was an emotive or rational process was far from settled during this period, and this is true even within the *Encyclopédie*. In fact, the instability of the concept among the Encyclopedists comes to the fore when we consider the entry for the adjectival form of "pardon," "PARDONNABLE" (forgivable). The unattributed article reads, "FORGIVABLE, adj. (Gramm.) able to be forgiven; it is said of an action for which one finds the excuse in the circumstances that either preceded, or accompanied, or followed it" (PARDONNABLE, adj. [*Gramm.*] qu'on peut pardonner; il se dit d'une action dont on trouve *l'éxcuse* dans les circonstances qui l'ont, ou précédées ou accompagnées, ou suivies).[10] Here, we see that the careful distinction between the excuse and forgiveness and between reason and sentiment that had been drawn in the previously cited entries is effaced, as the excuse is now presented as being *constitutive* of forgiveness. The reason: according to the definition the decision as to whether or not a particular deed is forgivable rests more firmly on extenuating circumstances (those that preceded, accompanied, or followed a misdeed) than on any sentiment originating in the heart. Rather tellingly, the article even employs the word "excuse" in clarifying the meaning of "forgivable." Accordingly, a highly rational weighing of circumstances must be carried out if a deed is to be considered within the bounds of forgiveness, at least according to this entry.

Here the influence of the Christian doctrine of forgiveness appears to be entirely absent, or, more correctly, it is limited only to the *function* that forgiveness serves. That is, the definition does not rely to any degree on the actual *content* of Christian doctrine. In fact, the only elements that resemble the Catholic model are those regarding the purification of the "sinner" and his reinsertion into a community, but even these similarities are limited. This is because, under the auspices of both the Catholic and Protestant models, such purification and reinsertion would necessarily be analogous to the negation of culpability and the reestablishment of fellowship with God (and, it follows, with those who believe in him). However, and this point is key, within the *Encyclopédie* article this purification is completely revised as to both its significance and origin, as it occurs thanks to a purely rational process that points only to extenuating circumstances. As a result, it is not the sinner's moral fabric that is purified—it can't be, as it is not even called into question. What is purified is the offense itself. This is done through a diminution of the significance of the crime and thus the degree to which the sinner's character is revealed therein. Accordingly, the act of forgiveness brings about a change only in the *victim's* perception of the misdeed, without actually affecting the wrongdoers themselves. Appropriately, such forgiveness is bestowed with ambivalence toward the emotional state of the perpetrator. Such a rationalization of the misdeed is entirely absent from the Christian understandings of forgiveness.[11] What we have, then, is a purely secular presentation of forgiveness (or, perhaps more correctly, of "forgivable" actions).

When understood in these terms, this particular definition grossly contradicts the distinction between forgiveness and the excuse that was so cautiously forged within the definition for "pardon" I described earlier. The heart and sentiment are no longer invoked, as forgiveness is here wholly circumscribed within the domain of reason. Thus, whereas these entries do highlight how unstable and confused the concept was within the circles in which Voltaire, Diderot, and Holbach were circulating, many of these same articles also testify to the fact that the Enlightenment's treatment of forgiveness was not merely limited to illegitimately appropriating Christian content, as has often been assumed.[12] There were sincere efforts—however flawed—to create an entirely new definition.

The longest and most detailed entry for forgiveness is "PARDONNER," which *is* attributed to Denis Diderot. And it is Diderot's approach to forgiveness that Rousseau will contest. The article begins innocently enough: "It is to renounce punishment, sacrifice one's resentment, and promise to forget a misdeed" (C'est remettre le châtiment, sacrifier son ressentiment &

promettre l'oubli d'une faute). As was customary at the time, Diderot admits the necessity of forgiveness to the existence of flawed, terrestrial creatures. He does so in a moralizing tone: "One forgives oneself so often, that one would to do well at times to forgive others" (On se pardonne si souvent à soi-même, qu'on devroit bien *pardonner* quelquefois aux autres).[13] That forgiveness is vital to a well-functioning society and that it is owed to all (or to most) men is taken as a foregone conclusion. This is not surprising given how active and thus antithetical to peace the emotion of anger was perceived to be at the time. Indeed, many of the most important early modern thinkers (Bacon, Hobbes, Descartes, Locke, Montesquieu, Butler, Holbach, Helvétius, Morelly, and Voltaire) were concerned with how exterior manifestations of anger (colère) could effectively be quelled to the extent necessary to maintain peace within civil society.[14] They were not concerned with the havoc that dissatisfied anger could wreak on the inner realms of the human heart.

Yet it is what follows that Rousseau would have found objectionable. It is worth quoting Diderot at length:

> There are qualities that one forgives less easily than offenses.
>
> One must have much modesty, meticulousness, and art in order to wrest forgiveness from those to whom one is superior.
>
> . . . Some men created a foolish work, that some imbecilic editors managed to spoil, and they never could forgive us for having suggested a better one. There is no variety of persecution that these enemies of all that is good spared us. We saw our honor, our fortune, our liberty, and our lives compromised in the span of a few months. We would have obtained from them a pardon for a crime; we could not obtain it for a good action. They discovered that the majority of those whom we did not judge worthy to contribute to our enterprise were all too disposed to espouse their hatred and jealousy. We could not imagine a crueler revenge for all of the evil they have caused us than to bring to fruition the good that we had started.
>
> That is the sole species of resentment that was worthy of us. Every day they sink lower and lower on account of their crimes; I see the opprobrium that advances over them. Time does not forgive evil; sooner or later it imposes justice.

> (Il y a des qualités qu'on *pardonne* plus difficilement que des offenses.
>
> Il faut bien de la modestie, bien de l'attention, bien de l'art pour arracher aux autres le pardon de la supériorité qu'on a sur eux.

THE MAGNANIMOUS PARDON   41

. . . Des hommes qui ont fait un sot ouvrage, que des imbéciles éditeurs ont achevé de gâter, n'ont jamais pû nous *pardonner* d'en avoir projetté un meilleur. Il n'y a sorte de persécutions que ces ennemis de tout bien ne nous ait suscitées. Nous avons vû notre honneur, notre fortune, notre liberté, notre vie compromises dans l'espace de quelques mois. Nous aurions obtenu d'eux le *pardon* d'un crime, nous n'en avons pû obtenir celui d'une bonne action. Ils ont trouvé la plûpart de ceux que nous n'avons pas jugés dignes de coopérer à notre entreprise, tout disposés à épouser leur haine & leur jalousie. Nous n'avons point imaginé de vengeance plus cruelle de tout le mal qu'ils nous ont fait, que d'achever le bien que nous avions commencé.

Voilà l'unique espèce de ressentiment qui fût digne de nous. Tous les jours ils s'avilissent par quelques nouveaux forfaits; je vois l'opprobre s'avancer sur eux. Le tems ne pardonne point à la méchanceté. Tôt ou tard, il en fait justice.)[15]

Notice here how the very definition of *pardonner* invokes a power dynamic and thus the degree to which amour propre is operative within the definition. The authors and defenders of the rival work to which Diderot refers (presumably the Académie Française's *Great Dictionary of the Arts and Sciences*) could not forgive the Encyclopedists because, by virtue of the superior quality of the *Encyclopédie*, their role as critics and scholars had been called into question. Instead, they were riddled with feelings of shame or "opprobre" (opprobrium). By claiming that it takes a lot of art and feigned modesty to wrest forgiveness from those to whom one is superior, Diderot reveals that forgiveness is something that must be granted from a (perceived or actual) position of superiority. Having created an inferior work, the *Encyclopédie*'s persecutors found themselves humiliated and thus unable to pursue anything other than vengeance. Diderot does not present this as a choice on his detractors' part but rather as part and parcel of the meaning of forgiveness (one to which he assumes the *Encyclopédie*'s persecutors also subscribe). Fortunately, Diderot is able to find solace in the superiority of his own work. This, he knows, bothers his persecutors immensely. For this reason, he maintains that bringing his project to fruition is the only worthy revenge. We can assume that if Diderot's persecutors were to admit the superiority of the *Encyclopédie* and therefore the illegitimacy of their accusations, Diderot would happily forgive them. Failing that, he claims, posterity will punish them, for as long as his persecutors refuse to admit their inferiority they remain, by definition, incapable of receiving any forgiveness that Diderot could grant.[16] In the meantime, readers who have opted to consult the *Encyclopédie* as opposed to one of those lesser dictionaries are both the witness and source of the work's (and its authors') superiority. They are an instrument with which Diderot further subjugates those who cannot forgive him (though who, in reality, should be groveling at his feet, as, again, forgiveness is in actuality Diderot's to bestow or withhold). To read the *Encyclopédie* is to affirm the success of the mammoth undertaking from which it was born and thus the right of the project's collaborators to eventually pardon those who—out of lack of confidence in their own work and therefore out of jealousy—had found themselves disposed to attack it. The resolutely polemical tone of "Pardonner" is indeed no accident; it is Diderot's means of putting a fine point on his critiques of the *Encyclopédie*'s detractors by affirming the supremacy of the project to which he had dedicated so much of his life.

It is worth noting that Montesquieu makes a similar point regarding the need for forgiveness to be bestowed in a top-down manner through the character of Usbek in the *Lettres persanes*. Usbek observes, "Universal approbation is more often bestowed upon the mediocre man. One is charmed to give to him, one is enchanted to take away from the [extraordinary man]. Just as envy is lavished on one and he is forgiven nothing, one speaks in favor of the other: vanity declares itself in favor of the mediocre man" (L'approbation universelle est plus ordinairement pour l'homme médiocre. On est charmé de donner à celui ci, on est enchanté d'ôter à [l'homme extraordinaire]. Pendant que l'envie fond sur l'un, et qu'on ne lui pardonne rien, on supplée tout en faveur de l'autre: la vanité se déclare pour lui).[17] Those who are of superior standing are, by such logic, seldom forgiven. As was the case for La Rochefoucauld and the character of Usbek, our amour propre prevents us from forgiving those who are above us. Mediocrity, on the other hand, finds favor everywhere, and its errors are easily overlooked.

Finally, the widespread approval of the hierarchical model of forgiveness among both Rousseau and the Encyclopedists' most immediate and influential intellectual precursors is also affirmed in Francis Bacon's essay, "On Revenge." Bacon provides numerous justifications for renouncing revenge and forgiving instead. One of his primary arguments is that it proves the superiority and wisdom of the forgiving individual: "Certainly, in taking revenge a man is but even with his enemy; but in passing it over, he is superior; for it is a prince's part to pardon. . . . That which is past is gone, and irrevocable; and wise men have enough to do, with things present and to come; therefore they do but trifle with themselves, that labor in past matters."[18] To pursue revenge is to dwell too long on one's own vulnerability and thereby to indulge weakness rather than strength. To forgive, however, is to imitate the patriarchs and prove the superiority of one's character over that of the offending party.[19] By appealing to the amour propre of his reader, Bacon makes forswearing vengeance an attractive and potentially self-enhancing action.

This brief overview of what forgiveness meant and the purposes it served during the period in which Rousseau composed his *Dialogues* hardly does justice to the concept's very rich history within the French or, for that matter, British traditions. There were other models available, and we certainly find other understandings of "pardon" and "pardonner" that either ignore or play down the action's possible connections to grandeur and are even outwardly hostile toward them. In this respect we may consider the entries for these terms in the 1762 edition of *Le dictionnaire de l'Académie Française*, in which we find no overt reference to magnanimity, generosity, or anything of the kind—and this even in those articles that seek to outline the concept's secular value.[20] As we have already seen, this was also the case with some of the entries in the *Encyclopédie*. Whether the hierarchical model was in fact the dominant tendency in secular ethics in the early modern period is impossible to prove with just this small handful of examples. However, it was the case that thinkers with whom Rousseau considered himself in dialogue often invoked it—and this approvingly. It is precisely the more magnanimous variety of forgiveness that Rousseau wished to challenge and that he was not only deliberately trying to refute but, furthermore, consciously trying to revise in *Rousseau, Judge of Jean-Jacques*, to which we will now turn.

2

THE PHILOSOPHES' PLOT AND
THE FRENCHMAN'S ANGER

Rousseau's treatment of forgiveness serves as a fascinating contrast to the models we have just discussed. When read in the context of his political philosophy, his comments on forgiveness in the *Dialogues* constitute an extension of his views on justice, the general will, and the good citizen. One of the central aims of the *Dialogues* is to distinguish between true and false forgiveness in a matter consistent with the ideal of civic virtue Rousseau championed. Rousseau thus presented a model of forgiveness whereby its arbiter forgives not with the aim of subjugating the perpetrator of a misdeed but rather with the intention of upholding the processes of justice and the principle of equality. In so doing, an individual does not forgive out of a desire for self-aggrandizement in the eyes of spectators but instead as a means of reaffirming one's respect for the law, one's allegiance to the dictates of justice, and, as a result, one's solidarity with compatriots. Although Rousseau did leave a space for third parties in conciliatory action, these third parties were neither called on to witness nor to ratify the superiority of the one who forgave. Rather, they were called on to actively participate in the dialectic themselves as the guarantors of justice. Placing the corrupt model of forgiveness they practiced at the heart of his objections, Rousseau casts the Messieurs not only as his own enemies but also as enemies of justice, of the general will, and of the state for having manipulated the public. I shall therefore contextualize the discussions of forgiveness in the *Dialogues* within the larger framework of Rousseau's political philosophy as presented in the *Second Discourse* and *The Social Contract*. It is this that will enable me to explore the productive capacities of anger and, in particular, the sentiment's capacity to intensify the citizen's bond to the state, while simultaneously exemplifying said citizen's commitment to justice and devotion to the state. In ideal circumstances, the citizen's anger is piqued only in response to legitimate violations of the social contract that are perceived as such by both the purveyors of justice and, in turn, by the general populace. But in instances of false accusations, infringements on due process, and corruption by particular interests, it is possible for the mechanizations of justice and, it follows, for public opinion to become debased, something that is very often revealed through conflict. According to my reading, the *Dialogues* explore the way that conflict can bring to light the discrepancies between theory and praxis when it comes to justice and, as a result, can lead to the alienation of those forced to see the arbitrariness with which that which passes for justice is often doled out. I see the change that occurs in the Frenchman's perspective as an evolution in his character from an emphatic citizen to a much more complicated and, arguably, enlightened individual who comes to the doleful realization that his inner self will not always be able to easily coincide with his civic identity and that he must determine a course of action that can reconcile the contradictions that arise.

Forgiveness is a major theme in the *Dialogues*, as it is a key component in the plot against J.-J. that the Frenchman describes. As the Frenchman early on admits, J.-J.'s true crime and that which initially got him ejected from the fold was not that he was wrong or disloyal. Rather, his transgression was that he had surpassed his fellow philosophes in both reputation and renown, largely on account of the wild success of Rousseau's opera, *The Village Soothsayer*.[1]

> Seduced by a decent and simple exterior, by a temperament thought then to be easygoing and sweet, by the degree of talents needed to sense theirs without pretending to be a rival, they sought him out, became attached to him, and would soon have subjugated him. . . . But when they saw that this man who was so simple and so sweet was suddenly taking wing and rising rapidly to a reputation they could not reach, they who had such well founded high pretensions soon began to suspect there was something beneath it that was not quite right. . . . They firmly resolved to find what they sought and spent time taking the surest means so their efforts would not be lost.

> (Séduits par un extérieur honnête et simple, par une humeur crue alors facile et douce, par la mesure de talens qu'il falloit pour sentir les leurs

sans prétendre à la concurrence, ils le recherchérent, se l'attachérent et l'eurent bientot subjugué. . . . Mais quand ils virent que cet homme si simple et si doux prenant tout d'un coup l'essor s'élevoit d'un vol rapide à une reputation à laquelle ils ne pouvoient pas atteindre, eux qui avoient tant de hautes prétentions si bien fondées, ils se douterent bientot qu'il y avoit là-dessous qui n'alloit pas bien. . . . Ils formerent la ferme résolution de trouver ce qu'ils cherchoient et prirent à loisir les mesures les plus sures pour ne pas perdre leurs peines.)[2]

Unable to accept that the unassuming *ingénu* could so quickly surpass the men of letters who had come to dominate the intellectual scene, the Messieurs sought out in J.-J.'s thought and person the means to condemn him. The Messieurs' anger at what was, ultimately, a personal slight that resulted from their own amour propre emboldened them to repackage J.-J. as an enemy of the state and of virtue. Their own particular interests thus directed their very public attacks on J.-J.[3]

But the public accolades that J.-J. had previously enjoyed could not so easily be reversed, as the character and life of J.-J. were to a large degree unassailable. As the Frenchman recounts, J.-J. had the courage to bring his behavior in accord with his principles.[4] For this reason alone, he had earned the admiration of an entire generation:

> His daring morality that he seemed to preach by example even more than in his books, and above all his apparent selflessness, of which everyone was then dupe, all these singularities which presupposed at least a resolute soul aroused the admiration even of those who disapproved of them. People applauded his maxims without accepting them and his example without following it.
>
> (1:34; 1:702–3; Son audacieuse morale qu'il sembloit prêcher par son exemple encor plus que par ses livres, et surtout son desinteressement apparent dont tout le monde alors étoit la dupe; toutes ces singularités qui supposoient du moins une ame ferme excitoient l'admiration de ceux-mêmes qui les desapprouvoient. On applaudissoit à ses maximes sans les admettre et à son exemple sans vouloir le suivre.)

Desperate to create inconsistencies where none existed to sway public opinion in their favor, the Messieurs in turn took advantage of J.-J.'s naïveté and trust to discover the means to best undermine his public image. J.-J.'s

THE PHILOSOPHES' PLOT   47

abandonment of his five children—a fact that he had confided to Diderot, Grimm, and others—in turn became useful fodder in assailing J.-J.'s character (Rousseau, *Confessions*, 1:375). The sincerity and transparency that J.-J. had demonstrated toward his friends were thus turned against him in the cruelest possible fashion.[5]

But personal attacks of this nature alone would not suffice. Banking on their collective credibility as critics, the Messieurs deemed it necessary to develop a carefully orchestrated interpretation of J.-J.'s oeuvre wherein the meaning and intention of his work became distorted.[6] His thought was in turn presented to the public in the form of a shamelessly inaccurate caricature. The Frenchman—who in the *First Dialogue* stands in as the personification of the uncritical, reading public that is dupe to the Messieurs' ruse—therefore sees himself not only as permitted but, moreover, obliged to dispense with actually reading the work of J.-J. (1:679). The Frenchman maintains that one does well to accept the judgment handed down by the learned Messieurs, lest one become infected by the venom that J.-J.'s writings contain (1:693). For the Frenchman, J.-J. is a dangerous, if somewhat seductive, enemy.

Notwithstanding their enormous credibility in the eyes of the reading public, the ultimate obstacle to discrediting J.-J. was the Messieurs' former association with him. This is because, in destroying J.-J.'s reputation, the Messieurs also had to account for the fact that J.-J. had been part of their inner circle. The Messieurs thus had to ensure that, in discrediting his philosophy and his person, they did not undercut their own reputation. The answer to this public relations conundrum was to forgive J.-J. for the very crimes they had accused him of committing against the general public. The Frenchman somewhat naively recounts:

> [The philosophes] wished to unmask him, but they did not want to lose him, and the one seemed to follow necessarily from the other. How could he be confounded without being punished? How could he be spared without their becoming responsible for the continuation of his crimes, for they well knew they should not expect repentance from him? They knew what they owed to justice, truth, and public safety, but they knew no less well what they owed themselves. After having had the misfortune to live intimately with this scoundrel, they could not deliver him over to public prosecution without exposing themselves to some blame, and their honest souls, still full of commiseration for him, wanted above all to avoid scandal and to make it

appear to the eyes of the world that he owed them his well-being and his preservation.

(1:33–34; 1:702; Ils devoient, ils vouloient le démasquer mais ils ne vouloient pas le perdre, et l'un sembloit pourtant suivre necessairement de l'autre. Comment le confondre sans le punir? Comment l'épargner sans se rendre responsable de la continuation de ses crimes: car pour du repentir ils savoient bien qu'ils n'en devoient point attendre de lui. Ils savoient ce qu'ils devoient à la justice, à la vérité, à la sureté publique, mais ils ne savoient pas moins ce qu'ils se devoient à eux-mêmes. Après avoir eu le malheur de vivre avec ce scelerat dans l'intimité, ils ne pouvoient le livre à la vindicte publique sans s'exposer à quelque blâme, et leurs honnêtes âmes, pleines encore de commisération pour lui, vouloient sur tout éviter le scandale, et fair qu'aux yet de toute la terre il leur dut son bien-être et conservation.)

Forgiving J.-J. was recognized to be advantageous in numerous ways. First and foremost, in granting it, the need for a trial and, eventually, punishment was circumvented. The philosophes were therefore spared the humiliation of admitting that they had—at one point in time—found in J.-J. a kindred spirit. Further, in forestalling actual punishment, the philosophes could present themselves as generous and empathetic individuals who maintained continuity in their dealings with J.-J. Finally, because such forgiveness was ostensibly bestowed out of compassion, if J.-J. were ever to refuse to accept the kindness and protection that the other magnanimous philosophes offered him, he would be and, indeed, was necessarily and automatically labeled ungrateful. Accordingly, the "grâce," "clemency" and "pardon"—the words are used interchangeably throughout the text, a fairly common practice at the time—that J.-J. received from the Messieurs is thereby presented as a means of maintaining the philosophes' authority and reputation.[7] It is presented as a means to subjugate J.-J.

The fact that, in the common parlance of the period, forgiveness very often constituted the affirmation of the superiority of the one who forgave (and that this was problematic) is reiterated as the text progresses. It is telling that the Messieurs are able to lend credence to their complaints against J.-J. precisely by forgiving him. The Messieurs essentially bestowed forgiveness just as they raised their complaints. By placing forgiveness at the heart of their plot against J.-J. and accompanying their attacks on J.-J.'s character always with the insistence that he be pardoned, the Messieurs were able to use the popular semantics of their time to their advantage: they sidestepped the need for an external review of his crimes, in which they would have been revealed as accomplices, hypocrites, or both. What is more, in their carefully orchestrated surveillance of J.-J., they took great pains to ensure that he could do no further harm. This, or so they claim, they did on behalf of the state and in the name of civic virtue. Accordingly, they presented themselves as deeply invested in protecting the greater good and as desirous to relieve the powers that be of what would have been an onerous task. In this manner they stood in as proxies for the legislative, judicial, and executive powers. Although he recognizes that the actions of the Messieurs were not fundamentally disinterested, the Frenchman nevertheless holds fast to the belief that all this was ultimately done in the interest of the public: truth, justice, and the public's security were at stake, and all were admirably served by the decisive actions of the Messieurs in question.

The character of Rousseau, a sympathetic reader of J.-J., is aghast at the injustice that pervades such a plot. No matter how horrendous the crime, no matter how ample the evidence, all criminals must be given the right to defend themselves, and this is true even if—particularly if—a pardon is to be granted. Rather than mounting a personal defense of J.-J., the character of Rousseau labors to point out the greater significance of what has gone on:

> The right of pardon presupposes the right to punish, and consequently the prior conviction of the guilty party.

> (1:56; 1:732; Le droit de faire grace suppose celui de punir, et par consequent la préalable conviction du coupable.)

And later:

> The clemency your gentlemen boast of . . . is deceptive and false; and when they count as a good deed the exemption they claim to give him from the harm he deserves, they . . . lie, since they have not convicted him of any punishable action. An innocent person who deserves no punishment needs no pardon, and such a word is nothing but an insult to him.

> (1:65, 1:743; see also 1:947; La clemence dont vos Messieurs se vantent . . . est trompeuse et fausse, et quand ils comptent pour un bienfait le mal mérité dont ils disent exempter sa personne ils . . . mentent,

puis'qu'ils ne l'ont convaincu d'aucun acte punissable, qu'un innocent
ne méritant aucun châtiment n'a pas besoin de grace et qu'un pareil
mot n'est qu'un outrage pour lui.)

Rousseau, in fact, continually underscores the link between justice and
clemency, forgiveness and indignation, punishment and grace. In so doing,
he repeatedly affirms the need for due process, not just in relation to J.-J.
but also in relation to all who are subject to the law. The fate of J.-J. and the
forgiveness he received thus serve as haunting examples of how powerful
the Messieurs have become. As the Frenchman finally learns in the *Third
Dialogue*, what happened to J.-J. is a cautionary tale indeed.

It is fascinating that the character of Rousseau also maintains that, even
after a conviction, the consent of the guilty party must be obtained before
grace can be bestowed.

> It would still be necessary to know from him whether he consented
> to preserve his life and his freedom at this unworthy price. For a par-
> don, like any other gift, is legitimate only with the consent, at least
> presumed, of the person who receives it; and I ask of you whether
> the conduct and discourse of J. J. permit us to presume this consent
> from him.
>
> (1:67; 1:745–46; Encore falloit-il savoir de lui s'il consentoit à conserver
> sa vie et sa liberté à cet indigne prix; car une grace ainsi que tout autre
> don n'est légitime qu'avec le consentement, du moins présumé, de
> celui qui la reçoit, et je vous demande si la conduite et les discours de
> J. J. laissent présumer de lui ce consentement.)

Forswearing punishment and vengeance is not—nor should it ever be—
regarded as a gift that comes from above and can be bestowed according
to the whims of the offended party. Much to the contrary, it requires the
consent of the individual who is to receive it, lest it become unjust and
tyrannical.[8]

Such statements constitute an explicit refutation of Thomas Hobbes,
who had maintained that a juridical pardon renders the need for due process moot. According to Hobbes, a man may "resist the sword of the commonwealth in defense of another man, guilty or innocent" only when one is
accused of the same capital crime and risks the same punishment. But once
an individual is pardoned for a crime that his accomplices are still to be tried

for, said individual no longer has the right to defend the other perpetrators: "But the offer of pardon taketh from them to whom it is offered the plea of self-defense, and maketh their perseverance in assisting or defending the rest unlawful." Hobbes thus implies that the pardoning of select individuals can be used as a means of breaking up alliances against the sovereign, insofar as, once a man is pardoned, he need no longer defend himself out of fear of death or punishment. From this it follows that the pardoned individual can no longer legitimately defend the interests of others who "have resisted the sovereign power unjustly" in the same way that he has.[9] Self-defense against accusations made by the public authority is necessary and permitted only when punishment is being considered. Once the possibility of punishment has been removed, one must no longer assert either one's own innocence or the innocence of others. Rather, one must remain silent, accept the judgment of guilty, and, we can assume, be grateful for the sovereign's generosity and wisdom. Ultimately, for Hobbes the juridical pardon constitutes nothing less than a gag order.

Rousseau finds such argumentation fundamentally flawed. He recognizes that punishment may take many forms and that a ruined reputation results in pain.[10] The pardon essentially constitutes one form of punishment among others. What is more, Rousseau had a soft spot for innocence, believing that it should always be exposed and defended as such when it was wrongly accused. Whereas Hobbes was indeed aware of the importance of maintaining a reputation of virtue and courage within the social realm, he did not believe that the sovereign should concern himself with restoring the ruined reputations of men unless the sovereign had a vested, political interest in doing so. This is precisely why Hobbes maintained that a man should not seek retribution for "words of disgrace . . . for which they that made the laws had assigned no punishment."[11] For Hobbes, concern for reputation was "phantastical" insofar as the law is concerned and therefore need not be protected by juridical process. Artfully, therefore, Rousseau reveals the Hobbesian nature of his detractors in vaunting the value of the forgiveness they had granted. And this is a stinging critique indeed.

But for all his disagreements with Hobbes as to how and under what conditions the pardon should be granted, Rousseau seems to agree that the granting of grace is risky business. As Peter E. Digeser has observed, one of Hobbes's objections to the systematic pardoning of breaches of the covenant was that it could undermine the office of the law, particularly if such pardons are granted on account of particular covenants. This is why, in the chapter of the *Leviathan* titled "Of Crimes, Extenuations, and Punishment,"

Hobbes recommends that the sovereign pardon only when he can do so in a manner consistent with the covenant that he has with all his subjects, the same covenant that serves to protect the sanctity and vigor of the commonwealth. Similarly, Rousseau maintains that granting forgiveness in instances where the law has been violated must be done very carefully and according to very specific prolonged and, arguably, public deliberations, deliberations that must prioritize the common good over and above the interests of the perpetrator and even the desires of the victim. Rousseau bolsters this argument by observing that the pardon leaves criminals to wander about freely without providing any certitude that moral rehabilitation has occurred. If a malefactor has not asked for forgiveness but is nevertheless made the object of it, then his crime may remain hidden even to himself. Such a man may therefore fail to see the evil of his ways.[12]

By invoking such legalistic terms and the greater good in discerning laudable conciliatory processes from corrupt ones, Rousseau suggests that the resolution of anger must accord with political practices and the general will wherever the interpersonal relations of citizens qua citizens are concerned. If this is the case, then anger itself must be regarded as an emotion that has political significance of one form or another. But how can this be the case, given what was a preponderant tendency of the period to cast personalized anger as a decidedly destructive and therefore apolitical passion?

The answer to this question can be found by analyzing key aspects of Rousseau's political philosophy that are at play within the text. It is therefore necessary to interrupt my discussion of the *Dialogues* to extricate those points within Rousseau's political contributions that address the interrelatedness of anger and justice. I will then resume my discussion of the *Dialogues*.

3

THE PRODUCTIVE CAPACITIES
OF THE CITIZEN'S ANGER

In the *Second Discourse* Rousseau nominates one of the distinguishing traits of Natural Man as his incapacity to experience any form of enduring anger: he cannot dwell on slight. Natural Man need not forgive—he cannot forgive—because he does not have access to the experience that would render forgiveness conceivable or even necessary. Of Natural Man, Rousseau writes,

> His soul, which nothing stirs, yields itself to the sole sentiment of its present existence, with no idea of the future, however near it may be, and his projects, as limited as his views, hardly extend to the close of the day.

> (Son ame, que rien n'agite, se livre au sentiment de son existence actuelle, sans aucune idée de l'avenir, quelque prochain qu'il puisse être, et ses projets bornés comme ses vûes, s'étendent à peine jusqu'à la fin de la journée.)[1]

Rousseau describes Natural Man as, experientially speaking, existing in a perpetual present and therefore as lacking any concept of linear time. The ramifications that this observation had for Rousseau's estimation of both anger and forgiveness cannot be understated, as Natural Man's experience of time renders him immune to the desire for redress for wrongs committed against him and thus relieved of the need to bestow forgiveness.

For Natural Man, the events of the past cease to resonate just as soon as their physical effects are no longer felt. The dissolution of the desire for punitive actions cannot and need not be willed, as the omission of past evils happens spontaneously; he is in a state of absolute ignorance of anything that could properly be considered forgiveness. Accordingly, in contradistinction to many of Rousseau's contemporaries discussed earlier, for Natural Man the suspension of the desire for retribution is not an act that is reflected on or intended for self-preservation, the desire to dominate, or any greater good, as Rousseau's Natural Man has no sense of the greater good and is indifferent to how he is perceived by others. It is, rather, a naturally occurring *process* that occurs on account of Natural Man's capacity to forget and, it follows, his inability to experience anger for an extended period. Natural Man may indeed initially experience rage at the injuries he receives. Further, he may   out of fear and on account of his instinct for self-preservation (amour de soi)—flee his malefactors, subsequently avoiding them in the future. But he is incapable of principled moral hatred on account of his proclivity to forget. So, whereas in the case of Natural Man the resolution of anger may indeed contribute to self-preservation, it does not arise on account of a felicitous calculation of the means necessary to achieve such an end.

Natural Man's inability to experience enduring anger is bolstered by his freedom from the processes of comparison that, for Social Man, provide the context for amour propre.

> Since they had no dealings of any kind with one another; since they therefore knew neither vanity, nor consideration, nor esteem, nor contempt; since they had not the slightest notion of thine and mine, or any genuine idea of justice; since they looked on any violence they might suffer as an easily repaired harm rather than as a punishable injury; and since they did not even dream of vengeance except perhaps mechanically and on the spot like the dog that bites the stone thrown at him; their disputes would seldom have led to bloodshed if they had had no more urgent object than Food.

> (154; 3:157; Comme ils n'avoient entre eux aucune espèce de commerce; qu'ils ne connoissoient par conséquent ni la vanité, ni la considération, ni l'estime, ni le mépris; qu'ils n'avoient pas la moindre notion du tien et du mien, ni aucune véritable idée de la justice; qu'ils regardoient les violences, qu'ils pouvoient essuyer, comme un mal

facile à réparer, et non comme une injure qu'il faut punir, et qu'ils ne
songeoient pas même à la vengeance, si ce n'est peut-être machina-
lement et sur le champ, comme le chien qui mord la pierre qu'on lui
jette; leurs disputes eussent eu rarement des suites sanglantes, si elles
n'eussent point eu de sujet plus sensible que la Pâture.)

Natural Man, because he does not see himself in relation to others, is not
threatened by what slight may symbolize in a larger social context.[2] As long
as his survival is assured and his amour de soi satisfied, his sense of self is
not jeopardized by the injuries he suffers. Further, because of the natural
abundance of the earth and the limited, physical needs of Natural Man, he
has no notion of personal property: should someone steal "his" clothing
or food, the earth shall provide a replacement almost automatically. This
further renders Natural Man immune to the conditions that would permit
feelings of anger to endure. His "anger" (if indeed we want to call it that)
is a visceral and immediate response to pain that entails nothing more and
nothing less than a desire to distance himself from the source of his pain.
Essentially, the evils that Natural Man either suffers or commits have no
more temporal duration or, for that matter, ontological significance than
stubbing one's toe.

It is now well established that it was by comparing the civilized to the un-
civilized states of man in the *Second Discourse* that Rousseau was able to shift
the blame for all of men's evil onto society itself, and this at the very beginning of his career.[3] Social Man is greedy and desperate for the approval of
others. He therefore spends his life pursuing objects that are unnecessary to
his survival, creating needs where there should be none, and thus making
himself miserable by obsessively pursuing the mirage of contentedness that
society holds out before him. This is a leitmotif in Rousseau's philosophy,
most explicit in the distinction between amour propre and amour de soi
that he makes in the following, oft-cited passage from book 4 of *Émile*.

> Self love, which regards only ourselves, is contented when our true
> needs are satisfied. But amour-propre, which makes comparisons, is
> never content and never could be, because this sentiment, preferring
> ourselves to others, also demands others to prefer us to themselves,
> which is impossible. This is how the gentle and affectionate passions
> are born of self-love, and how the hateful and irascible passions are
> born of amour-propre. Thus what makes man essentially good is to
> have few needs and to compare himself little to others; what makes

him essentially wicked is to have many needs and to depend very much on opinion. On the basis of this principle it is easy to see how all the passions of children and men can be directed to good or bad.

(13:364; 4:493; L'amour de soy, qui ne regarde qu'à nous, est content quand nos vrais besoins sont satisfaits; mais l'amour-propre, qui se compare, n'est jamais content et ne sauroit l'être, parce que ce sentiment, en nous préférant aux autres, éxige aussi que les autres nous préfèrent à eux, ce qui est impossible. Voila comment les passions douces et affectueuses naissent de l'amour de soy, et comment les passions haineuses et irascibles naissent de l'amour-propre. Ainsi, ce qui rend l'homme essentiellement bon est d'avoir peu de besoins et de peu se comparer aux autres; ce qui le rend essentiellement méchant est d'avoir beaucoup de besoins et de tenir beaucoup à l'opinion. Sur ce principe, il est aisé de voir comment on peut diriger au bien ou au mal toutes les passions des enfants et des hommes.)

This is not to say that amour de soi always degenerates into amour propre or that amour propre is necessarily entirely wicked.[4] To survive in society, man must take into account how the needs of others compare to and how they support or run perpendicular to his own. Only by doing so can he recognize how participating in the social contract serves his amour de soi by satisfying his physical needs, ensuring his own safety, and guaranteeing his survival. As Pierre Force points out, in both the *Second Discourse* and *The Social Contract* the "realization that love of well-being is the sole motive of human actions provides a solid foundation for the first social relations."[5]

But the productive capacities of comparative self-appraisal do not end there. Rather, they extend into the domain of amour propre, ultimately encompassing it: for an individual to experience benevolence and compassion and to understand and respect what is just, he must concern himself with how he is positioned in relation to others with regard to the moral law. He must therefore care about his moral reputation within the society in which he resides.

Such a reading of the positive value of amour propre within Rousseau's system can be extracted from the following passages from *Émile*.

Émile is a man of good sense, and he does not want to be anything else. One may very well try to insult him by this title; he will stick to it and always feel honored by it. Although his desire to please does not leave him absolutely indifferent to the opinion of others, he will concern himself with their opinion only insofar as it relates immediately to his person, and he will not worry about arbitrary evaluations whose only law is fashion or prejudice. . . . He loves men because they are his fellows, but he will especially love those who resemble him most because he will feel that he is good; and since he judges this resemblance by agreement in moral taste, he will be quite gratified to be approved in everything connected with good character.

(13:511, 4:670–71; Émile est un homme de bon sens et ne veut pas être autre chose: on aura beau vouloir l'injurier par ce titre, il s'en tiendra toujours honoré. Quoique le desir de plaire ne le laisse plus absolument indifférent sur l'opinion d'autrui il ne prendra de cette opinion que ce qui se rapporte immédiatement à sa personne sans se soucier des appréciations arbitraires qui n'ont de loi que la mode ou les préjugés. . . . Aimant les hommes parce qu'ils sont ses semblables, il aimera surtout ceux qui lui ressemblent le plus, parce qu'il se sentira bon, et jugeant de cette ressemblance par la conformité des gouts dans les choses morales, dans tout ce qui tient au bon caractère il sera fort aise d'être approuvé. Il ne se dira pas précisement: je me réjoüis parce qu'on m'approuve, mais: je me réjouis parce on approuve ce que j'ai fait de bien; je me réjoüis de ce que les gens m'honorent se font honneur; tant qu'ils jugeront aussi sainement il sera beau d'obtenir leur estime.)

And, in the vicar's "Profession of Faith":

There is some moral order wherever there is sentiment and intelligence. The difference is that the good man orders himself in relation to the whole, and the wicked one orders the whole in relation to himself. The latter makes himself the center of all things; the former measures his radius and keeps to the circumference. Then he is ordered in relation to the common center, which is God, and in relation to all the concentric circles, which are the creatures.

(13:455, 4:602; see also 4:547; Il y a quelque ordre moral par tout où il y a sentiment et intelligence. La différence est que le bon s'ordonne par raport au tout et que le méchant ordonne le tout par raport à lui. Celui-ci se fait le centre de toutes choses, l'autre mesure son rayon et se tient à la circonférence. Alors il est ordonné par raport au centre commun qui est Dieu, et par raport à tous les cercles concentriques qui sont les créatures.)

These passages show that comparison and thus amour propre are indispensable attributes to any moral being. It is only through amour propre that socialized man can recognize that a world composed of other moral beings exists and that it is a worthy endeavor to strive to feel at home and be accepted therein (*oikeiôsis*).[6] Put simply, our perceived value to others is important to our moral constitution. For Rousseau, it is thus not *if* a man relates to others that determines whether he is good or bad (indeed, once he is socialized, he cannot help but do so) but *how* he does so that determines his moral worth.[7]

The problem, of course, is that once amour propre has been awakened it has an unfortunate tendency to overwhelm its proper boundaries. It becomes, to use Christopher Brooke's term, "inflamed," and socialized man in turn becomes obsessed with unnecessary goods. He does not simply want to be respected as law abiding and ethical by his peers; he wants to surpass them in every realm where comparison is possible. He thus ardently desires to be considered wittier, wealthier, more beautiful, better dressed, and more powerful than his moral peers. In this way amour propre, a force that initially had led him to seek *oikeiôsis* as a moral being in the social milieu, paradoxically leads to Social Man's alienation from it. Further, it leads him into vice. This is why Rousseau considered society to be a corrupting force. For Rousseau, our natural passions are, by definition, limited and tend only to our preservation.[8] But our socially derived passions are in essence appropriations that, as Brooke observes, are "pernicious" and go well beyond the "call of nature."[9] Ultimately, these appropriations result in obsessive comparison with others, a flawed evaluation of one's true needs, and estrangement from one's self (*allotriosis*).[10]

It is on account of this alienation and the false belief that his value is derived from the opinions of others that Social Man widens the field on which he may be attacked, thereby multiplying the occasions at which he may experience anger. This is in large part because Social Man's obsession with his own reputation and his misguided desire to be superior to others in every realm in which comparison is possible makes him hypersensitive to forms of slight in a way that Natural Man cannot even conceive of: it is not just physical pain to which Social Man is susceptible. Rather, he is also capable of being pained by the unfavorable opinions of others, even when it concerns a trait or quality that is ultimately indifferent to his physical welfare or his moral character. As a result, the number of occasions and the possibilities of insulting Social Man are infinitely greater than they would be if his amour propre were directed only toward being at home in the moral order and at home with himself. Considering Rousseau's negative appraisals of certain varieties of anger and how they relate to the deleterious effects of "inflamed" amour propre therefore highlight Rousseau's intellectual indebtedness to Stoic thought.[11]

A solitary creature, Natural Man is immune to this disease.

> The Passions, in turn, owe their origin to our needs, and their progress to our knowledge; for one can only desire or fear things in terms of the ideas one can have of them, or by the simple impulsion of Nature; and Savage man, deprived of every sort of enlightenment experiences only the Passions of this latter kind; his Desires do not exceed his Physical needs.

> (142; 3:143; Les Passions, à leur tour, tirent leur origine de nos besoins, et leur progrès de nos connoissances; car on ne peut désirer ou craindre les choses, que sur les idées qu'on en peut avoir, ou par la simple impulsion de la Nature; et l'homme Sauvage, privé de toute sorte de lumiéres, n'éprouve que les Passions de cette dernière espèce; Ses desirs ne passent pas ses besoins Physiques.)

Natural Man, having no desires that extend beyond his actual, physical needs, is not subject to vice and, further, does not experience the misdirected amour propre that produces vice and alienation. All his actions are thus both automatically justified and limited by the desire for self-preservation. There are no evil intentions for Natural Man because he has no intentionality.

At the same time, it is for precisely this reason that Natural Man may not be considered a moral being properly speaking: for him the choice between good and evil does not exist. Further, he cannot concern himself with how he measures up to others morally speaking or how others compare to him.

> It would at first seem that men in that state, having neither moral relations of any sort between them, nor known duties, could be neither good nor wicked, and had neither vices nor virtues, unless these

words are taken in a physical sense and the qualities that can harm an individual's self-preservation are called vices, and those that can contribute to it, virtues.

(150; 3:152; Il paroît d'abord que les hommes dans cet état n'ayant entre eux aucune sorte de relation morale, ni de devoirs connus, ne pouvoient être ni bons ni méchans, et n'avoient ni vices ni vertus, à moins que, prenant ces mots dans un sens physique, on n'appelle vices dans l'individu, les qualités qui peuvent nuire à sa propre conservation, et vertus celles qui peuvent y contribuer.)

Duties and, it follows, morality emerge only with stable and consistent social relations; they neither precede such relations nor do they have any content or value independently of them. Prior to his entry into society, the actions of Natural Man are considered to be "good" or "bad" only to the extent that they contribute to self-preservation.

Once socialized, however, the ultimate purpose of all duties is to uphold whatever it is that passes for justice in the society in which one resides. Practicing morality, therefore, makes one regard oneself as worthy of the rights and privileges that the mechanizations of justice—be they social, political, or legal in the strictest sense—have been designed to protect. As an added advantage, the moral individual guarantees that his own role and, we may assume, reputation within the social order is preserved. Accordingly, for Rousseau morality is to a large extent other-directed, as it necessarily seeks the approval of others.[12] From this it follows that morality (at least the variety that can be considered practicable within the social realm) is relative to the cultural norms and laws in which one resides in ways that natural virtue is not.[13]

Rousseau's distinction between the amoral status of Natural Man and the moral status of Social Man obliged him to cast anger as an evil, certainly, but as a necessary one within society. On this point, Coleman's work is once again instructive. Coleman draws our attention to an episode early in the *Confessions* where Rousseau recalls a formative experience in his youth. Rousseau had been unfairly accused of having broken a comb belonging to Mademoiselle Lambercier. His denials fell on deaf ears, and the young Rousseau received a sound thrashing. This "first experience of violence and injustice" remained "deeply ingrained" in Rousseau's sensitive heart. The great significance of this event lay less in the victimization of Rousseau and the pain he himself had endured than it did in the righteous indignation that succeeded his initial rage. Coleman points out that the connection that Rousseau forges between individual slight and general injustice in this episode serves to bolster Rousseau's case that he could observe the moral life with both objectivity and enlightened sympathy, a vantage point that Rousseau believed extended even to slights against himself. Of this experience, Coleman writes, "The initial anger is depersonalized, so that Rousseau's reaction to unjust actions, while passionate, is detached from his own interests. . . . The anger is then re-personalized, not as an egotistical imperative but as a moral demand upon the self from outside. . . . He could make injustice to others his own because he had already been forced to do so in his own divided experience of self." The focus of Coleman's study is primarily on the anger that Rousseau experienced personally and the degree to which it contributed to establishing both the latter's independence and authority toward the other philosophes in moral matters. Coleman correctly observes that the indignation that Rousseau expresses in the *Second Discourse* toward those who, "precisely under the cover of philosophical equanimity, refuse to be moved by the suffering of others" is a case in point. Again, as Coleman notes, anger is not always pathological, as it can be "a healthy form of protest against complacency," "a sign of moral vigor, of commitment to truth."[14]

But is such depersonalized anger, such indignation, the purview only of Rousseau? Of the philosophes? Rousseau's political philosophy suggests that depersonalized anger—or what today we might refer to as righteous indignation—is not only the right of every moral being and a sign of moral vigor but also a fundamental duty of the virtuous citizen. I suggest that it is on this point that Rousseau most explicitly broke rank with the Lockes, Holbachs, and Morellys of his day, all of whom believed that, by carefully regulating the behaviors of the citizenry, philosophical rulers could ensure peace and contain man's natural impulse to anger by means of limiting the occasions for personal offense.[15] In what constitutes a striking contrast to this point of view, Rousseau maintains that the experience of being alternately both the object and the source of (appropriately depersonalized) anger is a step that is ontogenetically necessary to becoming both a moral subject and a virtuous citizen.[16]

This is certainly the case in *The Social Contract*. Whereas in the *Second Discourse* Rousseau casts anger as a byproduct of Social Man's desire for domination and therefore as a largely negative, socially derived sentiment, in *The Social Contract* and his *Considerations on the Government of Poland* he suggests that anger is necessary to the formation of political bodies and the creation of emphatic citizens. Within Rousseau's political philosophy, the capacity to experience anger is an indispensable component of the citizen's psychology. This becomes clearest in his discussion of war. Rousseau argues that anger at the enemy consists in recognizing the enemy as Other. This is possible only on account of constant contact with others whom one recognizes to belong to the same social contract and as therefore sharing the same values and laws. Rousseau reiterates the well-known argument from the *Second Discourse* regarding the natural passivity of Natural Man, which he contrasts with both political peace and the state of war.

> Men, from the mere fact that, while they are living in their primitive independence, they have no mutual relations stable enough to constitute either the state of peace or the state of war, cannot naturally be enemies. War is constituted by a relation between things, and not between persons; and, as the state of war cannot arise out of simple personal relations, but only out of real relations, private war, or war of man with man, can exist neither in the state of nature, where there is no constant property nor in the social state, where everything is under control of the authority of the laws.

> (2:11; 3:356–57; Les hommes vivant dans leur primitive indépendance n'ont point entre eux de rapport assez constant pour constituer ni l'état de paix ni l'état de guerre, ils ne sont point naturellement ennemis. C'est le rapport des choses et non des hommes qui constitue la guerre, et l'état de guerre ne pouvant naître des simples rélations personnelles, mais seulement des rélations réelles, la guerre privée ou d'homme à homme ne peut exister, ni dans l'état de nature où il n'y a point de propriété constante, ni dans l'état social, où tout est sous l'autorité des loix.)

Rousseau draws a line around war, claiming that it is applicable only to those who are beyond the reach of the law *and* who also present a clear and present danger to the state. The presence of an Other, whose ideals and interests are not compatible with those of the society in question, neither necessarily arouses the ire of the citizen nor should it. But if the Other acts in a manner that betrays a desire to destroy the society, then the citizen, when commanded by the sovereign to do so, must fervently work toward the destruction of the enemy of the state. It is in this manner that, by cultivating and maintaining a certain level of cool disdain for the Other through civic education, the sovereign can ensure that—when the situation requires it—his peaceful citizens will be capable of transforming into effective soldiers. In the relationship between the citizen and the Other, as Rousseau points out just a paragraph later, men of opposing sides are only enemies "accidentally" in their role as soldiers. In their roles as men, as citizens, as members of the homeland, they remain largely indifferent and only mildly disdainful toward others who are unlike them. In times of war, however, this disdain must morph into purposeful and unwavering hatred that can inspire the citizen to make the ultimate sacrifice should he be commanded to do so.

In the *Considerations on the Government of Poland*, Rousseau suggests that cultivating such indifference, such cool disdain, is a necessary component of public, civic education. Rousseau claims that "national institutions" (institutions nationales) are responsible for forming the character, the tastes, and the mores of the people. When successful, these institutions instill a love of country among the populace so ardent that, when one is forced to spend time abroad, one "die[s] of boredom" (mourir d'ennui).[17] This prevents a people from "dissolving, taking pleasure, uniting with" (2:175; 3:960; de se fondre, de se plaire, de s'allier avec), the members of other social systems. Essentially, a good civic education enables individuals to limit the scope of the ideals that they can consider legitimate when they assess their own moral worth: no longer is all of humankind ripe for comparison in moral matters but rather only those who issue from the same social system of the individual making the comparison. Civic education thus forces citizens to view their moral worth *not* in relation to humankind but rather in relation to those whose normative moral principles they have internalized.

But we misread Rousseau if we interpret this as meaning that he was recommending either militant xenophobia or vigilantism. He was certainly well aware that arousing collective hatred among a people is a very dangerous endeavor indeed. As Joshua Cohen has noted, "Rousseau does not hold that it is reasonable for a single person to have and to act on a general will under circumstances in which there is no assurance that others will do the same," regardless of an individual's certitude in his own individualized judgment or the collective anger that he has witnessed.[18] Only the sovereign can make the call to action.

Rousseau therefore recommends that the Poles celebrate their liberation from the Russians by paying homage to the heroes who fought on their behalf and who "had the honor of suffering for their country in the enemy's chains" (2:175; 3:961; ont eu l'honneur de souffrir pour la patrie dans les fers de l'ennemi). In so doing, he offers a word of caution about the type of emotion that these celebrations should elicit: cool disdain, *not* a visceral and unbridled hatred, should prevail among the populace at such events.

> I would not want any invective against the Russians to be permitted in these solemnities, nor that they even be spoken about. That would be honoring them too much. This silence, the memory of their barbarity, and the eulogy of those who resisted them, will say everything that needs to be said about them: you ought to disdain them too much to hate them.

> (2:176; 3:961; Je ne voudrois pourtant pas qu'on se permit dans ces solemnités aucune invective contre les Russes, ni même qu'on en parlât. Ce seroit trop les honorer. Ce silence, le souvenir de leur barbarie, et l'eloge de ceux qui leur ont resisté, diront d'eux tout ce qu'il en faut dire: vous devez trop les mepriser pour les haïr.)

At first glance, it is tempting to read these lines as Rousseau's way of saying that "living well is the best revenge." However, when read in the context of the rest of the essay, it is clear that they are also inspired by very pragmatic concerns. The Poland that Rousseau describes is anarchical and surrounded by hostile enemies on all sides. Indeed, Rousseau begins this particular section of the essay by speaking about how weak Poland is militarily and how, should the Russians wish to invade again, its only defense will be the homogenized nature and abiding patriotism of its people. The carefully crafted collective disdain that Rousseau recommends for the Poles is thus intended to function not only as a constant reminder of Russian barbarism but, more important, as an unmistakable and impenetrable barrier between "us" and "them," the self-same and the Other.

> You might not be able to keep them from swallowing you; at least make it so they cannot digest you. . . . If you make it so that a Pole can never become a Russian, I answer to you for it that Russia will never subjugate Poland.

> (2:174; 3:959–60; Vous ne sauriez empêcher qu'ils ne vous engloutissent, faites au moins qu'ils ne puissent vous digerer. . . . Si vous faites en sorte qu'un Polonois ne puisse jamais devenir un Russe, je vous réponds que la Russie ne subjuguera pas la Pologne.)

The best way to prepare to forestall the success of attacks on Poland's geographic integrity is to cultivate disdain among the populace for anything and anyone that is not quintessentially Polish. Given, again, Poland's lack of military might, Rousseau's assertion that the Poles "ought to disdain [the Russians] too much to hate them" underscores a certain truth about group psychology. The collective hatred of the masses—because of its intensity—quickly becomes frenetic, overwhelming its boundaries. But such energy can neither maintain nor contain itself indefinitely. Eventually it must either seek satisfaction through action or exhaust itself in frustration. Disdain, because it is an attitude more so than a passion, is quite different. As Sianne Ngai has observed, "unlike rage, which cannot be sustained indefinitely, less dramatic feelings like envy and paranoia have a remarkable capacity for duration."[19] Envy, paranoia, disdainful paranoia: all these emotions can be maintained across time, without risking to overreach their bounds or even needing to be acted on. To allow invectives against the Russians and to hate them would essentially amount to a battle cry that could have disastrous consequences for the Poles. It would either lead them into a war that they could not win or burn itself out, thus allowing the Poles to cease to recognize how fundamentally they differ from the Russians. But a profound and unwavering variety of *disdain* for the Russians renders it impossible for a Pole ever to be integrated by them. The Poland that Rousseau envisages will therefore be an undesirable (even though easy) target for the Russians. Artfully crafted and strategically seeded disdain among the people is therefore to be the primary weapon in Poland's defensive arsenal until such a time that it can develop the military might that it needs. A true and good Pole will experience such disdain not only as a duty but also as an integral and inexorable part of his own personality.

It is along similar lines that Rousseau maintained in *A Discourse on Political Economy* (1755) that members of other successful social systems often regard the justice of any other social system as arbitrary, misguided, and prejudicial.

> It is important to observe that this rule of justice, though certain with regard to all citizens, may be defective with regard to foreigners. The reason is clear. The will of the State, though general in relation to its own members, is no longer so in relation to other States and their members, but becomes, for them, a particular and individual will, which has its rule of justice in the law of nature. This, however, enters equally into the principle here laid down; for in such a case, the

great city of the world becomes the body politic, whose general will is always the law of nature, and of which the different states and peoples are individual members.

(Il est important de remarquer que cette regle de justice, sûre par rapport à tous les citoyens, peut être fautive avec les étrangers; et la raison de ceci est évidente: c'est qu'alors la volonté de l'Etat, quoique générale par rapport à ses membres, ne l'est plus par rapport aux autres Etats et à leurs membres, mais devient pour eux une volonté particulière et individuelle, qui a sa règle de justice dans la loi de la nature, ce qui rentre également dans le principe établi: car alors la grande ville du monde devient le corps politique dont la loi de nature est toujours la volonté générale, et dont les Etats et peuples divers ne sont que des membres individuels.)[20]

Whereas Rousseau admits that the universal law of nature binds all men in some absolute sense, he also notes that such laws are not the laws of man and are not typically conducive to the formation of political bodies. For the citizen to transform himself into a full-fledged member of the state, he must overlook the similarities that he shares with all of humankind and focus his attentions instead on the differences between his own state's laws, customs, and mores and that of the opposing state. The citizen qua citizen must therefore remain somewhat blind to the cultural and ethical relativism with which politics are shot through. This is the only way that he may see the will of his people as a general will and thus imagine it to be valid in an absolute sense. Political identities are always based on a fiction, but they are not for that reason any less vital to the fabric of society. The righteousness of the emphatic citizen may indeed be somewhat unfounded and, at times, misguided, but it is not for that reason any less necessary to the preservation of the state.

But if the state is to survive, this cool and relatively disdainful indifference must necessarily be shattered the moment that a real and present danger arises, a point that is raised repeatedly in *The Social Contract*. The indifference of the citizen must be transformed into active and purpose-driven anger when commanded to do so by the sovereign in response to an attack from outside the social system. This transformation must occur on account of and in response to the destruction of politics—ideological, cultural, political, or physical—that the enemy represents for the in-group. The ability not only to experience this type of anger but to act on it when faced with a threat from outside the social system to which one belongs is thus an indispensable quality of the good citizen.[21] Such anger entails viewing the enemy as an individual whose interests represent a corrupt and damaging particular will *and* whose actions present a palpable and very real threat. When the sovereign declares war and the magistrate deems it warranted, this disdain must transform itself into collective moral hatred so that it can drive cooperative action.

There is an objection to such a reading with which I must here contend, namely, the fact that Rousseau is quite clear that the general will must remain generalized with regard to its object. In *The Social Contract* Rousseau writes,

> The general will, to be really such, must be general in its object as well as its essence; that it must both come from all and apply to all; and that it loses its natural rectitude when it is directed to some particular and determinate object, because in such a case we are judging of something foreign to us, and have no true principle of equity to direct us.
>
> (La volonté générale pour être vraiment telle doit l'être dans son objet ainsi que dans son essence, qu'elle doit partir de tous pour s'appliquer à tous, et qu'elle perd sa rectitude naturelle lorsqu'elle tend à quelque objet individuel et déterminé; parce qu'alors jugeant de ce qui nous est étranger nous n'avons aucun vrai principe d'équité qui nous guide.)[22]

It seems to follow that public anger, since it is directed toward a particular object (the Other, the foreigner, what have you), cannot be the expression of the general will. Assuming that the citizens' anger were "depersonalized," which is to say not directed toward satisfying an individualized, particular interest, it could, for Rousseau, still be considered general in its essence. Nevertheless, it would still be particular in its object, which would run counter to what Rousseau actually wrote.

Such an objection is certainly valid. The contradiction is resolved, however, if one considers carefully the overall thrust of Rousseau's political philosophy, his abiding pragmatism, and the ambiguous nature of the word "object." As Patrick Riley has pointed out, "a 'general will' is a philosophical and psychological contradiction in terms; will is a conception understandable, if at all, only in terms of individual actions." Riley further observes that one does not get around this problem by simply calling it a "common ego" or viewing it as an "analogical forerunner to Kant's pure practical reason"; although such a view can account for "cohesiveness," it does not constitute "voluntarism" properly speaking. Riley thus suggests that Rousseau's contract theory was intended as a criticism of existing contract theories, which "dealt too much with the form of obligation, with will as it is, and not enough with what one ought to be obligated *to*, and with will as it might be." According to Riley's reading, Rousseau was able to set his contract theory apart by establishing that "will is not enough, that perfect polity alone is not enough, that will must be united to perfection, and that perfection must be the standard of what is willed."[23] In this way Rousseau was able to distinguish legitimate political authority from mere force, thereby creating a conceptual space in which the subjects' allegiance to the social contract could be considered sincere.

But Rousseau's notion of the general will, if it is to have any stake in action, would have to be able to do more than simply will unity. It would need to have a means of exemplifying that perfection is indeed its standard. To render itself palpable, the general will would at times have to apply itself to particular scenarios and thereby lead to collective action. Failing this, obligation would be nothing more than a theoretical construct existing in a hypothetical world and political life would be nothing more than an attitude or an intense sentiment of patriotism relegated to a sphere of mere contemplation. It would lack any stake in action.

Shklar's study is again instructive here. She points out that the general will is not merely creative of unity; it is also defensive of the values to which the society it directs adhere. This is true to such an extent that, when functioning properly, the general will takes precedence over the individual's particular, self-interested will, beating it into submission, whenever a course of action that concerns the collectivity is being deliberated on.[24] If Shklar is correct, then it is possible and, indeed, I would say indispensable for collective anger to be able to be experienced and deployed in a manner consistent with the general will. But this is possible only if collective anger can manifest itself in the world of appearances in the form of actions directed toward particular objects. Otherwise, such anger would have no content.

For the type of anger I am describing to accord with Rousseau's understanding of the general will, such anger would have to be wholly defensive of the values to which the society experiencing it subscribes, as opposed to merely antagonistic toward that which was regarded as different. Once that condition were met, such anger could then be directed toward obliterating the enemy in the name of collective self-defense. If experienced in this manner, then the Other would be viewed by the in-group as an individual or group of individuals who do not respect the general will and thus as individuals to whom the principles of equality, freedom, and justice do not apply. If this is the case, then one of the objectives of anger that accords with the general will would have to be to preserve the conditions that allow the general will of a particular social system to maintain the distinction between itself and the will of the Other (which could either be the particular will of an individual or the collective will of another social system). The magistrate gives content to this general objective, this collective anger, when he names an Other as an enemy and decides on a course of action for his people. In this manner, such anger remains general in the strictest sense with regard to its objectives, even though in manifesting itself it has become attached to a particular object *that is regarded as exterior to the system and thus as not privy to the equality of all citizens that the general will is obliged to defend.*

I take this to be Rousseau's point in his discussion of the general will in part 2, chapter 4, of *The Social Contract.* He does indeed note that, within the in-group, exceptional cases and quarrels may arise wherein neither general convention nor precedent offers guidance as to how best to resolve them. He further maintains that these unprecedented events risk jeopardizing the general will and the sanctity of the state, as it is extremely difficult in such scenarios to distinguish between the particular will of an individual or group of individuals and the general will. This is because discord among members of a society amounts to a "case in which the individuals concerned are one party, and the public the other" (un procès où les particuliers intéressés sont une des parties, et le public l'autre). Rousseau admits that there is no easy way to determine where the true general will lies in such unprecedented quarrels when he states, "I see neither the law that ought to be followed nor the judge who ought to give the decision" (28; 3:374; je ne vois ni la loi qu'il faut suivre, ni le juge qui doit prononcer). But in instances where a common interest *can* be identified with certitude, a decision can be reached, a judge can be nominated, and a judgment can be rendered. That is to say, collective anger directed toward a particular object (even if, in the case of crimes, that object is a member of the collective) can be sanctioned by the general will so long as it is aroused on account of the threat toward the common interest that the particular object poses. This is the point of the following passage:

> It should be seen from the foregoing that what makes the will general is less the number of voters than the common interest uniting them;

for, under this system, each necessarily submits to the conditions he imposes on others: and this admirable agreement between interest and justice gives to the common deliberations an equitable character which at once vanishes when any particular question is discussed, in the absence of a common interest to unite and identify the ruling of the judge with that of the party.

(28; 3:374; On doit concevoir par là, que ce qui généralise la volonté est moins le nombre des voix, que l'intérêt commun qui les unit: car, dans cette institution, chacun se soumet nécessairement aux conditions qu'il impose aux autres; accord admirable de l'intérêt et de la justice qui donne aux délibérations communes un caractère d'équité qu'on voit s'évanouir dans la discussion de toute affaire particulière, faute d'un intérêt commun qui unisse et identifie la règle du juge avec celle de la partie.)

Where common interest cannot be located with any degree of certainty, it is extremely difficult, perhaps impossible, to condemn any particular individual in a manner consistent with the general will. In such situations, justice is but a word and a veil behind which particular interests lurk. But if a common interest that supports the principles of justice and equity *can* be articulated, then anyone acting contrary to it can be declared an enemy and thus determined to be the appropriate object of collective anger. When understood in this light, it is possible for Rousseau's general will to be directed toward condemning specific individuals, so long as said individuals have proven themselves to not only be impervious to sharing in the common interest but, and this point is key, committed to destroying it.

The complex relationship between civic virtue and legitimate forms of collective indignation is clearest in Rousseau's discussion of Christianity. As we have just seen, the necessity for the magistrate to be able to gauge, cultivate, and control manifestations of anger among the populace is an issue that is addressed at length in both *The Social Contract* and *Considerations on the Government of Poland*. But this is dependent on the populace being receptive to such indignation and capable of maintaining it with a considerable degree of conviction. Because Christians are unable to internalize collective indignation, Rousseau was obliged to cast them as being fundamentally bad citizens.

As is often observed, the Christian's incapacity to transform into an avid defender of the state is, in fact, a large part of the reason why Rousseau dismissed Christianity as fundamentally pernicious to the state in *The Social Contract*, notwithstanding his admiration for Jesus's noble project, his unassailable behavior, and his "salutary use of use of moral fables" as expressed in such texts as the *First Discourse* and the "Letter to Franquières" (1769).[25] Rousseau does so for numerous reasons. First, being an adherent to an utterly spiritual religion oriented toward celestial pleasures, the Christian performs his duties with a profound indifference toward "the good or ill success of his cares" (le bon or mauvais succès de ses soins). Further, because he is concerned primarily with his existence after his death, the Christian will not be able to fight with passion in times of war. Indifferent toward victory, Christian soldiers who march into war "know better how to die than how to conquer" (119; 3:466; savent plutôt mourir que vaincre). Martyrdom is thus a much more appealing proposition for them than victory, which is hardly conducive to maintaining the integrity of the state.

The final and, for our purposes, most important reason that Rousseau banished Christianity from politics was that the Christian has difficulty experiencing anger: "Christian charity does not readily allow a man to think hardly of his neighbors" (119; 3:466; La charité chrétienne ne permet pas aisément de penser mal de son prochain). Much of this has to do with the fact that in Christianity, the similarities among men—and not differences—are stressed. Men are mortal, fallible, and finite. The differences in their characters and customs notwithstanding, for the true Christian, all men are all thus equidistant from God, which is to say infinitely removed. A distinction between the in-group and the out-group therefore does not exist. Furthermore, the belief that the righteous will be rewarded and the evil punished in a transmundane realm makes them care little for the paltry judgments of their fellow man. Vehement anger is thus an experience to which the true Christian does not have access and collective disdain an attitude that he cannot maintain with any degree of zeal.

The political ramifications of such an outlook are pernicious, as a society shot through with Christian charity enables the crafty, unbelieving individual to gain ascendancy by imposing himself as imbued with God's authority and therefore worthy of respect. Incapable of viewing others critically, the true Christian has no choice but to give his assent when such a man appears on the scene, even if he behaves in ways that are sanctioned neither by the law nor by social custom. The Christian therefore cannot recognize that the man who presents himself as a messenger of God is a usurper.[26] Or, rather, if he does recognize it, he minds very little: "True Christians are made to be slaves, and they know it and do not much mind: this short life counts for too little in their eyes" (120; 3:467; Les vrais chrétiens sont faits pour être esclaves; ils le savent et ne s'en émeuvent guères; cette courte vie a trop peu de prix à leurs yeux). The Christian measures his moral perfection and that of others in relation to divine perfection. Whereas it is quite possible that the Christian is aware of the faults and evil intentions of others, he just as easily finds fault with himself. For this reason the Christian holds steadfast to the belief that only God has the right to judge. So whereas he is not amoral in the way that Natural Man is precisely because he does have a moral standard (that of Christ) to which he compares himself, he is incapable of recognizing his own indignation as legitimate and thus worthy of action. He is not bound by the law of man but by the law of God, and God can and will take care of all violations at the Final Judgment.[27] In the end, therefore, the Christian is essentially as effective as Natural Man in enforcing moral standards, which is to say, worthless. In Rousseau's political imagination, the devout Christian figures among the living dead as far as morality is concerned because he cares so little for the duties that others have toward him and toward the political structure to which he belongs that he finds it impossible to pay much heed when terrestrial laws are broken. Only sin counts for him, and God will take care of that at the Final Judgment. Violations of the dictates of justice and attacks on the institutions that defend it do not arouse the Christian's righteous indignation. So it was that Rousseau concluded that Christianity was incompatible with civic virtue.

Rousseau's views on war and on the necessity of taking part in collective indignation did not extend only to enemies of an opposing state. In the wake of a crime, the citizen could, and often should, be ejected permanently from the fold:

> Every malefactor, by attacking social rights, becomes on forfeit a rebel and a traitor to his country; by violating its laws he ceases to be a member of it. In such a case the preservation of the State is inconsistent with his own, and one or the other must perish; in putting the guilty to death, we slay not so much the citizen as an enemy. The trial and the judgment are the proofs that he has broken the social treaty, and is in consequence no longer a member of the State. Since, then, he has recognised himself to be such . . . he must be removed by exile as a violator of the compact, or by death as a public enemy; for such an enemy is not a moral person, but merely a man; and in such a case the right of war is to kill the vanquished.

(31; 3:376; Tout malfaiteur attaquant le droit social devient par ses forfaits rebelle et traître à la patrie, il cesse d'en être membre en violant
ses loix, même il lui fait la guerre. Alors la conservation de l'Etat est
incompatible avec la sienne, il faut qu'un des deux périsse, et quand
on fait mourir le coupable, c'est moins comme citoyen que comme
ennemi. Les procédures, le jugement, sont les preuves et la déclara-
tion qu'il a rompu le traité social, et par conséquent qu'il n'est plus
membre de l'Etat. Or comme il s'est reconnu tel . . . il en doit être
retranché par l'exil comme infracteur du pacte, ou par la mort comme
ennemi public; car un tel ennemi n'est pas une personne morale, c'est
un homme, et c'est alors que le droit de la guerre est de tuer le vaincu.)

The lawbreaking citizen threatens the social pact that gives the state its form
and legitimacy. Breaking the law amounts to a declaration of war, because
in doing so one reveals that one neither loves the law nor views oneself as
obligated to behave in accordance with it. After due process is satisfied and
a judgment of guilt decided on, such a citizen must be viewed with the
same disdain and distance as the enemy who comes from afar. In the eyes
of the state and of all citizens, a malefactor who has been found to violate
the sanctity of the social contract and the laws that protect it can no longer
be considered a moral being properly speaking. Such an individual becomes
the absolute Other, and it is the virtuous citizen's duty to recognize this individual as such when a declaration of guilty has been made. In this sense,
Rousseau reiterates an argument that Joseph Butler himself had invoked
regarding the necessity of resentment toward vice and wickedness to group
formation. For Butler, such resentment "is one of the common bonds by
which society is held together; a fellow-feeling which each individual has in
behalf of the whole species as well as of himself."[28]

Rousseau is able to make such a statement about the perceived immo-
rality of the noncitizen on account of his views regarding absolute versus
relative good and evil in the section of The Social Contract titled "On Law."
Whereas he admits that there exists a transcendental order and a variety
of absolute justice that emanates from God, he immediately notes that socialized man is incapable of comprehending such justice.[29] Only laws and
conventions established by the general will of citizens relating to one another as citizens can approximate absolute justice. Because all rights and
duties are derived from the law that has received the consent of the governed, Rousseau concludes that the interrogation of metaphysical ideas

concerning justice and, therefore, rights and duties within the civic order must necessarily be regarded as non sequitur (3:378–79). From this it follows that, if a judgment of guilty has been made in accord with the state's laws, then the virtuous citizen must accept that judgment as a fact and in turn view the condemned as an enemy of the highest order. Just as is the case in the state of war, the virtuous citizen should be compelled to act out of indignation at the sight of the perpetrators of actions that have been judged to be crimes, as they represent a threat to the sanctity of law and thus to the integrity of the state.

Rousseau's views on this are unequivocal: only the sovereign can bestow grace in such instances, as only he is above the law. But even this, Rousseau points out, must be done rarely, as the frequent bestowal of grace ultimately weakens the power of the law in the eyes of the citizens.[30] Rousseau admits that this is a cold conclusion to come to: "But I feel my heart protesting and restraining my pen; let us leave these questions to the just man who has never offended, and would himself stand in no need of pardon" (32; 3:377; Mais je sens que mon coeur murmure et retient ma plume; laissons discuter ces questions à l'homme juste qui n'a point failli, et qui jamais n'eut lui-même besoin de grâce). The obvious reference here to Jesus Christ implies that the question of when grace is appropriate is one that, more often than not, cannot be answered by mere mortals.[31] Even for the sovereign, the satisfaction of collective anger by means of punishment—rather than its dissipation in the form of grace—is a surer means to maintain the integrity of the state.[32] As S. J. Perelman once punned, "to err is human, to forgive supine." Rousseau would most certainly concur, at least as far as the sovereign is concerned. When collective indignation has been aroused and legitimized by a judgment of guilty, grace sends a confusing message indeed to all who partake in it.[33] Because appropriately sanctioned collective indignation is such a powerful weapon when it comes to defending the sanctity of the state, it must never be ridiculed or put out of office. As we shall see in the discussion of *Rousseau, Judge of Jean-Jacques*, this was a fatal flaw in the Messieurs' plan to silence Jean-Jacques.

THE FRENCHMAN'S CONUNDRUM

With a better picture now in place of the need to be able to partake in collective anger—understood here as indignation—to the psychology of the Rousseauvean citizen, I can now resume my analysis of the *Dialogues*. I ended the earlier discussion of the *Dialogues* with the hypothesis that, by invoking legalistic terms in discerning laudable from corrupt conciliatory processes, the character of Rousseau suggests that, when publicized and legitimized by the assent of the citizenry, the resolution of anger must accord with the dictates of justice. I suggest that it is because of this that, in *Rousseau, Judge of Jean-Jacques*, the character of Rousseau is finally able to wrest the Frenchman from the grips of the prejudices that the Messieurs had cultivated.

To a large extent, Rousseau's options in converting the Frenchman were decidedly limited, given the latter's psychology. Banking perhaps on the fact that the Frenchman would be touched in the same way that he was, the character of Rousseau begins the conversation with the Frenchman by stressing the beauty of J.-J.'s philosophy. He describes an ideal world in which passions are limited, amour propre is absent, and natural freedom reigns. To this world, he compares French society, wherein amour propre abounds, and men chase after the illusion that happiness and contentedness are found in social ascendancy, thereby ultimately rendering themselves both evil and miserable (1:669–71). Rousseau therefore reproduces the arguments he made in the *Second Discourse* regarding the natural goodness of man, as compared to the evils of inflamed amour propre. Much to Rousseau's chagrin, the Frenchman remains unmoved after listening patiently to Rousseau's exposition. He responds, "I'm racking my brain unsuccessfully to see what these fantastic beings you describe have in common with the monster we were just talking about" (1:12; 1:672; Je cherche inutilement dans ma tête ce qu'il peut y avoir de commun entre les êtres fantastiques que vous décrivez et le monstre dont nous parlions tout à l'heure). Rousseau, who has yet to realize what he is up against, continues in his explication of J.-J.'s philosophy, at least for a time.

The Frenchman, wholly unimpressed, retorts by highlighting the fact that Rousseau mistakenly overlooks the abominations of J.-J. and "praises him to the skies" (1:13; 1:673; le plaçant dans les astres) solely on account of the fact that he wrote a couple of novels. It is at this point that the difference in Rousseau's and the Frenchman's perspectives is finally revealed. Rousseau observes, "The Author of the Books and of the crimes appears to you to be the same person. I believe I am correct to see them as two. That, Sir, is the key to the enigma" (1:13; 1:674; L'Auteur des Livres et celui des crimes vous paroit la même personne; je me crois fondé à en faire deux. Voila, Monsieur le mot de l'énigme). It is at precisely at this point that Rousseau turns the conversation toward J.-J.'s character, his alleged crimes, and the means by which he was condemned.

To fully grasp the nature of this shift in rhetorical strategy on Rousseau's part we must recognize that the defining aspect of the Frenchman's psychology is that he is an emphatic citizen, a fact with which even the author of *The Social Contract* and, certainly, of the *Considerations on the Government of Poland* would be obliged to concur. France may have been an ill-constituted state at the time Rousseau was writing. And he was unabashed about his low estimation of the "men of our days" (hommes de nos jours), whom he described as "Bourgeois" and thus as "nothing" (rien) (*Émile*, 4:250; see also 4:665). Be that as it may, this does not prevent the Frenchman from believing in the superiority of the French people and regarding the French state an example worthy of imitators. Much like the Poles that Rousseau describes in his *Considerations on the Government of Poland*, the Frenchman's cool disdain for those outside of his social system is steadfast. He therefore has difficulty seeing his own people and culture with a critical eye. He wholeheartedly rejects any and all accusations that the French justice system is either flawed or arbitrary. Indeed, a well-constructed delusion can hold up for a long time and withstand all sorts of attack. The Frenchman's identity as an emphatic citizen may very well be based on a fiction, but his patriotism is not for that reason any less powerful or sincere. This is precisely why he vehemently struggles to uphold the legitimacy of the condemnation of J.-J., as the latter was declared the enemy of the French people. As far as the Frenchman is concerned, the Messieurs did well to orchestrate a plot against him. That their condemnation of J.-J. won the public's assent is proof of this. This is why, even though he is aware of the questionable means employed to exile J.-J. and the particular interests in the name of which they were undertaken, the Frenchman nevertheless maintains that justice has been served. It is this that obliges him to refuse to distinguish between the author and the criminal: J.-J. is an enemy that must be absolutely eliminated. Such are the rules of engagement during times of war. Such is the faith that citizens must maintain in the judgment of their more enlightened leaders.

It was with his writings and his opera that J.-J. had won the acclaim of the public. Once he had been classified as a criminal, he had to be expelled absolutely from the public's imagination and esteem. To allow J.-J., an enemy, to continue to positively influence public opinion would have weakened the integrity of the state and in turn encouraged dissension (1:675). All of J.-J.'s contributions had to therefore be either exposed as pernicious or, in one important instance, reduced to plagiarism. The fact that the Frenchman has never read a word from J.-J.'s pen is therefore not the result of ignorance or a lack of intellectual curiosity on his part (1:679). It is, rather, the mark of his unwavering allegiance to his fellow citizens and his robust refusal to deviate from both public opinion and the dictates of the lawgivers. So confident is the Frenchman in the rectitude and unanimity of public opinion that he refrains from criticizing *The Village Soothsayer*. Instead, the Frenchman prefers to chalk J.-J.'s chef d'oeuvre up to plagiarism, just as the Messieurs have instructed the public to do. There is a very good explanation as to why the Messieurs would have adopted such a tactic in this one instance: the opera had elicited such "transports of admiration" (transports d'admiration) and immense enthusiasm from the public (1:681). To subsequently dismiss the work as unworthy of the public's esteem would be to ridicule public opinion by exposing it as potentially flawed. Given the great success of the opera, belittling the work would have undermined a cultural product that had the merit of creating a unified reaction and thus a sense of solidarity among the public.[1] Because, and I return to this point later, the Messieurs' authority rests on their ability to manipulate public opinion they could not expose it as capable of erring. Wisely, therefore, they attributed the opera to a work of another anonymous composer.

Because Rousseau recognizes that, as an emphatic citizen, the Frenchman cannot be swayed by a discussion of the merits of J.-J.'s work or character, he changes course. He does so by turning the discussion toward justice as a sacred and inviolable social ideal that must never be circumvented or ignored. In this respect, he opts to engage the Frenchman on the latter's own terms. As discussed earlier, Rousseau points out that the right to pardon presupposes the right to punish. He also argues that the right to punish presupposes a judgment of guilty. This enables him to launch into a discussion about due process in which the character of Rousseau maintains that men remain citizens up until the moment that a verdict is rendered. Prior to the moment that judgment of guilty is passed, the accused enjoy certain rights. One of these rights is the right to defend oneself. J.-J., as Rousseau points out, was denied this basic right because he was condemned without ever being formerly accused. To add insult to injury, J.-J. remains oblivious to the fact that he has been condemned and subsequently pardoned. Because he was never formerly accused, he was not allowed to answer for his crimes. Essentially, much of Rousseau's argumentation is geared toward making the Frenchman cognizant of the difference between public opinion and the general will. Whereas in ideal scenarios public opinion can be the mouthpiece for the general will, it very often errs on the side of particular interests.

Wishing to elucidate the greater danger that such practices represent when generalized, Rousseau encourages the Frenchman to imagine himself in J.-J.'s position:

> But if you were isolated on earth, without defense and without defender, and the prey of your enemies for twenty years as J. J. has been, one could easily prove to me in secret about you what you have proved to me about him, without my having anything to reply either. Would that be enough to judge you without appeal and without wanting to hear you?
>
> (1:58; 1:734–35; Mais si vous étiez isolé sur la terre, sans defense et sans defenseur, et depuis vingt ans en proye à vos ennemis comme J. J., on pourroit sans peine me prouver de vous en secret ce que vous m'avez prouvé de lui, sans que j'eusse rien non plus à répondre. En seroit-ce assez pour vous juger sans appel et sans vouloir vous écouter?)

Rousseau then proceeds to cite two current events to exemplify why justice must never be deliberated upon behind closed doors. In the first instance, a man was accused of a "flagrant offense" (délit notoire) that was supported by "public and unanimous testimony" (1:59; 1:735; un témoignage public et unanime). He was nevertheless acquitted of the crime when it was discovered that, on the same day that the crime took place, he was in fact tried for an identical crime some place else. The judges of both crimes were then forced to dig deeper and another guilty party was discovered.

In the second example, a man who had been condemned to death and was already up on the scaffold was saved when the true author of the crime for which the condemned had been accused came forward. The condemned man was in turn absolved, and the man who was actually guilty was pardoned for his "generosity" (1:59, 1:736; générosité). It is worth noting that this is one of those rare instances alluded to in *The Social Contract*, where the sovereign appropriately bestows grace. The true perpetrator of the crime, although he had formerly broken the law, proves through his admission that he respects justice to such an extent that he experiences righteous indignation against himself and is willing to act on it by confessing. The fact that by admitting to the crime he risked to take the condemned man's place on the scaffold proved that he was willing to die so that the integrity of the state's institution of justice could remain intact. This particular individual, guilty though he is, does not view either the laws or justice instrumentally; he truly loves them. In confessing, the guilty party demonstrated that he was the type of citizen who can and will transition into the role of a soldier when a threat to the social system presents itself. In this particular instance, the guilty party recognized that the crime he had committed and the ill effects that resulted from it constituted a threat to the state and was antithetical to justice. When faced with this reality and the sight of one of his compatriots being executed in his stead, the citizen within him was moved to compassion and denounced the culpable individual (himself). He in turn was willing to sacrifice himself so that innocence and justice could prevail. The absolution of the true perpetrator who willingly (and publicly) confessed his crime and thus reaffirmed his own devotion to justice and the law thus had pedagogical attributes from which other citizens could benefit, and the sovereign did well to pardon him.

Such last-minute absolutions occur with more frequency in England, where the trials are conducted publicly. In France, unfortunately, trials are conducted behind closed doors. The result is that "the weak are subjected to the revenge of the powerful without scandal, and the procedures—always unknown to the public or falsified to deceive it—remain" (1:60; 1:736–37; les

foibles sont livrés sans scandale aux vengeances des puissans, et les procédures, toujours ignorées du public ou falsifiées pour le tromper, restent).

Whereas the Frenchman recognizes the legitimacy of Rousseau's complaint, he nevertheless maintains that due process would have been super-
fluous in J.-J.'s case. First, there is unanimity among all those who know
him that he is a scoundrel. Second and, for our purposes, more important,
the Frenchman reiterates the fact that J.-J. has escaped actual punishment.
Because of this, J.-J. is subject only to the moral hatred of the public: "He is
not being punished for one offense or for another, but he is abhorred. . . . I
see nothing that is not just in that. The horror and aversion of men is due
to the wicked person whom they allow to live when their clemency leads
them to spare him" (1:62; 1:740; On ne le punit ni d'un délit ni d'un autre,
mais on l'abhorre. . . . Je ne vois rien là que de juste. L'horreur et l'aversion
des hommes est düe au méchant qu'ils laissent vivre quand leur clémence
les porte à l'épargner).[2]

The Frenchman's response is strange indeed. For a man who is so consciously aware of the importance of public opinion, he seems to be very
little concerned with how it is formed or how closely it approximates the
general will. His role as a good citizen being the definitive aspect of his
identity, he blindly adheres to public opinion. His disdain for J.-J. is thus an
article of faith to which he ascribes on account of the public's approval of
the legitimacy of the sentiment. The Frenchman, although he has never
read J.-J., is almost instinctually aware of the dangers that peering through
societal delusions presents. Accordingly, if he initially resists the argumentation of Rousseau, it has less to do with the strength or weakness of the latter's arguments than it does with his own fear of becoming alienated from
the society from which so much of his identity is derived.

The Social Contract, and in particular its discussion of particular versus
general wills, is again instructive in understanding the Frenchman's initial
obstinacy in accepting the due-process argument that Rousseau offers. Particular wills attend to the interests of individuals or groups of individuals.
They do not regard the greater good of the entire community. The general will, on the other hand, seeks out justice and equality for all citizens.
For Rousseau, the ultimate good is a society in which, thanks in large part
to civic education, public opinion always tends toward upholding the law
and thereby maintaining the integrity and legitimacy of the social contract.
When functioning in accordance with the general will, public opinion is
subject to the laws espoused by a public composed of private individuals rationally deliberating the common good. Its validity is enforced and

maintained through public censure and the subject's desire to be recognized as a virtuous, law-abiding citizen.[3]

But the general will, as Rousseau goes to great lengths to point out, is not simply a majority-rules mentality. For the will of the masses to constitute a general will properly speaking, it must have as its object the "common good" (intérêt commun) and, as such, must in principle oppose arbitrariness, pure prejudice, and private interests. Failing that, one is left only with "the will of all" (la volonté de tous) under the rubric of which a large number of particular wills mesh together and masquerade as the general will. It is thus that public opinion can err: "Of itself the people wills always the good, but of itself it by no means always sees it. The general will is always in the right, but the judgment which guides it is not always enlightened" (1:34; 3:380; De lui-même le peuple veut toujours le bien, mais de lui-même il ne le voit pas toujours. La volonté générale est toujours droite, mais le jugement qui la guide n'est pas toujours éclairé).[4] In periods where factions and partial associations succeed in amassing large numbers of adherents, the risk that the "will of all" replaces the "general will" increases (1:3:371–72). In such circumstances, public opinion, or the porte-parole for the general will in ideal situations, becomes corrupt and leads the people astray. When this happens, it is the duty of the legislator—not the magistrate, not the sovereign, not the citizen, as Rousseau stresses—to step in to ensure that laws are created and enforced in accord with the general will, regardless of the direction popular opinion may be oriented in, even if this means short-term, material losses for the majority (1:3:380).

But if, in his political philosophy, Rousseau admitted that public opinion could and often did become corrupt, he just as readily acknowledged that going against it was a dangerous endeavor:

> Once customs have become established and prejudices inveterate, it is dangerous and useless to attempt their reformation; the people, like the foolish and cowardly patients who rave at sight of the doctor, can no longer bear that any one should lay hands on its faults to remedy them.
>
> (1:39; 3:385; Quand une fois les coutumes sont établies et les préjugés enracinés, c'est une entreprise dangereuse et vaine de vouloir les réformer; le peuple ne peut pas même souffrir qu'on touche à ses maux pour les détruire, semblable à ces malades supides et sans courage qui frémissent à l'aspect du médecin.)

To expose public opinion as corrupt is to invite the wrath of the masses and to run the risk of being declared an Other. At the same time, the failure to do so is to stand idly by as the state approaches its ruin, as when particular wills gain ascendancy, the "social bond begins to be relaxed" (le noeud social commence à se relâcher). Those who recognize that the general will has been replaced by the will of all can no longer believe that the common good (l'intérêt commun) is served by the laws, customs, and opinions of the masses. The citizen in them therefore becomes alienated from the very society from which this part of their identity is derived: "Each man, in detaching his interest from the common interest, sees clearly that he cannot entirely separate them; but his share in the public mishaps seems to him negligible beside the exclusive good he aims at making his own" (1:91; 3:438; Chacun, détachant son intérêt de l'intérêt commun, voit bien qu'il ne peut l'en séparer tout à fait, mais sa part du mal public ne lui paroît rien auprès du bien exclusif qu'il prétend s'approprier). Individuals who have peered through the veil of public opinion and have seen that the face of the general will has been gravely disfigured cannot help but begin to see the state instrumentally. Whereas individuals so enlightened may not separate themselves entirely from the community or seek to destroy the state, they cannot help but prioritize their own selfish interests over and above those of the community. Worse still, they cease to truly love and respect the laws by which they are governed and no longer act (or, if the option exists, vote) in a manner advantageous to the sanctity of the state.[5] They in turn become citizens in name only.

If one understands the Frenchman's definitive characteristic as his genuine love for the state, his faith in its laws, and his belief that public opinion is synonymous with the general will, one begins to see just how much of a threat the character of Rousseau's defense of J.-J. poses for him. Although the Frenchman has never read the work of J.-J., he senses the risk that he runs if Rousseau wins the argument. It is revealing that, at numerous points in the conversation, the Frenchman cites the potential threat that J.-J. poses. In so doing, he underscores Rousseau's imperviousness to feelings of French patriotism. He does so by citing the latter's staunch refusal to cease and desist in his study of J.-J.'s life and works, despite what has been the Messieurs unequivocal condemnation and the public's ratification thereof: "You must admit that you are very obstinate, very tenacious in your opinions. Given the little authority that public opinion has over you, it is easy to see that you are not French" (1:26; 1:692; see also 1:759; Il faut avouer que vous êtes un homme bien obstiné, bien ténace dans vos opinions; au peu d'autorité qu'ont sur vous celles du public, on voit bien que vous n'êtes pas Français). As an emphatic citizen, the Frenchman's existence has always been marked by the suppression of his particular will, his own inclinations, and his personal opinions wherever affairs of public interest were concerned, and these affairs were always dictated to him through public opinion.[6] He therefore defends the judgment against J.-J. on the basis of his own national identity. Rousseau—because he is not a Frenchman—is not expected to concur with him. But he is expected to respect and appreciate the authentic patriotism from which the Frenchman's arguments are born.

The Frenchman's anxieties become even more apparent when Rousseau asks him what he would do if, "after attentive and impartial research" (d'attentives et impartiales recherches), he were to find a "simple, sensible, and good man" (un homme simple, sensible, et bon) in place of the "infernal soul" (l'âme infernale) the latter sees in him (1:78; 1:761). The Frenchman responds,

> Cruelly, you can be sure. I feel that while respecting him and doing him justice, I would then hate him more, perhaps, for my errors than I hate him now for his crimes. I would never forgive him for my injustice toward him. I reproach myself for this disposition, I blush for it; but I feel it in my heart despite myself.
>
> (1:78–79; 1:761; Cruellement, soyez-en sûr. Je sens qu'en l'estimant et lui rendant justice, je le haïrois alors peut-être encore pour mes torts que je ne le hais maintenant pour ses crimes: je ne lui pardonnerois jamais mon injustice envers lui. Je me reproche cette disposition, j'en rougis; mais je la sens dans mon coeur malgré moi.)

Jeremiah Alberg analyzes this particular scene in some detail in his theological study, *A Reinterpretation of Rousseau: A Religious System*. He concludes that in the phrase, "I will never forgive him for my injustice toward him," Rousseau expresses "not only an incisive psychological fact, but also a profound theological mystery. In the presence of someone who has wronged a person, that person's heart can harden." According to Alberg, this feeling arises in the Frenchman on account of the fact that the question Rousseau poses to him makes him recognize that the hatred he rightly felt toward the public image of J.-J. mistakenly "got transferred to the person of J.-J. himself." Alberg continues, "In other words, it is one thing for the Frenchman to hate the vices of the scoundrel, whose portrait was presented to him, but to let it be carried further, not through any judgment but rather through an impetuous passion that dominated him without him knowing it, is something else."[7]

There are a few objections that one can make to such an interpretation. First and foremost, Alberg argues that Rousseau's quarrel with forgiveness stems ultimately from the latter's quarrel with the Christian model of absolution and what Alberg takes to be Rousseau's subsequent rejection of the notion of original sin. He therefore fails to consider that the Christian model of forgiveness was not necessarily the only (or even principal) point of reference for Rousseau's thoughts on forgiveness, the insertion of the words "almost invincible error" (une erreur presque invincible) at one point in the text (1:215, 1:937) and their theological tenor withstanding. We have already seen how, in the eighteenth century, forgiveness was more often discussed in relation to social hierarchies than in relation to religion, particularly among the Messieurs to whom the *Dialogues* are addressed. Arguably, the centrality of forgiveness to affirming social (and intellectual) hierarchies was a leitmotif in Enlightened writing. For Rousseau, therefore, it is certainly possible that the repeated references to (and critiques of) the hierarchical model of forgiveness prevalent in his day arose out of his political thought more so than his views on religion and original sin. If this is the case, then we must look toward Rousseau's political philosophy to better understand the significance of the Frenchman's utterance when understood in terms of his eventual conversion. The Frenchman fully respects and approves of the Messieurs' authority, not only as critics and philosophers but, at least as far as J.-J. is concerned, as proxy legislators, magistrates, and sovereigns and as the arbiters of public opinion. It is therefore safe to assume that—at least in the *First Dialogue*—the Frenchman by and large ascribes to their philosophy and, we may assume, their understanding of forgiveness.[8]

The other problem with Alberg's interpretation is that the Frenchman has yet to meet or even read J.-J. at the time this phrase is uttered. His anger, therefore, is utterly depersonalized. The Frenchman does not despise J.-J. for having mounted a personal attack against him in his capacity as an individual. He despises J.-J. because he has been declared the enemy of the state on account of the crimes he allegedly committed. The Frenchman's anger ultimately stems from the fact that J.-J.—both as an individual and an author—presents a threat to French state, of which the Frenchman is the emphatic citizen that Rousseau idealized in *The Social Contract* and in his *Discourse on Political Economy*. The Frenchman has been imbued with the laws of the state and the maxims of the general will; he doesn't simply follow the laws—he loves them. He views the existence of the state as inextricably bound up with his own. Because of this, no moral hatred, no amount of rage, and no efforts to expel J.-J. from the fold can be seen as excessive when the threat of J.-J. becomes manifest, which is the case when Rousseau defends him. Faulty though the public's judgment may sometimes be, the Frenchman's vehement defense of it is and always shall be laudable so long as he continues to view his relationship to J.-J. as constituting one between a citizen and an enemy of the state (and not between two individuals).[9]

The portion of the *Dialogues* cited earlier cannot fully be understood unless one comprehends the magnitude of the gauntlet that the character Rousseau has thrown down in asking the Frenchman how he would react if he were to discover an upstanding man in J.-J. in place of the monster the Messieurs depict. Here, Rousseau essentially asks the Frenchman whether he would be willing to break rank and reject public opinion if he were to discover proof in J.-J.'s favor. The fact that the Frenchman responds by saying that his hatred for J.-J. would augment rather than diminish in such a scenario and that he would be incapable of forgiving J.-J. for having been the object of the Frenchman's own injustice shows just how desperately the citizen in him clings to his belief in the rectitude of public opinion. Morality, justice, and the law are always relative to the civic order in which they are practiced. It therefore follows that enemies are enemies, not in any absolute sense, but only relatively speaking. As an emphatic citizen, the Frenchman desires to maintain his faith in the well-constructed delusions on which public opinion rests, which allow him to easily distinguish between his enemies and his fellow citizens. The alternative to him is terrifying, as discovering the fallacy of J.-J.'s alleged crimes would destroy his confidence in the state that he loves and to which he has pledged his allegiance. It would reveal that the collective indignation in which he shares is unfounded. Worse still, it would expose the gulf that separates public opinion from the general will in the society in which he resides. Such a realization would force him to forge an alternate identity as an individual who viewed the state, the law, and what passes for the general will only instrumentally and in relation to his own selfish interests. He would no longer be the Frenchman but simply a man who happens to reside in France. He therefore maintains that his rage would be amplified at the discovery of J.-J.'s innocence, as J.-J. would have been the ultimate cause for his loss of faith in the sanctity of the state and the justice it practices.

This causes him shame on numerous levels. First and foremost, the Frenchman fancies himself a man who loves justice in his capacity as a citizen. To recognize that the justice of the state is not in accord with the very principles on which it is ostensibly based would threaten the legitimacy of the social contract. Second, and more important, the discovery of J.-J.'s innocence would place him in the awkward position of either challenging public opinion on the basis of it being composed of particular wills (the will of all) in the hopes of reforming or being forced to become complicit with injustice and therefore insincere in his role as a citizen. Because he claims that he would not forgive J.-J. his own injustice, we may assume that he believes he would take the latter route. In this way, the Frenchman is confronted with his own lack of courage: he is no worthy protector of the state after all. In refusing to forgive J.-J., even if he were found to be innocent after due process were satisfied, the Frenchman admits that he is potentially capable of following the faulty dictates of public opinion out of laziness, fear, and self-interest. Yes, even the Frenchman could look at his role as a citizen with disdain and nevertheless perform it most admirably. Yes, he would prefer to uphold the mere appearance of justice if it wins the public's approval than to challenge public opinion in the name of due process. Yes, he could turn a blind eye toward inequality. Yes, he could knowingly let his fellow citizens continue to be led astray by a band of usurpers. In addition to shame, this spawns in his heart a very personalized variety of anger: in the hypothetical scenario that Rousseau presents, J.-J.—granted, by no fault of his own—would bring to the fore and render excruciatingly palpable all the tensions between the individual and the citizen that reside in his heart. And that would be unforgivable.[10]

Robert Osmont notes that, in this moment of sincerity, the Frenchman gives voice to a truth of which Rousseau-as-author would only become more convinced with time, namely that a key component to injustice is the inability for socialized men to forgive others on account of amour propre's tendency to act as a barrier to reconciliation.[11] But when read in the context of other eighteenth-century discussions of forgiveness, we must see the Frenchman's admission not as a discovery on his part (or, for that matter, Rousseau's) but rather as adherence to what was another dominant tendency at the time. It is likely no accident that the phrase "I would never forgive him for my injustice toward him" (1:78-79; 1:761; je ne lui pardonnerois jamais mon injustice envers lui) and other phrases like it are dispersed throughout the work.[12] These statements are intended to recall to mind a widespread belief during the period, one that eventually found its way into the *Encyclopédie*'s entry for "PARDONNER," wherein Diderot claims of the detractors of the collaborative project that "we could have obtained from them forgiveness for a crime, but we could not obtain it for a good action" (11:933–34; Nous aurions obtenu d'eux le *pardon* d'un crime, nous n'en avons pû obtenir celui d'une bonne action). As discussed in chapter 1, Diderot bases this argument on the observation that "one must have much modesty, meticulousness, and art in order to wrest forgiveness from those to whom one is superior" (11:933–34; Il faut bien de la modestie, bien de l'attention, bien de l'art pour arracher aux autres le pardon de la supériorité qu'on a sur eux). For Diderot and many of Rousseau's contemporaries and intellectual precursors, the question as to who can forgive whom depends on who is recognized to be in a position of superiority—be it moral, intellectual, or tactical. Accordingly, to "wrest forgiveness" from another to whom one is superior by virtue of one's innocence, one must pretend to a position of inferiority to fool the other into a false sense of security.

Rousseau was not alone in realizing this but rather was simply reiterating a common belief at the time. Hobbes, for example, had also described in *The Leviathan* the disdain for the victim that arises in the malefactor's heart following a misdeed: "To have done more hurt to a man than he [the doer] can, or is willing to expiate, inclineth the doer to hate the sufferer. For he must expect revenge or forgiveness, both of which are hateful." As Edmund S. Morgan has observed, it was for similar reasons that Benjamin Franklin would claim that "Great Britain has injured us too much ever to forgive us." Morgan quotes Franklin as having said, "Even if it were possible for Americans to forget and forgive what the British had done to them, 'it is not possible for *you* (I mean the British nation) to forgive the People you have so heavily injured; you can never confide again in those as Fellow Subjects, and permit them to enjoy equal Freedom, to whom you know you have given such just Cause of Lasting Enmity.'"[13] For the Enlightenment thinker, the revelation of one's moral inferiority was an unbreachable obstacle to forgiveness, as requesting forgiveness constituted—by definition—the affirmation of a hierarchy.

Under such a model, if the Frenchman had been unjust to J.-J., then his former injustice would bear witness to the fact that he had fallen prey to the Messieurs' plot, had very limited knowledge of justice, and, worst of all, was in fact more of a slave than a citizen. Accordingly, the grounds on which he would be unable to forgive himself if J.-J. were innocent would be accompanied by the recognition that he had failed to live up to some ideal image of himself. Inferior now to the previous image of himself from which his own certitude in his judgment and moral worth and thus his capacity to forgive others had been grounded, he would no longer have any claim to a position of superiority from which forgiveness could be bestowed. Indeed, the very system by which superiority and inferiority, soldiers and enemies, are distinguished from one another would be revealed to be nothing other than arbitrary. The Frenchman would be left with incertitude in his own relative moral worth and the knowledge that his own, revised notion of justice conflicts with that which is being practiced. His complacency—if it were to continue—would render him no better than those who had devised the plot to begin with. Finally, it would render him inferior to J.-J., who, at the very least, had dared to challenge these usurpers. If the Frenchman conceives of forgiveness as being a top-down notion, he could never forgive J.-J. in a manner that he could articulate.

Appropriately, the character of Rousseau says he appreciates the Frenchman's frankness in admitting this. He highlights the fact that, in at least one respect, the Frenchman would not be utterly alienated from the society he calls his own in refusing to forgive J.-J.: "Moreover, console yourself about this disposition, which is merely one of the most natural developments of amour-propre. You share it with all judges of J. J., with the difference that you are perhaps the only one who has the courage and frankness to admit it" (1:79; 1:761; consolez-vous de cette disposition qui n'est qu'un development des plus naturels de l'amour-propre. Elle vous est commune avec tous les juges de J. J. avec cette différence que vous serez le seul peut-être qui ait le courage et la franchise de l'avouer). In what can perhaps best be described as a backhanded compliment, Rousseau notes that it is courageous to admit that one would lack the courage to stand up for justice in a hypothetical situation.

But even if, as mentioned earlier, the Frenchman is not here making a discovery about the necessity of amour propre being served by forgiveness rather than trumped by it, the Frenchman does add an interesting twist. In all the examples that we have discussed thus far, the act of forgiving has always been exteriorized. What is more, the perpetrator of the misdeed has always been the object of forgiveness. In the hypothetical scenario that Rousseau presents, the Frenchman claims that he would be both the perpetrator of the misdeed *and* the agent of forgiveness, which, again, he would refuse to bestow.[14] The Frenchman would be unable to forgive J.-J. for the Frenchman's injustice toward him. How can this be?

The answer to this question may very well reside in the split subject that is so central to Rousseau's political philosophy. In forging a strict division between the individual and the citizen, Rousseau was able to set up the neat distinction between exteriority, or a subject's socially determined role, which denies the idiosyncratic subject any individuated authority in the public sphere, and interiority or, a subject's true essence, which is accorded absolute authority in the private sphere. It was, of course, thanks to this very distinction, however tenuous, that Rousseau was able to conduct his protracted project of self-justification—a project that was explicitly apolitical—without undermining the political theory he had elaborated in *The Social Contract* and his *Encyclopédie* article "POLITICAL ECONOMY."[15] Jean Starobinski's *Jean-Jacques Rousseau: La transparence et l'obstacle* remains an authoritative text on this issue, as he notes that, within his autobiographical works, the judgment that Rousseau seeks is one that will not be made according to social norms or customs but rather one that will be made independently of, and even in direct opposition to, them. For Rousseau to engage in his project of self-justification in the way that he felt he needed to without overthrowing his political theory, such a distinction was vital.

In this sense, Rousseau deviated greatly from John Locke's views on public opinion. Whereas Locke cast that which ran counter to the law of public opinion in decidedly negative terms by referring to it as madness, Rousseau found an intrinsic value in those beliefs that were individualized and independent from social norms and customs, so long as they did not interfere with the duties of the citizen.[16] As Richard Sennett rather eloquently put it, Rousseau's system is founded on the apparently paradoxical belief that "political tyranny and the search for individual authenticity go hand in hand" insofar as the former isolates the latter from all social duties and obligations. Ironically, political tyranny therefore sets the individual free by closing one in on oneself.[17] Of all the tensions internal to Rousseau's work, the ramifications of such a view are what have most puzzled scholars, as it remains unclear what one is supposed to do when the demands of authenticity run counter to the demands of social utility and cultural norms.[18]

The Frenchman comes up against this problem head-on when he discovers in the *Third Dialogue* that J.-J. is indeed innocent. Ultimately, he is left with the choice of waging a noble war against public opinion that he is sure to lose and therefore practically guarantee his expulsion from society.[19] In such a scenario, he would therefore be reduced to being an ideal citizen for whom no existing state would correspond. Public opinion would designate him as an enemy, and the Frenchman would lose his claim to the very rights and privileges that he would be defending. He would not forgive J.-J. for his own injustice because the distinction between citizen and enemy would no longer hold between them. This is because the Frenchman, too, would be regarded to be as much of an Other to the citizens of France as J.-J. already is. From this it follows that the conceptual distinction that the Frenchman has always employed and, at the moment that these lines are uttered, still depends on in identifying and experiencing the social system to which he belongs would be lost. With it, the grounds by which he could recognize justice and crimes and, it follows, articulate either civic indignation or political forgiveness would dissolve.

Another option would be to maintain only his appearance as a citizen for personal gain and, in so doing, to remain complicit in a crime that undermines the very state to which he pledges allegiance. In this respect, he would be a bad citizen at heart, though his outside behavior would bare no trace of this.[20] Sensing, at least in the *First Dialogue*, that he would go with this option, the Frenchman claims that he would not forgive J.-J. for having been the ultimate source of his loss of faith in the judicial system and the people charged with upholding it and, it follows, his sincerity in his role as a citizen.[21] With such a perspective, he would not be able to forgive J.-J. on the grounds that he would no longer have a system by which good and evil, just and unjust, legal and illegal, could have any significance for him. On the upside the dissolution of the Frenchman's loss of faith in the pronouncements of justice would also entail the automatic dissolution of J.-J.'s (perceived) crime. On the downside, instead of being the Other that formerly had helped the Frenchman identify more firmly with his compatriots, J.-J. would now stand in as the force that alienated the Frenchman forever from the society from which his identity had previously been derived. Because the Frenchman claims that he would not forgive J.-J. at a moment where he still adheres most completely (if somewhat desperately) to his identity as an emphatic citizen, the hypothetical situation that Rousseau presents to him renders J.-J. unforgivable in his mind. This is because the situation Rousseau describes announces the possibility that the Frenchman could himself become an Other to the citizen he believes himself to be—in thought if not in deed. Because J.-J. would be the ultimate source and catalyst of the alienation (and identity crisis) that the Frenchman thinks is likely to ensue, J.-J. would remain forever unforgiven, even (especially) should he be found innocent.

A third option, but one that the Frenchman could not possibly be considering in the *First Dialogue*, as he has yet to read J.-J., consists in renouncing his identity as a citizen absolutely and in becoming an individual, wholly and completely. Much like the Savoyard vicar and, for that matter, J.-J., the Frenchman would be forced to live at the fringes of society. In such a scenario, he would lose the comforts of society and renounce all the rights and duties that being a citizen entails. On the upside, all his behavior would be in perfect accord with his individuated principles, tastes, and opinions. Because he could assume as his only identity his identity as an individual, the Frenchman would no longer have to base his own moral code on the cultural norms and laws of the state. He would be only an observer of the injustice against J.-J. but would no longer be one of its perpetrators. As far as his past actions toward J.-J. are concerned, he could then shift all the blame onto society itself and, much like a certain autobiographer we all know, he would have no need for forgiveness because his true self would be revealed to have always remained insulated from the misdeeds his social self performed.

Of course, in the end J.-J. is found to be innocent, and the text concludes by essentially cutting the baby in half (or, perhaps, more appropriately, in thirds). The Frenchman refuses to speak publicly on J.-J.'s behalf. This refusal—which he himself describes as a "confession"—is rooted in the knowledge that he, Rousseau, and J.-J. stand to gain little and lose everything in challenging public opinion. The Frenchman claims that, in accusing the Messieurs directly, he would run the risk of becoming a pariah and condemning himself and his family to ruin:

> That would be undertaking a step as imprudent as it would be useless, to which I don't want to expose myself. I have a status, friends to preserve, a family to support, patrons to satisfy. I don't want to play Don Quixote in this and fight the powers in order to be the center of attention for a moment and be lost for the rest of my life.
>
> (1:221–22; 1:946; see also 1:939; Je ferois en cela une démarche aussi imprudente qu'inutile à laquelle je ne veux point m'exposer. J'ai un état, des amis à conserver, une famille à soutenir, des patrons à ménager. Je ne veux point faire ici le Dom Quichotte et lutter contre les puissances pour faire un moment parler de moi et me perdre pour le reste de ma vie.)

On the other hand, the Frenchman is hardly ready to simply play along with the plot to destroy J.-J. out of self-interest. He therefore takes the resolution to no longer contribute to the myth regarding J.-J., as he shall no longer speak against his own convictions regarding J.-J.'s innocence. The Frenchman thereby resolves to be a conscientious objector in the war against J.-J. (1:945).

On the surface it appears as though—in so doing—the Frenchman renounces his identity as a citizen and therefore goes with something closely akin to option three, as outlined earlier. But a closer reading reveals that the Frenchman still maintains a certain, indissoluble loyalty to France, even as he leaves it to join J.-J. in his exile. Indeed, he resolves to continue to serve his country in some very important capacities. First, he expresses a desire to repair the wrongs that he committed against J.-J. in his role as a citizen (1:946). He thus wishes to assume the role of a messenger of sorts for the—now silenced—general will that he alone carries in his bosom.[22] Just as the Messieurs had stood in as proxies for the legislative, judicial, and executive bodies in condemning J.-J., the Frenchman will make the reparations on behalf of a corrupt but nevertheless innocent public.[23] In the Frenchman, who shall request it, J.-J. will have an object on whom he can bestow forgiveness for the evils that he has suffered. Thus, the citizenry—through the Frenchman— shall voice its love of justice and prove itself deserving of grace.

What is more, and it is here that we arrive at what will be his positive contribution to the people he calls his own, the Frenchman will ensure that J.-J.'s works are preserved for posterity. The Frenchman takes such a resolution because he is firmly convinced that it is impossible at present to alter public opinion in J.-J.'s favor. Nevertheless, he is optimistic that true justice will again direct public opinion at some point in the future. The Frenchman realizes that becoming the depository of J.-J.'s work is not without its dangers. But he also recognizes that it is the only means to guarantee that those works that J.-J. has composed but not yet published shall not be altered after his death in an effort to further propagate an unfavorable image of him. It is also the means by which the Frenchman ensures that truth and justice may someday circulate freely in the society he still loves in spite of itself. The Frenchman ends his part of the conversation with the following statement:

> I offer to share with you the risks of this trust, and I promise to spare no effort in order to have it appear someday for public viewing just as I received it, enlarged by all the observations I have been able to amass that tend to unveil the truth. That is all that prudence allows me to do for the sake of my conscience, for the interest of justice, and for the service of truth.
>
> (1:245; 1:975; Je m'offre à partager avec vous les risques de ce dépôt, et je m'engage à n'épargner aucun soin pour qu'il paroisse un jour aux yeux du public tel que je l'aurai receu, augmenté de toutes les

observations que j'aurai pu recueillir tendantes à dévoiler la vérité. Voilà tout ce que la prudence me permet de faire pour l'acquit de ma conscience, pour l'intérest de la justice, et pour le service de la vérité.)

With these words, the Frenchman declares his enduring allegiance to the general will by maintaining that he shall henceforth act in the service of justice. Because he claims that one day it will appear to the eyes of the public in all its glory, the justice of which he speaks is not a variety of personalized justice. It is, rather, one that will accord with the general will of the public when it reemerges from its slumber. At that point in time, the Frenchman will be the mouthpiece for J.-J.'s justified indignation. The fact that J.-J. has won the respect of the Frenchman, not on account of any personal inclinations or affections on the latter's part but rather on account of the fact that J.-J.'s "destiny is perhaps a unique example of all possible humiliations" (sa destinée est un exemple peut-être unique de toutes les humiliations possibles) in a corrupt system, serves as proof that the Frenchman sees J.-J. through the lens of *fraternité* more so than through that of love (215; 1:937). The Frenchman is thereby able to remain the Frenchman (as opposed to simply a man who resides in France) by freeing himself from the grips of a corrupt and corrupting plot and by conceiving of the general will as silenced, certainly, but by no means arbitrary.

This is not to say that the individual in the Frenchman does not also derive some satisfaction from such a resolution. In his final exchange with Rousseau, he invokes his conscience and thus the faculty that had miraculously survived in spite of the blindness into which public opinion had formerly led him. Conscience, and we shall speak more of this later, is that aspect of the individual that cannot be corrupted by amour propre and the clamor of society. It can only be silenced. As John Charvet has observed, conscience is a sentiment that is "awakened" once the good has been appropriately identified through reason. The conscience is less a continuing process of judging in particular circumstances than it is a change in perspective. Charvet notes that it is "a once-and-for-all development or reorientation of the individual towards a different conception of what is the good for him, a conception of his relation to the moral order, to which he is then held by the voice of conscience infallibly telling him when he is or is not living up to it."[24] The Frenchman's newly aroused conscience is satisfied by the resolution to preserve J.-J.'s work, as in taking it he commits himself to correcting the wrongs that he had carried out in his capacity as a citizen. After all, it was his conscience that, once awakened by Rousseau's argumentation, enabled him to undertake his careful study of J.-J.'s writings in the first place. In this regard, he voluntarily reimburses the debt he incurred as a citizen for his former injustice toward J.-J. But because he also resolves to act not only on behalf of himself and J.-J. but also on behalf of France and in the name of justice and the spirit of the laws, his conscience does not result in the creation of a new, personalized moral order.[25] He remains the Frenchman who waits in the wings for France to return to itself.

When read in the context of Rousseau's political philosophy, the *Dialogues* serve as a commentary on the capacity of anger to inspire law-abiding citizens to zealously defend the interests of the state. But just as the text explores the productive capacities of collective indignation when justified, it also offers a warning to those who would employ such a powerful tool. Collective indignation—once publicized—necessitates an objective review of the misdeed and of the victim's reaction to it. Such a review must neither take into account the particular interests of either party nor may it consider the rank, talents, or fame of either the victim or the perpetrator. Instead, in reviewing the crime one must maintain one's focus on the general will and the common good. Accordingly, the review of the crime must consider only the laws of the state, under which all citizens are equal. Because of this, once a judgment of guilty or innocence has been passed, the citizen-victim has no choice but to comply with the ruling. In publicizing one's anger one therefore abandons an exclusive claim to it.

As a result, the individual who publicizes his anger also renounces the right to forgive should the malefactor be found guilty. Like punishment, in such circumstances forgiveness must be granted in accord with the general will, and it must be bestowed by the sovereign. To do otherwise is to undermine the sanctity of the state, the generality of the law, and the very notion of justice, all of which render the social contract legitimate. By invoking what was his unjust condemnation, Rousseau-as-author holds his fate up as an example of how dangerous the philosophes have become on account of their ability to sway public opinion. He does so by highlighting how easily due process was cast aside in his case, both with regard to J.-J.'s condemnation and his subsequent and phony pardon. Forgiveness, like anger, should not be thrown around so easily, as it risks to alienate and to confuse all those who have internalized the collective indignation that the crime inspired. And, as we have seen, this is precisely what happens with the Frenchman.

The resolution of the Frenchman's conundrum does raise some very interesting questions about what Rousseau anticipated in the way of an affective response from his readers and how that response coincides (or not) with his political thought. On the one hand, in *The Social Contract* Rousseau suggests that the ideal citizen or, rather, the emphatic citizen must never be able to discern the gulf that oftentimes separates the general will from public opinion, and theory from praxis. As discussed earlier, he is also vehement in his belief that individuals must not feel at liberty to throw off the yoke of the law and of public censure, no matter how corrupt or misguided they may be revealed to be. The reaction of the Frenchman, however, suggests that there are instances where freeing oneself from social constraints and even acting in ways that undermine them can be laudable. If this is the case and the reader is supposed to sympathize and identify with the Frenchman's conundrum, then the text constitutes a drastic revision or all-out contradiction of what Rousseau actually wrote in his straightforwardly political texts. I do not pretend to be able to explain or resolve these tensions. I bring them to light simply because they demonstrate that there are very real ramifications to reading the *Dialogues* politically, ramifications of which Rousseau may have been more or less aware but that nevertheless reveal limitations and new possibilities within Rousseau's system.[26]

In many respects, the Frenchman's evolution foreshadows what Kant wrote in his famous essay, "What Is Enlightenment?" (1784). As Kant maintained, "Enlightenment is man's release from his self-incurred tutelage," tutelage that prevents him from making "use of his understanding without direction from another." But, as Kant is quick to point out, enlightenment is not something that can be achieved without both "resolution and courage." Leaving the state of ignorance and the comfort that is to be found there is, as Kant observed, a terrifying endeavor indeed. What is more, and this may be a way to at least partially resolve some of the tensions between the *Dialogues* and the rest of Rousseau's political philosophy, it is not something that can quickly be attained by the populace. Kant's speaks of "independent thinkers" who "after throwing off the yoke of tutelage from their own shoulders" (slowly) disseminate the "spirit of the rational appreciation of both their own worth and every man's vocation of thinking for himself."[27]

The Frenchman, with his resolution to wait in the wings until the timing is right before revealing the truth to the public, certainly seems to adhere to this ideal of thinking for oneself and the notion of gradual and cautious progress among the masses. Again, within Rousseau's political philosophy, it is explicitly prohibited that such freethinking occur among the masses wherever political or juridical matters are concerned. Furthermore, he is adamant about the fact that, wherever the public good is concerned, individuals do not have the right to act in ways that run perpendicular to the law, public opinion, or whatever it is that is masquerading as justice. But one cannot help but notice that the ending of the *Dialogues* allows for the possibility that, in certain circumstances, individual civilians have not only the right but the duty to buck the system, and in essence it anticipates Kant's ideal of Enlightenment (and all the risks that such Enlightenment entails).[28] The *Dialogues*, I suggest, therefore complicate the distinction between the man and the citizen and the respective rights and duties of each that Rousseau so cautiously forged over the course of his career. In this sense the text is, as James F. Jones so eloquently put it, an example of how the Rousseauvean self must constantly redefine itself to exist within the social milieu. As Jones observes, "perhaps the ultimate truth of the *Dialogues* is that there is no truth to be perceived, that the truth of the self is always a fiction, always in need of being endlessly created."[29] Indeed, the ending of the *Dialogues* certainly leaves the reader with the sense that the resolution that the Frenchman makes at the conclusion of the text is just the beginning of what will be an ongoing struggle to reconcile the demands of his bifurcated existence, and it is yet another example within Rousseau's corpus of an ending that is, in essence, a nonending.[30]

Another issue with which we must contend is that the *Dialogues* do not address what should be done in instances where violations of the law lead to anger that is unworthy of being publicized. Surely, Rousseau is not recommending that the citizen's anger—even when depersonalized and justifiably awakened—need always be publicized. After all, part of living in society entails accepting that minor violations of the law, of custom, of politesse, and of bienséance arise on a fairly regular basis. As discussed earlier, the response of many of Rousseau's contemporaries to this reality was to cast the anger of the average individual as an immediate and rather base physiological reaction that could be contained and, in some cases, eliminated by invoking the deleterious effects of pursuing vengeance. To varying degrees, therefore, they capitalized on self-interest to make a case for forgiveness.

As we have already seen, Rousseau had quite a different assessment indeed. Whereas he believed that in an ideal state the opportunity for slight would be reduced significantly and thus the occasions for anger less frequent, he did not believe that it was possible or recommendable to delegitimize anger entirely. Even he realized that citizens who are always encouraged to suppress their anger cannot be expected to adopt a soldier's mentality during times of war or, for that matter, in the wake of crimes against the state. This is, again, because collective indignation toward the enemy is what enables the citizen to overcome any pity the citizen may feel when pondering the pending destruction of the enemy or the punishment of the guilty party. Disdain directed toward potential enemies is, moreover, an important element of group formation, as patriotism can exist only with a clearly defined Other that is perceived as outside the system and, for that reason alone, regarded as inferior.

Unfortunately, the *Dialogues* do not address the question of if and when anger can be justified and subsequently resolved in instances wherein there is no recourse to either the law or public opinion. A brief look to *Émile*, however, offers a glimpse as to what Rousseau's views may be on this. Alberg draws our attention to a scene in book 2, wherein Émile learns just how it easy and, indeed, inevitable it is—through ignorance or, we may assume, bad intentions of one variety or another—for an individual to violate the social order.

The scene of which I speak is that which describes how Émile was first exposed to the notion of property and, more specifically, his interactions with the gardener whose melon seeds Émile had unknowingly plowed up to plant some beans on the same plot of land. After weeks of cultivating the land and seeing his bean sprouts emerge, Émile begins to understand the Lockean notion of property by which investing one's labor in a piece of land transforms it into one's personal property. When Émile returns one day only to find his sprouts torn up, he is justifiably angry: "This young heart is aroused. The first sentiment of injustice comes to shed its sad bitterness in it. Tears flow in streams. The grieving child fills the air with moans and cries. I partake of his pain, his indignation" (13:232; 4:331; Ce jeune coeur se soulève; le premier sentiment de l'injustice y vient verser sa triste amertume. Les larmes coulent en ruisseaux; l'enfant desolé remplit l'air de gémissemens et de cris. On prend part à sa peine, à son indignation). So it is that the notions of justice and of due process enter Émile's consciousness and indignation into his heart.

But Émile is not left to relish in his indignation for very long. After some investigation, it is discovered that it was in fact Émile who had initially violated the gardener's rights in plowing up the latter's rare Maltese melon seeds. This property had been worked by Robert's family for generations. It was vested with the labor of his ancestors. To add insult to injury, Robert, the gardener, had the intention of sharing these melons with Émile once they had ripened. The situation is resolved when Robert grants Émile the right to use a small corner of his property on the condition that Émile promise never to ruin his work again.

Alberg correctly points out that, for Rousseau, the insertion of an individual into the moral world requires knowledge of justice and that "the first sentiment of justice that a person develops is a feeling of what is owed to him or his rights." The tutor therefore recognizes that the notion of property—because it is tangible and clearly delineated—is an excellent means of welcoming Émile into the world of rights and duties. And the lesson is duly learned. As Alberg notes, there is a reason that Rousseau "begs" the reader to pay particular attention to the gardener affair, as its pedagogical attributes are numerous and vast: "The story ends with Émile learning about injustice by both experiencing violation and then realizing that he is already guilty of the same violation," writes Alberg. "With the injury received comes knowledge of the injury given. . . . Such is the world that Émile is being raised to inhabit. . . . The child awakes to the moral world as a guilty person."[31]

For our purposes, what is particularly instructive about this example is that it demonstrates how due process can and at times must be practiced privately. Due process is cast within the text as applying not only to the public sphere but also to the private, interpersonal sphere in certain types of scenarios (i.e., those in which civic virtues or laws are violated), and this is a big part of what Jean-Jacques tries to impart to his pupil. It is therefore telling that, initially, the tutor and Émile act like police; they "investigate" (on fait des perquisitions) and discover the culprit, then summon him (13:232; 4:331; on le fait venir). They hear the gardener out, and then they deliver the verdict: Émile, not the gardener, was in fact guilty.[32] Jean-Jacques immediately offers to make reparations on behalf of both himself and Émile by having new melon seeds imported. Alberg concludes from this scene and another that he analyzes in some detail that, in *Émile*, "there is reconciliation without forgiveness."[33] This reading is, of course, itself derivative of Alberg's larger argument that Rousseau had no thoroughgoing notion of forgiveness because he had denied the legitimacy of original sin and therefore absolution within a Christian context.

But if we consider just how broad the semantic field was with regard to the word "pardon" in the eighteenth century and, moreover, the frequency with which it was used interchangeably with other words, such as "clemency," "grâce" and "tolerance," it becomes difficult to make such a blanket statement. The affirmation of hierarchies and, secondarily, the invocation of social utility were very often cited as the motivating factors behind forgiveness, and Christianity was rather far from having a monopoly on the concept.

Further, because for Rousseau righteous indignation can arise only on account of the violation of laws, it necessarily follows that the remedy for such anger must be characterized by the satisfaction of human (and not divine) justice in the form of punishment or, in instances where it will not run counter to the common good, of forgiveness. Because Robert and Émile's reconciliation is carried out in accordance with standards of justice, it appears as though what occurs can indeed be regarded as constituting a—albeit modified—form of forgiveness by the eighteenth-century reader.

Again, upon discovering the truth of what actually occurred, the tutor offers to import new melon seeds for Robert. Admittedly, Robert does not respond either positively or negatively to Jean-Jacques's offer to import new melon seeds, so it remains unclear whether he accepts reparations. One thing is certain, however: the offer does not succeed in placating Robert, as Robert wants some sort of assurance that this will never happen again. The tutor then requests that his pupil be granted a small corner of the property where he may cultivate his beans, provided he reimburse Robert for the use of the land.

> Couldn't we propose an arrangement with the good Robert? Let him grant us, my little friend and me, a corner of his garden to cultivate on the condition that he will have half the produce.

> (13:233; 4:332; Ne pourroit-on proposer un arrangement au bon Robert? Qu'il nous accorde, à mon petit ami et à moi un coin de son jardin pour le cultiver, à condition qu'il uara la moitié du produit.)

The irony of the proposed arrangement, of course, is that Robert is most likely employed by Émile's father. Thus, what the tutor ultimately proposes is that the child become the tenant farmer of his own gardener.

What is fascinating, though often overlooked, is that Robert *refuses* this arrangement and instead grants the land to Émile without accepting anything in return: "I grant it to you *without condition*" (13:233; 4:332; Je vous l'accorde *sans condition*; italics mine).[34] It is the pedagogical significance of Robert's refusal to accept anything in return that is particularly relevant. Because all incidents described in *Émile* are premeditated and are designed to bestow on the pupil life-enduring lessons from the child's own experiences, it is fairly safe to assume that Robert was to a large extent in on the ruse. Whatever the case, in granting the corner of the property to Émile, Robert does demonstrate that he has forgiven him in two important respects. First,

Robert does not publicize his anger and his rightful complaint against Émile and the tutor, which he would be sure to have ratified in any court of law (or at least in the court of public opinion). One could make the argument that Robert therefore undermines justice and the common good by not giving due credence to the importance of property in forgiving in an instance where punishment, or at least seeking reparations, would have been more appropriate. Of course, the offender is a child and the magnitude of the "crime" quite small, so one can chalk his decision not to assert his rights in a court of law to mere pragmatism and common sense. Again, in actuality, all the land belongs to Émile's family anyway.

But Robert's dealings with Émile do not end there. And we must be mindful to distinguish between the actual state of affairs and Émile's perception of these events, as the lesson is to be found not in what actually is but in *how* Émile interprets what he is exposed to. Robert *gives* a small piece of land to Émile when the latter laments the fact that he does not have a garden. This gesture is extremely significant for our purposes. Whereas initially Robert acts unmoved by Émile's complaint, he quickly realizes that the best way to ensure the sanctity of his melons is to let Émile cultivate beans, lest Émile grow to resent the social contract with which he has just become acquainted and in so doing become an enemy of the state.[35] Robert thus forgives Émile and renounces both his claim against him and a portion of his land in the interest of the greater good. It is better to create citizens than enemies. It is better for men to give their assent through freedom rather than by force. It is best for men to love the law and the rights and obligations it establishes rather than resent them. This scenario is what makes Émile capable of internalizing the law of property as a sacred inviolable pact that defends the common interest and, by extension, his own personal interests. In allowing Émile to enjoy property and thus to have certain rights and certain claims in their interpersonal relationship that were previously lacking, Robert expresses his desire to relate to Émile not as an Other, not as an individual or friend, but rather as a fellow citizen. It is precisely for this reason that he refuses to accept half of Émile's harvest: to do so would be to undermine the very conditions of the equality that Robert's bestowal of the land has newly established. In this respect, Rousseau picks up on a theme outlined in his political works:

> All civil rights being founded upon property, as soon as the latter is abolished no other can subsist. Justice would be but a chimera, and

government a tyranny, and public authority lacking a legitimate foundation; no one would be obliged to recognize it except to the extent by which he was constrained to do so by force.

(Tous les droits civiles étant fondés sur celui de propriété, sitôt que ce dernier est aboli aucun autre ne peut subsister. La justice ne seroit plus qu'une chimère, et le gouvernement qu'une tyrannie, et l'autorité publique n'ayant aucun fondement légitime, nul ne seroit tenu de la reconnoitre, sinon en tant qu'il y seroit constraint par la force.)[36]

Émile must be able to feel that he has an absolute right to the beans he cultivates if he is to abide by the law that defends them. He must own his beans outright if he is to consider himself a participant in civic virtue. Similarly, if he is to understand that Robert too has rights and claims against him in their mini civil society, he cannot know that, in fact, the land actually belongs to his family in its entirety, for such a realization would render Robert's rights ridiculous in Émile's eyes. As Coleman notes, "Property not only restrains others from seizing what is mine, it also, and perhaps primarily, acts as a curb on my aggressive activity."[37]

As was the case in the *Dialogues*, one of the lessons that the gardener episode imparts to Émile is that, among citizens qua citizens, the resolution of anger must always be practiced in connection with and in support of justice. And it must be resolved in the interest of the common good under which all citizens are equal. It cannot just be doled out on account of whims, the desire to master others, or with the objective of forcing the perpetrator of a misdeed to incur a debt toward the victim. What is striking about this particular example is that it shows that forgiveness can be employed as an effective means of integrating those who, at the time of their misdeed, had seen themselves as existing outside the social contract, as was the case with Émile on account of his ignorance of it. The renunciation of anger of this variety is the means by which citizens can both renew and recreate the ties that bind them to one another. It is also the means by which prospective members of a community can gain admittance.

What remains to be seen is how forgiveness and anger function in relationships constituted by individuals relating to one another as such. This is the task to which I now turn.

PART 2

Private, Interpersonal Forgiveness

The Rousseauvean Intervention

For there is no man, that imparteth his joys to his friend, but he joyeth the more;
and no man that imparteth his griefs to his friend, but he grieveth less. . . .
A man cannot speak to his son but as a father; to his wife but as a husband;
to his enemy but upon terms: whereas a friend may speak as the case requires,
and not as it sorteth with the person. But to enumerate these things were endless;
I have given the rule, where a man cannot fitly play his own part;
if he have not a friend, he may quit the stage.
—FRANCIS BACON, "Of Friendship"

Le bonheur n'est pour vous ni sur la même route ni de la même espèce que celui
des autres hommes: ils ne cherchent que la puissance et les regards d'autrui;
il ne vous faut que la tendresse et la paix.
—ROUSSEAU, *Julie*

If, for the Rousseauvean citizen, legitimate anger was a decisively political passion that could be experienced only when conceiving of oneself within specific types of social relations wherein generalized laws of reciprocity and of rights and duties obtain, then we are left to ponder if and how anger was experienced by individuals relating to one another as such.

As argued in part I, the citizen's anger—be it of the more petty or righteous variety—becomes laudable only at the moment at which it references a generalized code of conduct and is publicized, and subsequently recognized and legitimized, by a third party. What this means is that, according to Rousseau, agents in the throes of anger reasonably expect that the emotion will be recognized by exterior observers as legitimate, provided that the emotion is aroused on account of the violation of certain social codes of conduct and, further, expressed in a manner appropriately depersonalized. As a result, the citizen's deliberations concerning the appropriateness of forgiveness for any particular malefactor in response to any specific misdeed can neither take into account extenuating circumstances (that is the job of the magistrate) nor pay much heed to said malefactor's remorse or lack thereof. Instead, for the emphatic citizen, the decision as to whether or not to renounce anger and forgive must rely solely on the degree to which a particular misdeed threatens the sanctity of the state's laws and mores and the extent to which any particular instantiation of forgiveness can be expected to serve to either reaffirm or undermine the (perceived) general will. Even when considering the bestowal of grace, we recall, the sovereign is not called on to contemplate the emotions and sentiments of the malefactor but rather is obliged to focus wholly on the needs of the larger community and the message that the bestowal of grace is likely to send to the general populace with regard to the sanctity and immutability of the law. Both anger and forgiveness as experienced by the citizen-acting-as-such are thus related primarily to a sphere of legality and only secondarily and potentially to morality in any absolute or transcendental sense within Rousseau's political thought.[1] It is for precisely this reason that, once anger is publicized, its resolution—be it in the form of either forgiveness or punishment—can and indeed must be ratified by public opinion and enacted in accord with the law and the general will. Such is the understanding of anger that emerges from Rousseau's works, such as his *Social Contract* and *Discourse on Inequality*, that deal explicitly with how human, moral impulse should function within the political social realm. With such an understanding of anger in place, punishment and, most important for our purposes, forgiveness are in essence political solutions to what is at base a political problem, hence the Frenchman's predicament in *Rousseau, Judge of Jean-Jacques*.

In Rousseau's literary and philosophical imagination, however, just as a person enjoys certain freedoms in one's capacity as an individual that one does not in one's capacity as a citizen, relationships characterized by love and true friendship are free of many of the constraints that apply to other, more politicized social relationships.[2] This is largely because sincere, intimate relationships and, in particular, friendships consist in adopting (and sharing) a particular perspective that neither calls for nor tolerates the mediation of either a third party nor pays much heed to social norms. It is for this reason that, as Thomas M. Kavanagh has noted, "true friendship" exists for Rousseau "outside any law of reciprocity, any even implicit *do ut des* dictating that each party remain either a creditor or a debtor in his relation as something else." The result is that "the discovery of the true friend is the election of an imaginary double in whom the self encounters the most

PRIVATE, INTERPERSONAL FORGIVENESS   105

profound sense of its own identity." For Rousseau, as Kavanagh concludes, "true friendship . . . had to be nothing less than a beatific transfixion of mutually elected doubles."[3] Because true friendship functions independently of accepted social norms, it is not subject to the same rules of social decorum, bienséance, and concerns for rank that define the social sphere, as are other types of relationships. It remains to be seen if and how such a view may have influenced Rousseau's views on how conflict could be resolved among friends, which is the task to which we shall now turn.

Given Rousseau's peculiar understandings of both friendship and anger, it would seem that, for him, the appearance of anger in private, interpersonal relationships—at least as it was popularly defined at the time—must either be a logical impossibility or, at the very least, serve as proof that the relationship is itself insincere. What is more, it must also signify that the means of articulating anger to outside observers are essentially obliterated wherever genuine friendship is concerned. This is because, by their very nature, such relationships fly in the face of any generalized code of conduct that is enforceable by a third party. As a result, no one from outside an intimate relationship could be called on to ratify whether any anger that may be expressed in the wake of a perceived or actual personal slight constituted a violation of the peculiar obligations and expectations that define said relationship. From this it follows that not only the acknowledgment and legitimization but even the mere perception of anger's resolution by a third party is utterly forestalled wherever friendship is concerned. Given that the overwhelming tendency of Rousseau's philosophical interlocutors was to cast forgiveness and, for that matter, anger as responses that had political significance and thus required the approbation of a third party if they were to be regarded as legitimate, it would seem that forgiveness within authentic intimate, interpersonal relationships must not occur with any degree of frequency or, at least, visibility within Rousseau's thought that would merit prolonged discussion.

Yet Rousseau's autobiographical and literary works reveal that he did indeed believe that forgiveness of a certain kind was an indispensable (if rare) component to private, interpersonal relationships. Within his oeuvre we find numerous examples where forgiveness is both requested and bestowed (and, yes, rejected) following personal slight within the context of love relationships and friendship. In these instances forgiveness is presented in a manner that is not only emotive but also fundamentally apolitical. The task before us, then, is to outline the constituent processes of such forgiveness and elucidate the significance that the action entails when practiced among individuals relating to one another as such.

I want to suggest that, for Rousseau, anger as experienced by individuals relating to one another as individuals was processed, articulated, and resolved much differently than it was for the citizen qua citizen, and this is true within both the public and political realms. Accordingly, Rousseau's understanding of forgiveness as practiced within private, interpersonal relationships evidences a dramatic break with other secular accounts of forgiveness that circulated in his day. For this reason he can be credited with having anticipated and, arguably, laid much of the conceptual groundwork for more contemporary accounts of forgiveness insofar as he distinguished between a political variety of forgiveness that entailed broader social and often legal significance on the one hand and, on the other, a more intimate and eminently personalized variety that attended to and arose from the emotions of the individuals involved.

There is one instance in the *Confessions*, which I discuss in detail, wherein personalized forgiveness and anger are contrasted to the more political varieties as outlined in the preceding chapters. It is Rousseau's reconciliation with Jean Francois de Saint-Lambert and Sophie d'Houdetot, an event that is itself juxtaposed with the (failed) reconciliation between Rousseau and Madame d'Epinay, Diderot, Grimm, and others. When read in the context of literary representations of personalized (as opposed to politicized) forgiveness within *Julie* and *Émile and Sophie*, this particular episode reveals that Rousseau envisaged a variety of interpersonal forgiveness that could be practiced within the confines of the intimate realm. Further, when felicitous, such forgiveness entails an emotional reorientation on the part of the agent vis-à-vis the perpetrator in a way that the more politicized variety did not.

Before I begin, it is worth stating explicitly that one of the primary aims of the following analysis is to problematize the widespread view that Rousseau's thoughts on forgiveness within interpersonal relationships were limited only to transferring misdeeds into a realm of nonculpability by means of pointing to the corrupting influences of the social order. Whereas such an observation certainly holds for much of Rousseau's autobiographical project, it does not do justice fully to the dialectical nature of Rousseauvean forgiveness as exchanged within the private, interpersonal relationships he describes. Further, such an interpretation does not accord due credence to just how dramatic Rousseau's intervention in the development of secular notions of forgiveness really was. It is this dialectic and its broader significance in the history of ideas that is the focus of what follows.

5

SAINT-LAMBERT'S AND ROUSSEAU'S
MIRACULOUS RECONCILIATION

On account of the exculpatory nature of the *Confessions* it is often assumed that Rousseau was largely indifferent—if not hostile—toward forgiveness when applied to his own person.[1] From the very beginning of the *Confessions* it is clear that Rousseau is undertaking the laborious task of recounting the minute details of his past to set himself not so much apart from his would-be moral peers but rather above them and thus beyond the reach of their moral judgment. Although ostensibly addressed to God, Rousseau is explicit about his desire to be seen as he truly is, not by God but by his fellow man, and judged fairly (and favorably) by them: "Let each of them in his turn uncover his heart at the foot of thy throne with the same sincerity; and then let a single one say to Thee, if he dares: '*I was better than that man*'" (1:5; Que chacun d'eux découvre à son tour son coeur aux pieds de ton trône avec la même sincérité; et puis qu'un seul te dise, s'il l'ose: *je fus meilleur que cet homme-là*).[2] That God knows the truth, senses the depth of Jean-Jacques's remorse, and recognizes his good character is, of course, a foregone conclusion for Rousseau, hence his relative indifference toward divine forgiveness.[3] But just as quickly as Rousseau extends an invitation to the yet-to-be-born ideal reader to determine the quality of his moral character in relation to others, he essentially rescinds it. To judge Jean-Jacques, one must be able to speak with the same sincerity and candor that he has. For this to happen, one must correctly determine the significance of every experience in one's life, no matter how seemingly insignificant. One must also be willing to examine, describe, and reveal the most shameful actions of one's life and in turn allow one's own conscience to judge the ethical significance of one's moral failings. This must all be done freely and without the influence of self-interest. Only then will any reader be able to claim with credibility that he has "show[n his] fellows a man in all the truth of nature" (montrer à mes semblables un homme dans toute la vérité de la nature) and thus be able to adequately determine whether he was a better man than Rousseau (5:5; 1:5).

It is Rousseau's pursuit of self-knowledge both in spite of and because of his awareness of individual repression and of the history of a universal instinctual repression within society that has, for so many scholars, established him as the precursor to psychoanalysis par excellence.[4] Regardless of one's own appraisal of psychoanalysis and its applicability to Rousseau's project of self-vindication (I myself am dubious), it is hard to deny that he was the first to so tirelessly interrogate and commit to paper the secrets of his personal motives, character, behaviors, and, most important, his sentiments with such racking candor. And, unlike his predecessors and contemporaries who took utter self-transparency somewhat for granted as being easily attainable, Rousseau maintained that the self was notoriously elusive. Uncovering one's true self was, for him, a daunting task indeed. As Margaret Ogrodnick observes, "[Rousseau's] autobiographies represent an unprecedented attempt to painstakingly retrieve and reveal the hidden self. He apprehends self-understanding as a travail to accommodate contradictory character traits and actions inconsistent with what he believes of himself."[5]

Rousseau presents the task of acquiring such thorough self-knowledge as essentially Herculean. Who could withstand such a severe review of one's most vulnerable, humiliating, and shameful moments? Who else could muster the courage to put such a confession out into the world in the form of the written word? From a strictly pragmatic standpoint, who could find the time? It is for precisely this reason that Rousseau opens the *Confessions* with the proclamation that he has embarked on a project that is both without a previous example and will never be imitated: "I am forming an undertaking which has no precedent, and the execution of which will have no imitator whatsoever" (5:5; 1:5; Je forme une entreprise qui n'eut jamais d'exemple, et dont l'exécution n'aura point d'imitateur). A large part of the identity that Rousseau's autobiography constructs consists in his tireless commitment to revealing the truth of what occurred in his life and in articulating the generative forces behind his intentions, actions, and sentiments. In this way Rousseau preemptively deflects any accusations that may be leveled against him. He does so on the basis that self-justification is to be found in self-accusation, an approach that was itself both a response and a challenge to the cool rationality demonstrated by his fellow philosophes and what he viewed as their overconfidence in their own abilities to adequately judge the worth of other men.

As the narrative of the *Confessions* progresses, Rousseau quickly announces that—notwithstanding his wholesome, early upbringing and his natural sensitivities— there is a strict disjunction between what he had done in his lifetime and who he knew himself to be.[6] And it is here where a problem arose: how can one's enduring innocence be asserted when the events that have made up one's existence contradict even the most liberal of moral standards and, moreover, were pernicious to others? Further, how can one exemplify the perfect unity of desire and principle and yet be so often led astray? The internal logic of the *Confessions* revolves around resolving these contradictions, which—Rousseau repeatedly assures us—are merely apparent.[7] One of the primary aims of the *Confessions* and one of the text's most impressive feats is that the author utilizes a form of logic that simultaneously establishes both his status as a victim and as that of a moral subject of the highest caliber whose freedom had miraculously never been compromised.

Jean Starobinski's *Jean-Jacques Rousseau: La transparence et l'obstacle* remains one of more the enduring articulations of just how Rousseau went about resolving this tension within his autobiographical works by erecting a distinction between interiority (who he truly was) and exteriority (what he did within the social milieu and how he was perceived by others). Rousseau's solution to this predicament is by now well known: Man is by nature good. Evil is produced by history and society. It consists in adhering to the requirements of decorum, in constantly reflecting on our own rank in relation to others, in pretending to be other than one truly is, and in stifling the voices of compassion and conscience. For Rousseau, however, the true essence of the individual remains intact even in face of such evil, though it is only rarely recovered and, even more rarely, given the opportunity to manifest itself through action.[8] The ultimate goal of the *Confessions* is thus to purge Rousseau's life of the evil actions he performed by means of committing his authentic self to paper. In so doing he stresses the disjunction between the actions he undertook and the feelings he had experienced (and still experiences) on account of them. Ultimately, after detailing the external pressures that caused him to act in the ways that he did, Rousseau is finally able to place the blame for his misdeeds squarely on the shoulders of society. As Starobinski notes,

The spontaneous fidelity that links expressive language to emotion ensures the truthfulness of everything else; the immediate truth of language guarantees the truth of past experience such as it was lived. Retrospectively, language propagates its purity, its innocence, its evidence. The lies and vices of Jean-Jacques's life are absorbed and purified by the immediate transparency of the confession.

(Par surcroit, cette fidélité spontanée qui lie la parole à l'émotion sert de garant à tout le reste: la vérité immediate du langage garantit la vérité du passé tel qu'il a été vécu. Elle propage rétrospectivement sa propre pureté, son innocence, son évidence. Tout ce qui, dans la vie de Jean-Jacques, fut mensonge ou vice se résorbe et se purifie dans la transparence de la confession.)[9]

In the *Confessions* Rousseau thus repeatedly underscores the conflicts that arose over the course of his life between his true feelings and beliefs, on the one hand, and societal demands, expectations, and prejudices on the other. From this was born Rousseau's "great maxim of morality" (grande maxime de morale):

to avoid situations that put our duties in opposition with our interests, and which show us our good in the harm of someone else: certain that whatever sincere love of virtue one brings to such situations, sooner or later one weakens . . . and one becomes unjust and bad in fact, without having ceased to be just and good in the soul.

(5:47; 1:56; d'éviter les situations qui mettent nos devoirs en opposition avec nos intérets, et qui nous montrent nôtre bien dans le mal d'autrui: sûr que dans de telles situations, quelque sincére amour de la vertu qu'on y porte, on foiblit tôt ou tard . . . et l'on devient injuste et méchant dans le fait, sans avoir cessé d'être juste et bon dans l'âme.)

In Rousseau's mind, his greatest achievement was that he alone had recovered his true essence and was in turn able to—no, *forced* to—lead an authentic existence. He had overcome the scandal of deceit and freed himself from perverse illusions. Whereas his contemporaries had always strove for obstruction in the form of well-constructed societal delusions, Rousseau had always strove for transparency in the form of self-knowledge.[10] What is more, he did not ignore the pangs of his guilty conscience for his failings but rather embraced them as the proof of his inherent goodness. Reinhart Koselleck states Rousseau's aims in this regard quite well when he writes that his *"Confessions* are the first modern 'confessions' in which shameless revelation turns truth into lies and make it impossible to tell truth from falsehood."[11] In the *Confessions* Rousseau essentially undermines the premises on which a condemnation of his character could be considered sound. In so doing, he moves himself beyond the realm of judgment and, or so it would seem, forgiveness. On this point Rousseau is unequivocal, for anyone who refuses to acknowledge Rousseau's candor, sincerity, and the enduring innocence and purity from which they spring forth is a man who, as Rousseau put it, is "fit to be stifled" (5:550; 1:656; un homme à étouffer).

The exculpatory nature of the text being what it is, it is tempting to end one's analysis of forgiveness in the *Confessions* right here, and indeed many have. This is doubly true if we accept Starobinski's claim that Rousseau's great failure was that he failed to confront the Other: "He was the first to live in a manner that exemplified the dangerous pact between the ego and language, that 'new alliance' in which man renders himself the Word incarnate" (Il a été le premier à vivre d'une façon exemplaire le dangereux pacte du moi avec le langage: la "nouvelle alliance" dans laquelle l'homme se fut verbe).[12] In avoiding an encounter with the Other in which he could have understood both the world and his place in it, Rousseau lost touch with the world that could have provided a mirror for his true self, or so it is often assumed. He in turn was incapable of cultivating a perspective that would have permitted the Other to figure into his ethical outlook.

Yet even with such a structure in place, some questions remain. First, is all discussion of forgiveness within the *Confessions* truly exhausted in the exculpatory and isolating nature of the text? Further, does Rousseau always succeed in resolving his misdeeds—perceived or actual—in a sphere of utter interiority, or are there moments where he suggests that a dialectic with another individual is instrumental to overcoming his past failings? Admittedly, the moments in the text wherein Rousseau admits culpability and thus the possibility that he could be or had been forgiven for anything are the exception more so than the norm. Be that as it may, at least one of these moments does exist within the *Confessions*, and it merits sustained analysis. This is doubly true if, following Christopher Kelly, we read Rousseau's *Confessions* as a series of moral fables that seek to foster imitation and reform the world by providing an immediate effect on the feelings of the lay reader and a delayed effect on the more contemplative mind of the philosopher through the presentation of less perfectly moral examples with which corrupt civilized humans can hope to identify and in turn mimic.[13] The story of Rousseau's reconciliation with Saint-Lambert and Sophie d'Houdetot is one such story, an example of how paradigmatic forgiveness can and should be exchanged and enjoyed among true friends.

Rousseau's relationship with both Saint-Lambert and Sophie d'Houdetot is recounted in books 9 and 10 of the *Confessions*. This particular series of events constitutes one of the rare occasions within the text wherein Rousseau casts himself as an individual who had, at least once in his life, genuinely participated in a felicitous bestowal of forgiveness. An analysis thereof elucidates how anger is experienced in intimate, interpersonal relationships and how it may resolved in a manner consistent with Rousseau's system within his autobiographical works.

The story is as follows: Sophie, though not beautiful in the classic sense and technically married, embodied the natural virtues and sincerity that Rousseau so respected and admired and to which he had paid homage when he created both the heroine of *Julie* and Sophie of *Émile*. Sophie d'Houdetot's purity and unaffectedness, coupled with her immunity toward the sentiment of hatred and her laudable indifference toward the approval of polite society, quickly won over Rousseau's heart (1:439). Saint-Lambert, Sophie's lover, confidant, and friend, was an agreeable man with talent, virtue, and wit (1:440). Upstanding and wise beyond his years, Saint-Lambert was greatly admired by Rousseau; he in turn respected and adored Rousseau. The three became fast friends. According to Rousseau, so eager was Saint-Lambert to establish an amicable "society of three" that existed in perfect friendship that he exhorted Sophie to spend more time with Rousseau.[14] Quickly, and by no fault of his own, Rousseau fell for Sophie: "She came, I saw her, I was intoxicated with love without an object, that intoxication fascinated my eyes, that object became fixed on her, I saw my Julie in Mme d'Houdetot, and soon I no longer saw anything but Mme d'Houdetot" (5:370; 1:440; Elle vint, je la vis, j'étois ivre d'amour sans objet, cette ivresse fascina mes yeux, cet objet se fixa sur elle, je vis ma Julie en Madame d'Houdetot, et bientôt je ne vis plus que Madame d'Houdetot). Rousseau claims that he had fought against his passion with everything that he possessed. Unfortunately, his morals, his shame, and his great respect and affection for Saint-Lambert were no match for such a passion. Rousseau's extreme sensitivity—his most enduring virtue—had, in this instance, compromised him by leading him into a passion from which he could not recover. Vice had worn a mask, and Rousseau had once again been led astray (1:441–42).

Rousseau soon revealed his feelings to Sophie during one of Saint-Lambert's extended absences (1:441). While made uneasy by the revelation, she wished to maintain a close friendship with him. She therefore continued to see Rousseau regularly, all the while maintaining that she loved Saint-Lambert and that she had hoped that Rousseau would overcome his passion for her in the name of friendship. This only further enlivened Rousseau's passion, of course. Still, Rousseau maintains that—on account of her virtue and his respect and esteem for both her and Saint-Lambert—their relationship remained chaste (1:445–46). In fact, so confident were Sophie and Rousseau in their abilities to overcome the latter's passion that they began to spend inordinate amounts of time together. During this time they pontificated on duty, morality, and love and spoke at length about their affection both for Saint-Lambert and for each other. Failing to realize that they were being watched and judged by onlookers, Sophie and Rousseau inadvertently thumbed their noses at societal norms.

> Since Mme d'Houdetot had the most tender friendship for me which she did not reproach herself at all, since I had an esteem for her all the justice of which no one knew better than I; she being frank, heedless, giddy, I being true, clumsy, proud, impatient, touchy; in our deceptive security we exposed ourselves much more than we would have if we were guilty.

> (5:375; 1:446; Comme Madame d'Houdetot avoit pour moi l'amitié la plus tendre qu'elle ne se reprochoit point, que j'avois pour elle une estime dont personne ne connoissoit mieux que moi toute la justice; elle franche, distraite, étourdie; moi vrai, maladroit, fier, impatient, emporté; nous donnions encore sur nous dans nôtre trompeuse sécurité beaucoup plus de prises que nous n'aurions fait si nous eussions été coupables.)

As Kelly observes, the apolitical character of this little society of three had constituted its charm, but it also entailed certain insurmountable vulnerabilities. The demands of normal domestic and political life cannot so easily be escaped, as the trio soon discovered.[15] D'Holbach and Madame d'Epinay soon suspected that a love affair existed between Rousseau and Sophie, and Saint-Lambert was labeled a cuckold.

According to Rousseau, throughout this entire ordeal he wavered between feelings of culpability and innocence, between action and inaction.

He then goes on to describe how an internal divide about the best course of action arose once his affection for Sophie was revealed. His remorse was intense and the indignation he felt against himself unparalleled: Rousseau should have been Sophie's "Mentor" but instead had secretly and against his better judgment hoped to seduce her. Normally, his shame alone would have been enough to help him to renounce his passion and thus enable him to distance himself from Sophie. Nonetheless, the fact that Sophie was the victim of a false accusation on account of what was ultimately Rousseau's own carelessness aroused his compassion. Shame and compassion are thus initially presented as dictating two alternate courses of action.

Rousseau claims that his shame dictated that he flee the scene of the crime, while his "compassion" motivated him to action. As Bernard Williams notes, shame is one of those emotions that "embodies conceptions of who one is and how one is related to others" (*Shame and Necessity*, 94). Guilt, on the other hand, is concerned with the victims and our feelings about them. It may extend to actions we have committed involuntary. However laudable guilt might be, according to Williams, shame is more instructive and can render our feelings of guilt more productive, as it inspires one to reflect on and improve one's ethical identity in relation to one's moral peers. In this passage, however, Rousseau seems to suggest that—because of amour propre and his fear of being perceived negatively—shame inspired him to recoil within himself. At this particular moment, Rousseau therefore suggests that it is only compassion for those we have wronged that will inspire us to overcome our shame and in turn act on our victims' behalf and right our wrongs (or at least try to). This is not to say that, within Rousseau's oeuvre, such guilt-ridden compassion always inspires individuals to act. Much to the contrary, it appears as though compassion is able to do so only for those with whom he has a deep attachment (hence the reason why Rousseau fled Marion, as he did not know her intimately). But I do want to draw attention to the fact that, in this particular incident involving Sophie, Rousseau suggests that—in the confidence of friendship—one does not feel aversion for the victim but rather seeks that victim out to resolve the pangs of culpability through rectificatory action. Indeed in this instance, Rousseau's shame stimulated a desire to isolate himself from the object to which it was attached, while his remorse and self-reflexive indignation inspired him to act on Sophie's behalf.[16]

> That was the first moment I was sensitive to the shame of seeing myself humiliated by the feeling of my fault in front of a young woman

whose just reproaches I was suffering. . . . The indignation I felt against myself from this perhaps would have been enough to overcome my weakness, if the tender compassion which its victim inspired in me had not softened my heart again.

(5:377; 1:448; Ce fut là le prémier moment où je fus sensible à la honte de me voir humilié par le sentiment de ma faute devant une jeune femme dont j'éprouvois les justes reproches. . . . L'indignation que j'en ressentis contre moi-même eut suffi peut-être pour surmonter ma foiblesse, si la tendre compassion que m'en inspiroit la victime, n'eut encore amoli mon coeur.)

It was Rousseau's compassion for Sophie—here cast as a "weakness"—coupled with his indignation at such an unjust accusation that initially carried the day, and Rousseau decided to defend her. Certain that it could have been only Madame d'Epinay who had been the source of the rumor about Rousseau and Sophie's alleged affair, Rousseau had lashed out against her in a series of letters that he composed over the course of a day. This only made matters worse, of course. What is more, it constituted yet another betrayal of Sophie, to whom he had promised that he would remain calm while allowing her to handle the situation (1:453).

Recognizing the need to quiet the scandal and appease Epinay, Rousseau quickly found himself in the awkward position of having to engage in damage control by apologizing to her for "graver faults of which I was incapable, and which I never committed" (de fautes plus graves dont j'étois incapable, et que ne commis jamais). When he arrived to deliver his apology, however, he was surprised to find that Epinay embraced him warmly and broke down in tears. Over dinner, she said nothing of the affair or his letters. Her silence on the issue continued throughout the next day. Rousseau found this behavior rather strange indeed. But since "she alone was offended, at least according to the formalities" (5:381; 1:454; elle étoit seule offensée, au moins dans la forme), he concluded that he did not have the right to ask for any clarification of what actually went on.[17] Naively, Rousseau considered the affair resolved and their friendship intact:

Continuing to live with her as before, I soon forgot this quarrel almost entirely, and I stupidly believed that she forgot it herself, because she did not appear to remember it.

(5:381; 1:454; Continuant au reste à vivre avec elle comme auparavant, j'oublia bientot presque entiérement cette querelle, et je crus bête- ment qu'elle l'oublioit elle-même, parce qu'elle paroissoit ne s'en plus souvenir.)

Such an easy resolution to this particular quarrel proved both fictive and fleeting, a fact that Rousseau soon discovered when he refused to ac- company Madame d'Epinay to Geneva. He was seen as ungrateful for the magnanimity Epinay had so recently demonstrated toward him in forgiv- ing him, a fact that—as Rousseau soon realized—she had already publi- cized. Rousseau in turn attracted the ire of Diderot, Holbach, and Grimm (1:455–61). Presumably out of spite for Rousseau's ingratitude, Epinay later revealed to others outside of their immediate entourage that Rousseau had abandoned his five children.[18] It is on account of such public humiliations that, in a letter to Epinay dated November 23, 1757, Rousseau definitively ended his friendship with her (*Correspondance*, vol. 4, no. 580).

Somewhat surprisingly, in the midst of all of this and just prior to his definitive rupture with Epinay, Rousseau felt compelled to defend himself against his friends' accusations of ingratitude. He did so in a letter dated Oc- tober 28, 1757, addressed to—of all people—Saint-Lambert (vol. 4, no. 547). In this letter he calls into question the sincerity of Epinay's reconciliation with him, maintaining that once one begins to speak of obligations and du- ties in friendship, the friendship itself ceases to exist. This conversation was itself an outgrowth of a conversation in the correspondence between Saint- Lambert and Rousseau that had started a month earlier about the meaning of friendship and the resolution of conflict among friends. A look to this correspondence is therefore instructive in better understanding the events recounted in the *Confessions* and, most important for our purposes, Rous- seau's understanding of paradigmatic forgiveness within private, interper- sonal relationships.

What happened between Saint-Lambert and Rousseau—both in the *Con- fessions* and in Rousseau's correspondence—acts as a marvelous contrast to the failed reconciliation between Epinay and Rousseau. It is, in fact, one of the rare moments in the *Confessions* where Rousseau casts himself as having successfully participated in a dialectic of forgiveness. Rousseau de- scribes how he went to see Saint-Lambert and Sophie following the scandal. Sophie's, Rousseau's, and Saint-Lambert's unwavering love and respect for one another ultimately led Rousseau to realize that the friendship and es- teem that he had for these two individuals exceeded and even trumped his

passion for the latter. While both Sophie and Saint-Lambert received Rousseau amicably, Rousseau quickly realized that the relationship had cooled.[19]
It is Rousseau's presentation of the passage from anger to forgiveness, from
coolness to warmth, and from betrayal back to perfect friendship that—at
least as far as Rousseau was concerned—I want to explore.

Depending on how one approaches the events I have just described, one
comes away with quite a different view as to how this event was resolved
and what it signifies in the larger context of Rousseau's thought and life.
There are, to be sure, moments in which Rousseau steadfastly denies any
culpability in much the same way that he does elsewhere in the text. He
does so (in the way that perhaps only Rousseau could) by transferring his
own error into a realm of nonculpability. Indeed, at one point he goes so far
as to blame both Sophie and Saint-Lambert for the scandal that erupted, as
they had brought the temptation toward him and thus opened themselves
up to the false accusations and rumors that followed. The society of three,
or so Rousseau maintained, had in fact been Saint-Lambert's brainchild:
"They alone had done the harm, and it was I who had suffered it" (5:388;
1:462; Eux seuls avoient fait le mal, et c'etoit moi qui l'avois souffert).[20]

If we stop our analysis here, we do indeed come away with a view of
Rousseau's conscience in which he builds a rampart of innocence around
himself that silences the harsh judgments of both the world and his conscience.[21] What is more, we can also detect an isolation of the perpetrator
(Rousseau) from the victims (in this case, Sophie and Saint-Lambert): not
only do the feelings of the victims no longer figure into Rousseau's understanding of what went on but they are at one point presented as having
ultimately been responsible for what was a crime against Rousseau. They
had failed to follow the dictates of polite society in insisting that Sophie
pass time alone with Rousseau. Rousseau had merely obliged the requests
of this strange couple. Rousseau, or so it would seem, therefore did in this
instance what he did best: he blamed others and, most important, society
for what was ultimately his own moral failing. Forgiving Rousseau was not
only unnecessary but also markedly inappropriate. This is, incidentally, Bernard Gagnebin and Marcel Raymond's interpretation of this event: "Everything happens as though he wanted to project his failing outside of himself,
on those closest to him (just as the ribbon's thief accused Marion)" (Tout
se passe comme s'il voulait projeter sa faute hors de lui, sur ses partenaires
immédiats [de meme le voleur de ruban accusait Marion]).[22]

A look to Rousseau's correspondence with Saint-Lambert, however, provides us with quite another version of the events and, to a large extent,

backs up Rousseau's story as recounted in the *Confessions*. By this I mean that what transpires between Rousseau, Sophie, and Saint-Lambert is not as similar to that event involving that infamous ribbon as it appears at first glance.[23] In a letter dated October 11, 1757, it is Saint-Lambert—not Rousseau—who expresses remorse at having ever suspected Rousseau of wishing to steal Sophie from him. In this letter Saint-Lambert recognizes that it was he who had sought to forge a connection between Sophie and Rousseau and, in so doing, had encouraged them to spend time together alone in his absence. What is more, he admits to having experienced a certain degree of unjustified jealousy and paranoia in his relationship with Sophie, which in turn skewed his appraisal of Rousseau when he had been confronted with vicious rumors of an infidelity:

> During my last voyage I thought I detected in her a change. I love her too much to lose anything in her heart without looking upon it with abhorrence and without feeling it most cruelly. I admit that I believed that you were the cause of what I imagined I had lost.
>
> (*Correspondance*, vol. 4, no. 534; Je crus a mon dernier Voiage Voir en elle quelque changement, je l'aime trop pour rien predre dans son Coeur sans m'en appercevoir d'abor & sans le sentir cruellement, je Vous avoüe que je Vous crus la Cause de ce que j'imaginois avoir perdu.)

Saint-Lambert then goes on to offer what can best be described as an unqualified apology:

> I made three people miserable. I am the only one who still experiences pain because I am the only one who could have remorse. I have, for some time now, tried to repair my injustice toward her. I want to repair those injustices I committed against you. Neither one of us has ceased to esteem or love you. Forgive us. Love us. We deserve your heart, and you will be satisfied with our hearts. I shall retain, however, the promise you made not to speak out against our relationship.
>
> (*Correspondance*, vol. 4, no. 534; J'ai fait Trois malheureux, je suis le seul a qui il reste des peines puisque je suis Le seul qui puisse avoir des remords, il y a déja du Tems que je cherche a reparer mes injustices pour elle, je Veux reparer mes injustices pour Vous. Nous n'avons

ni L'un ni l'autre cessé de Vous estimer ni de Vous aimer, pardonnés nous & aimés nous, nous méritons Votre Coeur & vous serés Content des nôtres, je retiens cependant La parole que Vous me donnés de ne lui parler jamais contre nos liens.)

Here, Saint-Lambert essentially requests that the relationship continue in its unhindered course. He expresses remorse for having suspected Rousseau of malicious intent. He also expresses a desire to make reparations. Admittedly, Saint-Lambert ends his apology by reminding Rousseau that the latter has given his word not to jeopardize Saint-Lambert's relationship with Sophie, perhaps betraying some residual traces of suspicion. At the same time, he is willing to accept the bulk of the blame for the cooling that has occurred between Rousseau and Sophie and Saint-Lambert and takes it upon himself to rectify the situation.

In his request for forgiveness, Saint-Lambert neither makes mention of social norms nor of tactical superiority, as many others in his situation and era may have been wont to do. Rather, he focuses on the extraordinary character of the friendship that they had shared and his intimate knowledge of both Rousseau and Sophie's true character. This is no small detail. Given the circumstances and Rousseau's socially inappropriate behavior toward Sophie, this letter from Saint-Lambert demonstrates that—like Rousseau—Saint-Lambert wishes that their little society continue to exist independently of generalized standards of social decorum. That Saint-Lambert could have reasonably expected all of those in the extended entourage who were privy to what had happened to condemn Rousseau and Sophie's alleged dalliance and, in so doing, legitimize the anger he had initially experienced proves this. Nevertheless, in keeping with what was the extraordinary nature of their friendship, he instead opted to request forgiveness.

In this letter, therefore, Saint-Lambert picks up on a theme that Rousseau had himself put forward in earlier correspondence, thereby revealing himself to be a kindred spirit. In the preceding letter from Rousseau to which this citation was a response, Rousseau emphasizes how condemnable the latter's relationship to Sophie is in the eyes of the world (she was, after all, married to another). In his letter from September 15, 1757, Rousseau wrote,

Do not think that you have seduced me with your reasons: I see the honesty of your heart and not your justification. I find your relationship blamable. Indeed, you yourself would not approve of it, and as long as both of you remain dear to me, I shall never accord to you in your present state the security of innocence. But a love such as yours also deserves certain consideration, and the good that it produces renders it less culpable.

(*Correspondance*, vol. 4, no. 527; Ne croyez pas m'avoir seduit par vos raisons: j'y vois l'honnêteté de vôtre ame, et non vôtre justification. Je blame vos liens, vous ne sauriez les approuver vous meme, et tant que vous me serez chers l'un et l'autre, je ne vous laisserai jamais dans vôtre état la sécurite de l'innocence. Mais un amour tel que le vôtre mérite aussi des égards, et le bien qu'il produit le rend moins coupable.)

Whereas Rousseau admits that Sophie and Saint-Lambert's relationship renders them worthy of blame, Rousseau nevertheless claims that their love for each other entitles them to special consideration, consideration that Rousseau—as a true friend—is all too happy to provide them with. Rousseau thus reveals that he adopts a somewhat bifurcated view of Sophie and Saint-Lambert's relationship. As a citizen who believes that the sanctity of marriage is vital to the continuation of society, he condemns their relationship as adulterous. He therefore maintains that they must not regard themselves as enjoying the security that innocence provides: public opinion and the general will would condemn their relationship were it to be rendered public and, in Rousseau's eyes, rightfully so. But as an individual who loves Sophie and Saint-Lambert as individuals and partakes in their happiness, Rousseau approves of their love. This is true to such an extent that, later in the letter, Rousseau establishes himself as a guarantor of sorts for the relationship. He maintains that, although he is willing to overlook social norms in this one instance, he would not approve of Saint-Lambert taking up with any other woman in a similar fashion. Only Sophie and Saint-Lambert's love for each other and the apolitical nature of their society of three entitles them to Rousseau's special consideration. The tensions between Rousseau's identity as a citizen and that of an individual are thus brought to the fore when he is confronted with the circumstances surrounding Sophie and Saint-Lambert's adulterous relationship. Rousseau's decision to forgive the technically "sinful" nature of their liaison comes from his vehement insistence to view the couple not through the eyes of a citizen but rather through those of an individual who relates to them as such. Rousseau's acceptance of the adulterous nature of their relationship is ultimately dependent on his ability to adopt an individuated and utterly personalized perspective that, as even he himself claims, no amount of argumentation could convince members of the general public to accept.

Saint-Lambert expresses his willingness to provide a similar variety of special consideration to Rousseau in his turn when he apologizes to Rousseau for having fallen prey to what was essentially a rumor that was itself born of generalized societal standards. Rousseau's behavior was inappropriate and, we may assume, humiliating to Saint-Lambert within the social realm. This does not appear to be up for debate. But as an individual who believes that the couple's friendship with Rousseau "shall constitute one of the greatest charms in his life" (fera un des plus grands charmes de [sa] vie), Saint-Lambert's initial anger and his coolness toward Rousseau represented a violation of the very foundation on which their friendship had been built. Realizing this, Saint-Lambert opts to abandon any feelings of rancor that he may have been experiencing on account of amour propre and concern for how he was perceived by others, however justified those feelings were in the eyes of those aware of the situation. He apologizes to Rousseau for having fallen prey to petty social prejudices (vol. 4, no. 534). Both Rousseau and Saint-Lambert thus reconcile themselves with each other and with their perceived misdeeds on the basis that the two men (and, for that matter, Sophie) relate to each other in a manner in which generalized standards of conduct and amour propre are voided of their influence. Feelings of rancor are automatically dissipated when this is recalled to mind, and Saint-Lambert's anger need no longer be expressed.

Admittedly, it is tempting to discount the correspondence surrounding this event as disingenuous. After all, in the *Confessions* Rousseau recounts how Sophie had gone to great lengths to hide from Saint-Lambert the "insane love" (5:376; amour insensé) that Rousseau had felt for her (and that he had professed in his correspondence to her) (1:448).[24] According to Rousseau, after their dalliance had been discovered, Sophie said the following to Rousseau: "My letters were as full of you as my heart was: I have hidden from him only your insane love of which I hoped to cure you and which I see that he is making into a crime of me without speaking to me about it" (5:376; 1:448; Mes lettres étoient pleines de vous ainsi que mon coeur: je ne lui ai caché que votre amour insensé dont j'esperois vous guérir et dont sans m'en parler je vois qu'il me fait un crime). Sophie had confessed only her own thoughts and actions to Saint-Lambert, while downplaying or denying that Rousseau had admitted having fallen in love with her and stolen a kiss.

Saint-Lambert was therefore not fully apprised of exactly what went on. Accordingly, it is not entirely surprising that Rousseau would remain somewhat vague on these details in his initial letter to Saint-Lambert.

But this does not mean that we have nothing useful to learn from this about the greater commentary on anger in friendship that Rousseau wished to make. Indeed, the "facts" are somewhat immaterial for Rousseau, and so they must be for us. More important is how Rousseau recounts these events in the *Confessions*; how they play out in Saint-Lambert's and Rousseau's correspondence; and what they reveal about the latter's views on reconciliation in the wake of personal slight within private, interpersonal relationships.

Particularly relevant in this regard is how Rousseau describes Saint-Lambert's subtle expressions of anger throughout the entire ordeal and the emotion's subsequent dissolution within the *Confessions*. In his capacity as a member of a larger social milieu, Saint-Lambert was angry that Rousseau had put Sophie in a compromising position socially. Nevertheless, from the very beginning, the honorable Saint-Lambert recognized that the personalized anger he was experiencing on account of a publicly humiliating series of events must remain within certain bounds. He "punished" Rousseau, but he did so "with indulgence" (je fus aussi le seul puni et même avec indulgence); he was tough on him, but amicably so (5:388; 1:462). Rousseau, for a time anyway, lost Saint-Lambert's esteem but the latter always maintained at least the appearance of friendship for external observers. The proof of this resides in the fact that Saint-Lambert refrained from expressing his indignation publicly. He might have fallen asleep and snored while Rousseau read a letter to him in private and, in so doing, injured Rousseau's pride. Nevertheless, he continued to treat Rousseau with respect and esteem in public and before other members of their entourage who were apprised of the situation, a fact that Rousseau underscored: "Such were my indignities, and such were his acts of vengeance; but his generosity never allowed him to give vent to them except among the three of us" (5:388; 1:463; Telles étoient mes indignités, et telles étoient ses vengeances; mais sa générosité ne lui permit jamais de les éxercer qu'entre nous trois). It is Saint-Lambert's discretion that proved the sincerity of his friendship and enabled Rousseau to present the forgiveness that was subsequently enacted between him and Saint-Lambert—once the latter's anger abided—as felicitous.[25]

I want to suggest that the lesson that one is supposed to come away with is that it is a noble soul that recognizes that the dictates of friendship extend beyond publicized personal slight and that, even in the wake of a misdeed, one maintains a debt to a former friend. Saint-Lambert epitomized this view in his dealings with Rousseau throughout the entire scandal insofar as he steadfastly refused to publicize his anger, which we may assume would have been—and, indeed, to a large extent had already been—ratified by others (in particular, Grimm, Holbach, Epinay, and Diderot). Feelings of pain may be inevitable in the wake of personal slight. Its expression, however, must be carefully calibrated. As discussed in part 1, only depersonalized anger or indignation at the violation of generalized laws, principles, and codes of conduct may be expressed publicly (again, for the citizen acting as such expressions of anger are often a duty). But in relationships such as friendships, wherein neither the dictates of law nor of social custom obtain, no variety of anger that meets the criteria for public expression may be admitted. In the correspondence, Saint-Lambert admits that his initial anger was rooted in adhering too vehemently to social norms and, in so doing, losing sight of both Rousseau's and Sophie's true character and the nature of their bond. His amour propre, we may assume, was also injured. Ultimately, and after some time to think it over, he recognized that he had violated the sacred pact of friendship by experiencing anger on account of what were generalized norms of conduct. It is this that puts him in need of Rousseau's forgiveness, hence Saint-Lambert's apology. To his credit, however, Saint-Lambert did not publicize his anger beyond the confines of their "society of three." It is this that makes it possible for Rousseau to forgive him and for their friendship to continue.

At the height of the scandal concerning Rousseau and Sophie's alleged affair, Saint-Lambert had tried to broker a reconciliation between Rousseau and Epinay for the latter's rumor mongering. In this letter, dated November 21, 1757, Saint-Lambert observes that Rousseau is "the craziest of the lot" (le plus fou de Tous). But he just as quickly points out that he is also "the least culpable" (le moins coupable) for precisely this reason (*Correspondance*, vol. 4, no. 579). Saint-Lambert then goes on to note that Rousseau's friends will quickly forgive Rousseau for having accused Epinay (and Holbach and Grimm) of having spread the vicious rumor to begin with.

> Your friends shall easily forgive you. They gave you the fever, and it is not to them to reproach you for what you did in your transports. . . . Do not break with Madame d'Epinay. I am certain that she still has friendship to offer you. Perhaps she was wrong. Take pleasure in forgiving her. . . . All that you have said against her since your fit of anger has not gone beyond the small circle of your friends. They will silence it, and you will repair it.

(vol. 4, no. 579; Vos amis doivent Tout aisément Vous pardonner, ils Vous ont donné La fiévre & et ce n'est point a eux de Vous reprocher ce que vous avés fait dans le Transport. . . . Ne rompés point avec Mde d'Epinai, elle a de L'amitié pour vous j'en suis sur, elle a peutétre eu des Torts, aiéz le plaisir de les lui pardoner. . . . Tout ce que Vous avés dit Contre elle depuis Votre Colere, n'est point sorti du petit cercle de Vos amis, ils le Tairont, & Vous reparerés.)

In his appeals to Rousseau, Saint-Lambert notes that his friends recognize Rousseau's tendency toward irascibility, his inherent weaknesses, and his difficulty in controlling his impulses.[26] His friends will therefore easily forgive Rousseau for the vehemence of his accusations on account of the fact that they appreciate and comprehend his singular nature. Worth noting here is that one of Saint-Lambert's arguments in favor of letting bygones be bygones is that Epinay's anger has not been publicized outside of the immediate entourage nor, he promises, will it ever be. Reconciliation is presented as a distinct possibility largely on account of this fact: whatever Epinay's feelings, she has not violated the sanctity of the friendship in requesting an external review of Rousseau's actions. This fact alone testifies to her enduring affection for Rousseau. Such is Saint-Lambert's argument. That he ended up being wrong about this was why Rousseau would eventually end his friendship with Epinay, a point that we shall discuss in more detail momentarily.

Rousseau renders this lesson about the need to refrain from publicizing anger in friendships even more explicit in book 10 of the *Confessions*. When Rousseau broke definitively with Diderot, it was Saint-Lambert who reminded him that their rupture did not entitle Rousseau to attack Diderot in public; on this point Saint-Lambert was unequivocal. A letter from Saint-Lambert that Rousseau reproduced in the *Confessions* reads as follows: "After our conversations of this summer, you appeared to me convinced that Diderot was innocent of the so-called indiscretions you imputed to him. I do not know whether he may have committed some wrongs toward you; but I do know very well that they do not give you the right to give him a public insult" (1:498; *Correspondance*, vol. 5, no. 705; Après les conversations de cet été vous m'avez paru convaincu que Diderot étoit innocent des prétendues indiscretions qu vous lui imputiez. Il peut avoir des torts avec vous, je l'ignore; mais je sais bien qu'ils ne vous donnent pas le droit de lui faire une insulte publique).[27] On account of the friendship he had formerly enjoyed with Diderot, Rousseau could not publicly rescind his approval of Diderot or violate Diderot's confidence now that the friendship had been terminated; such was Saint-Lambert's argument. Rousseau was initially devastated and angered by such a response. But he eventually came to appreciate the goodwill and wisdom from which it came, once he realized that it had been offered not out of disdain but rather out of affection (*Confessions*, 1:500–501). Rousseau too could fall victim to petty and very personalized anger. He too could be tempted by amour propre to publicize such anger under the pretensions that it had larger social relevance. The challenge was to overcome such temptations and in so doing maintain one's respect for friendship as a concept and as an ideal that exists independently of generalized codes of conduct, even after a particular friendship has come to a close. Saint-Lambert did well to remind Rousseau of this basic truth.

The upstanding nature of Saint-Lambert and his refusal to render public the failings and weaknesses of Rousseau are contrasted to the duplicitous dealings of Epinay, Grimm, Holbach, and others. This is brought to the fore at the dinner at the Chevrette that took place on October 27 and that immediately followed Rousseau's reconciliation with Sophie and Saint-Lambert. In addition to Sophie and Saint-Lambert, many of Rousseau's closest friends attended, as well as some important members at the periphery of his entourage. Among those present included Madame d'Epinay, Madame de Francueil, Madame de Blainville, and the Count d'Houdetot, Sophie's husband. Rousseau notes how, upon arriving, he was treated amicably: "I have never received a more affectionate welcome. One would have said that the whole company felt how much I needed to be reassured" (5:419; 1:500; Je n'ai jamais recue d'acceuil plus caressant. On eut dit que toute la compagnie sentoit combien j'avois besoin d'être rassuré). Unfortunately, over the course of the dinner, the count and his sister, Madame de Blainville, began to make cheap shots at Rousseau's expense, thereby rendering their "resentment" (ressentiment) apparent. In so doing, they had also made it clear that Epinay's anger had not remained as much of a secret as Rousseau had been led to believe. Indeed, her anger had been publicized within Rousseau's extended entourage. Epinay's failure to accord Rousseau the individuated concern and the utter discretion that true intimacy demands effectively put the nail in the coffin in which their friendship had for some time been resting.

In the midst of all this, only Saint-Lambert came to comfort Rousseau and treat him with respect and affection, thereby thumbing his nose at the exterior judgment that had been passed on Rousseau on account of his past behaviors. It is this that reassures Rousseau that he had genuinely been reconciled with Saint-Lambert and Sophie, even if the Epinays,

Blainvilles, Grimms, and Diderots of the world had shown themselves to be against him:

> The feelings of Mme d'Houdetot and of St. Lambert were less changed than I had believed, and I finally understood that there was more jealousy than low esteem in his keeping her separated from me. That consoled me and calmed me. Now that I was certain of not being an object of disdain to those who were the object of my esteem, I worked on my own heart with more courage and success. If I did not succeed entirely in extinguishing a guilty and unfortunate passion in it, at least I ruled what was left of it so well that it has not made me commit a single fault since that time. . . . The reciprocal behavior of all three of us, when our dealings had ceased, can serve as a model of the way decent people separate when it no longer suits them to see each other.
>
> (5:419–20; 1:501; Les sentimens de Madame d'Houdetot et de St. Lambert étoient moins changés que je n'avois cru, et je ne compris enfin qu'il y avoit plus de jalousie que de mesestime dans l'éloignement où il la tenoit de moi. Cela me consola et me tranquilisa. Sûr de n'être pas un objet de mépris pour ceux qui l'étoient de mon estime, j'en travaillai sur mon proper coeur avec plus de courage et de success. Si je ne vins pas à bout d'y éteindre entiérement une passion coupable et malheureuse, j'en réglai du moins si bien les restes qu'ils ne m'ont pas fait faire une seule faute depuis ce tems-là. . . . La conduit réciproque de tous les trois, quand notre commerce eut cessé, peut servir d'éxemple de la maniére dont les honnêtes gens se séparent quand il ne leur convient plus de se voir.)

Rousseau here describes both his own experience of forgiveness and what he takes to be Sophie's and Saint-Lambert's. They had maintained their affection for Rousseau throughout the entire ordeal and in spite of the maliciousness demonstrated by Rousseau's other acquaintances, just as Rousseau had maintained his affection for Saint-Lambert and Sophie in spite of the adulterous nature of their relationship. Even though, again, it was officially Saint-Lambert who had apologized, Rousseau here admits that he had on some level committed a wrong against Saint-Lambert in having fallen for Sophie. This becomes even clearer when he observes that, upon being reconciled with Saint-Lambert and witnessing the latter's dedication during the ill-fated conciliatory dinner with Epinay, Rousseau's conscience had obliged him to actively begin to work on his heart in an effort to overcome his passion for Sophie. He may not have succeeded in quelling it completely. Nevertheless, his actions toward Sophie were—at least as Rousseau recounts it—irreproachable from that time forward. If he could not control his heart, he could at least control his behaviors out of a sense of affection and dedication. Both Rousseau and Saint-Lambert's faults were outgrowths of the apolitical nature of the relationship between Sophie, Saint-Lambert, and Rousseau and, as a result, the impossibility of others from outside the relationship to fully understand or even perceive the peculiar obligations and expectations that these friends had toward one another. All three individuals were therefore responsible for what had occurred. As Rousseau recounts the story, the trio's dedication to one another was renewed and strengthened once this realization had been made, even as the scandal took on a life of its own outside their sacred society of three.

I bring this particular series of events to light because they illustrate that, for Rousseau, forgiveness as practiced among friends is an affair of the heart that operates independently and even against societal pressures. What is more, such forgiveness does not entail a felicitous calculation of ends and means, pulling rank, or reflection on social mores as its more political counterpart. It is able to preserve true friendship because forgiveness of this variety is itself the remedy for anger and feelings of rancor that had—out of respect for friendship—refused to seek their own public ratification. Forgiveness of an eminently personal variety is thus portrayed as having been allowed to intervene in Rousseau's relationship with Saint-Lambert and Sophie on account of the fact that, at least for all those directly involved, their relationship remained circumscribed within an utterly intimate sphere, even in the wake of a personal slight that had been rendered public. The forgiveness that Sophie, Saint-Lambert, and Rousseau practice in the midst of this semipublic scandal consists in adopting a perspective in which all three members staunchly refuse to see the relationship as susceptible to exterior judgments or generalized codes of conduct.

John Charvet's notion of "inner withdrawal" is helpful in imagining this. According to Charvet, for Rousseau "inner withdrawal" arises "out of the moral necessity to make oneself independent of the opinions and judgments of others in one's relations" and consists in detaching oneself from "one's external appearances for others."[28] The trio's enduring friendship and the forgiveness they in turn practice functions similarly but with an expanded scope: such an inward retreat can and, indeed, need be carried out collectively in the wake of misdeeds committed among those connected through true friendship. When such inner withdrawal is achieved among friends, the empirical fact of culpability (in this case, Rousseau's socially inappropriate behavior toward Sophie) is shown to have no bearing on the relationship and the individuated perspective that true friendship demands.

It is because their forgiveness of one another is brokered in such a fashion that Saint-Lambert need not feel "disdain" (mépris) or humiliation for having requested forgiveness from Rousseau, as it was not bestowed in a manner that publicly debased Saint-Lambert. What is more, Rousseau does not feel superiority toward Saint-Lambert in having granted it. It is telling that Rousseau does not discuss in the *Confessions* how Rousseau and Saint-Lambert's reconciliation was regarded by others: what happened between the two men and Sophie concerned only those involved and, as such, need not and could not be ratified by others. Far from establishing or reaffirming a hierarchy, Rousseau and Saint-Lambert's reconciliation affirms their equality in the eyes of the other. It is a dialectic in which each becomes guilty, remorseful, forgiven, and reassured in his turn. It is a dialectic in which each man's commitment to the other is renewed in a sphere of utter interiority.

It is worth noting that in Rousseau's treatment of Sophie and Saint-Lambert in the *Confessions* he does not discuss their definitive (and somewhat nasty) rupture in the spring of the following year in any detail. Instead, he chooses to focus on the reconciliation that took place in the fall of 1757. He merely alludes to the rupture that soon followed on account of Rousseau's extreme susceptibility to Sophie's critiques and handling of *Julie* and, ultimately, his own paranoia. When, as cited earlier, Rousseau observes that what followed between these three individuals "can serve as a model of the way decent people separate when it no longer suits them to see one another," he reiterates the notion that anger between friends should never be publicized. Not only does publicized anger oblige one to practice a more political variety of forgiveness but it also calls into question one's capacity to experience and appreciate the ideal of true friendship. To his credit, or so we are to assume, Rousseau practices what he preaches in remaining vague about the details of the rupture that occurred in the spring of 1758.[29] As Rousseau recounts the story, Saint-Lambert and Sophie did the same. They parted ways and ceased to be friends while, simultaneously, remaining loyal to the ideal of perfect friendship that they had once shared and in which they had—for a time anyway—taken so much pleasure.

PUBLICIZED ANGER AND THE UNFORGIVABLE

If Saint-Lambert and Rousseau's reconciliation is an allegory of both perfect friendship and felicitous reconciliation within the intimate realm, then his rupture with Epinay is the negative example that serves to reaffirm the ideal. Whereas this episode is often read as a further example of Rousseau's refusal to accept responsibility, I would like to suggest that the story he recounts is just as much (if not more) a means by which he grapples with the notion of the unforgivable.

In book 7 of the *Confessions* Rousseau addresses his paternity. Here, he recounts how embarrassed he was when Thérèse's first pregnancy declared itself (1:343). Some "dinner companions" (5:289; companions de table) who were "very amiable, and at bottom very decent people" (1:344; des gens très aimables, et dans le fond très honnêtes), recommended that he put the child in the Foundling Hospital; Rousseau acquiesced (1:344). In so doing, he even won favor among these same companions and was applauded for his decision. When in the following year Rousseau was faced with the same "inconvenience" (inconvenient), he disposed of the child in the same manner (5:289; 1:345). Later, after he won the prize from the Academy of Dijon for his *Discourse on the Sciences and the Arts*, Thérèse became pregnant for a third time. This time around, however, Rousseau did not simply follow the advice of some dinner companions but rather "philosophized" (philosophois) on the duties of men and the laws of nature, justice, reason, and religion (5:299; 1:356). He concluded that this child must also be abandoned in the same manner that the first two had. The next two children he fathered would meet the same fate. Whereas Rousseau expressed doubt as to the rectitude of his logic and, at times, longing for his abandoned children, he did find a way to rationalize his decision: had he kept his children, they may have grown to hate him. Besides, in all probability he would have been forced to abandon them sooner or later. It was therefore better that he remain unknown to his children: "but I am sure that they would have been brought to hate, perhaps to betray their parents: it was a hundred times better that they never knew them" (5:300; 1:357; mais je suis sûr qu'on les auroit portés à haïr, peut-être à trahir leurs parens: il vaut mieux cent fois qu'ils ne les aient point connus). So goes the thrust of Rousseau's argument.

Margaret Ogrodnick analyses these same scenes at some length in *Instinct and Intimacy: Political Philosophy and Autobiography in Rousseau* in an effort to clarify Rousseau's personal experience of conscience. According to her, Rousseau's decision to abandon his children demonstrates "the suppression of compassion by reason." Ogrodnick supports this claim with the observation that Rousseau's "reflection has no remedial effect on his moral judgment." Taking what is an avowedly psychoanalytic approach, Ogrodnick then notes the "self-defensive stance" that Rousseau takes vis-à-vis his guilty conscience. She further observes that the position that Rousseau adopted on his children is a case in point, where feelings of guilt result in both the isolation of the self and in a renunciation of the compassionate instinct and for humankind more generally:

> Conscience is a punishing faculty based in the dichotomy of innocence and evil, and so calls forth a defensive reaction. It is the correlate of suppression, and is therefore incompatible with the true self-awareness essential to moral sensitivity. . . . The rampart of innocence built against the internal judge also must defend against the censure of any real or projected external judges. The adversarial position thus entailed is incompatible with compassion: to the extent that conscience evokes a protective shield of innocence around the self, it results in a renunciation of the compassionate instinct and its empathetic identification with the other. Conscience also erodes the *amour de soi* that is the basis for the compassionate extension of the self. Associated with conscience is reproachful self-hatred, or what Nietzsche calls "this species of gnawing worm."[1]

Because it is beyond the scope of the present work, I refrain from commenting on whether, generally speaking, the conscience necessarily calls forth both an internal and external defensive reaction against censure in the name of protecting a "rampart of innocence." This is also the case with regard to questions as to if and how conscience may potentially lead to isolation within certain contexts and according to certain methodological approaches. Suffice it to say that, both within and without the psychoanalytic context, it has often been observed of the modern subject that, far from solidifying our connection to others, feelings of guilt often form an intractable barrier between ourselves and our victims by reducing the latter to a mere abstraction. Empathy is in turn limited in its powers to bring about action, if not suppressed entirely.[2]

Admittedly, it is tempting to interpret Rousseau's experience of conscience only in these terms, particularly on account of his protracted project of self-justification and the fact that, in spite of his misdeeds, he so vehemently maintained both his innocence and inherent goodness. What is more, the account of conscience offered by the Savoyard vicar in the "Profession of Faith" certainly leaves one with the impression that the victims figure minimally—if at all—into the vicar's experience of conscience. Certainly, that Rousseau possessed a remarkable capacity to insulate himself from his victims and the empirical fact of his culpability is a fairly common and, I would add, legitimate complaint leveled against him for his treatment of Marion and that pesky ribbon.

I have my reservations, however, as to whether the view of conscience that Ogrodnick presents accords with other, more explicit discussions in the *Confessions* of Rousseau's feelings of guilt and remorse toward his own misdeeds. Put simply, I am not so sure that we can reach many conclusions about Rousseau's own experience of the guilty conscience through an analysis of his treatment of his children. This is largely because it is not readily apparent that the incident regarding the abandonment of his children actually aroused either Rousseau's guilty conscience or any feelings of compassion that he subsequently reasoned away, particularly when compared with other events he relates elsewhere in the text.

In fact, in this particular confession Rousseau goes to great lengths to highlight just how much his conscience approved of the decision to abandon his children. Whereas, as Gagnebin and Raymond observe, Rousseau appears to have longed for the happiness he missed and the joys of paternity that he could have otherwise known, this hardly constitutes anything that could be considered a guilty conscience properly speaking.[3] However much we in the twenty-first century may disapprove of Rousseau's decision, he remains firmly convinced that it was "so good, so sensible, so legitimate"

(5:300; 1:357; si bon, si sensé, si légitime), or so he says.[4] Should we take him at his word?

It is of course hard to pronounce on this definitively. But it is worth considering that it was fairly common practice to place one's children in the foundling hospitals during the period. In 1750, for example, out of 19,035 children baptized in Paris, 3,785 were placed in one of the two foundling hospitals. In 1768 the proportion was 18,756 baptisms to 6,025 placements.[5] The frequency with which such placements occurred thus explains the somewhat nonchalant and, arguably, cold attitude that Rousseau's says his companions assumed toward the practice (1:344). It also serves to bolster Rousseau's claims that he felt neither remorse nor shame for having abandoned his children. He could be free of remorse because he had done what was best for them. He need not feel shame because, in relation to others, his actions made him neither better nor worse than those who had found themselves in a similar situation.[6] There is, after all, a certain degree of moral solace to be found in the nefarious actions of the masses when they resemble our own.

Rousseau's confidence in the prudence of his decision is further confirmed in a letter to Suzanne Dupin de Francueil, dated April 20, 1751. Rousseau opens the letter by citing the pain he still experiences for having missed out on the joys of fatherhood: "If my misery and my suffering deprives me of my power to fulfill such a sacred duty, it is a misfortune that one should pity me for and not a crime for which I should be reproached" (*Correspondance*, vol. 2, no. 757; Si ma misere et mes maux m'otent le pouvoir de remplir un soin si cher, c'est un malheur dont il faut me pla[i]ndre, et non pas un crime à me reprocher). Rousseau then proceeds to outline no less than seven justifications for having abandoned his children, such as he was having enough difficulty feeding himself as it was; he believed at the time that his death was imminent; and he felt that being a writer and a father was incompatible. In this letter he also claims that, in the foundling hospital, the children "are not brought up delicately" and thus end up more robust than their legitimized counterparts (see also *Confessions* 1:342n1). He closes the letter by reproaching Madame de Francueil for attributing to the "dishonor of vice" (le deshonneur du vice) what was in fact dictated by that of poverty.

I do not mean to suggest by all of this that it is an absurd proposition to characterize Rousseau's discussion of his abandoned children as evidence of his tendency to reason away both compassion and guilt and, in the case of his letter to de Francueil, defend himself against outside censure. Admittedly, it is likely that many of us—perhaps particularly if we are parents—would today find such rationalizations rather paltry and in turn suspect that

whoever offered them protested just a little too much for it to be believable
that their conscience was completely clear. But if we approach this particular confession with the assumption that Rousseau necessarily experienced
guilt that he quickly tried to dispel, are we not imposing the dictates of our
own conscience and cultural norms onto him?[7] What is more, if we take this
particular confession as indicative of Rousseau's experience of conscience
(as Ogrodnick does), are we not giving short shrift to the more prolonged
and explicit descriptions of guilt that he provides in his narrations of his
dealings with other individuals, such as Marion and Claude Anet?[8]

How one answers these questions clearly depends on how much relevance one accords to authorial intent (and Rousseau's capacity for deluding
himself). My own view—and it may very well strike those in the psychoanalytic camp as naive—is that the answer to both these questions is yes. I
therefore propose that we take Rousseau at his word when he claims that
he never doubted the morality of his choice to abandon his children and,
therefore, that in recounting the story of his children, his guilty conscience
is not reasoned away for the simple reason that he presents it has having
never been aroused. This is precisely why he underscores the fact that, even
after having philosophized on the duties of man, he still opted to abandon
the children that Thérèse bore for him.

I realize that in interpreting Rousseau's treatment of his children in this
manner I run the risk of being accused of having become the dupe to Rousseau's ruse. But my primary reason for wanting to bracket a discussion of
conscience in relation to Rousseau's abandoned children is that, at least as
he tells it, the significance of his abandoned children resides less in what it
says about Rousseau's character and more in what it reveals about Rousseau's views on both friendship and anger and, more important, anger in
friendship. So whereas I do not pretend that Ogrodnick's interpretation of
Rousseau's experience of these particular events can be easily confirmed or
refuted, I want to suggest that, if we focus too heavily on what this story
reveals about Rousseau's experience of conscience, we risk overlooking the
larger rhetorical point of this particular confession. Essentially, what I want
to focus on here is the lesson that Rousseau *intended* for the reader to take
away from the story of his paternity, more so than on Rousseau's actual
feelings at the time he abandoned his children, which are impossible to discern with any degree of certitude.

One of the strangest aspects of this particular confession and what sets it
apart from many others is that Rousseau underscores how eager he was *at
the time the events were unfolding* to share the story of his children's fates with

his friends. In his mind, he not only did what was best for his children; he also did what was socially prudent for Thérèse (and, for that matter, beneficial to philosophy). This is, in fact, one of the rare occasions of Rousseau's life recounted in the *Confessions* where interiority and exteriority, reason and sentiment, and morality and desire are presented as having been almost perfectly in accord with one another, and this even in spite of the fact that, when the truth was publicized years after the events unfolded, Rousseau was accused of having neglected his duties.

It is telling in this respect that Rousseau notes that he was so very proud of his decision as to how to handle Thérèse's pregnancies that had to restrain himself from boasting about it out of respect for her. Accordingly, only those individuals who were already aware of his relationship with Thérèse and thus would not have judged her any differently had they known of her pregnancies were privy to the truth: "That arrangement appeared so good, so sensible, so legitimate to me that if I did not openly boast about it this was solely out of regard for the mother, but I did tell it to everyone to whom I had declared our relations" (Cet arrangement me parut si bon, si sensé, si légitime que si je ne m'en vantai pas ouvertement ce fut uniquement par égard pour la mére, mais je le dis à tous ceux à qui j'avois déclaré nos liaisons). Voluntarily, therefore, Rousseau recounted the story of his children to Diderot, Grimm, Madame d'Epinay, and Madame de Luxembourg and to Madame Dupin, Madame de Chenonceau, and Madame de Francueil. He did so "freely, frankly, without any sort of necessity, and being able to hide it easily from everyone" (5:300; 1:357; librement, franchement, sans aucune espéce de necessité, et pouvant aisément le cacher à tout le monde). According to Rousseau, the decision to confide the truth to his friends was not a means of preemptively forestalling judgment. Rather, it was a means of demonstrating—through his sincerity—how much he valued these relationships and in turn trusted his friends not to betray him to the public who would (and indeed did) judge him more harshly. Rousseau's revelation of his paternity was a testament to the transparency he wished his friends to partake in and his faith in the notion that, in true friendship, generalized standards of conduct do not come into play: "In a word, I made no mystery of my conduct, not only because I have never been able to hide anything from my friends, but because in fact I saw nothing evil in it" (5:300; 1:358; En un mot, je ne mis aucun mistére à ma conduite, non seulement parce que je n'ai jamais rien su cacher à mes amis, mais parce qu'en effet je n'y voyois aucun mal). Just as Rousseau had accepted and forgiven Saint-Lambert and

Sophie's adulterous relationship, Rousseau had assumed that his friends would do the same with regard to his paternity.

To the fact that he was forthcoming about his children with his friends, Rousseau contrasts his silence on the issue before the public. At first glance, it would seem that Rousseau's admission that he kept his paternity a secret from the public necessarily undermines the claims to transparency that the text so vehemently defends. It would also seem that, because he had hidden the truth from the public, he must have experienced at least some degree of shame, if not guilt, on account of his decision. Yet, if we consider Rousseau's views on public knowledge as expressed in *Letter to Beaumont* (published between 1762 and 1765) and his *Letter to d'Alembert* and the dangers of scientific knowledge as per the *First Discourse*, *Émile*, and the "Profession of Faith," we find that Rousseau had a preemptive defense in place against such accusations. A recurring theme in Rousseau's works is the idea that one has an obligation to speak the truth only if the truth itself is useful.[9] As Leo Strauss observes, "From this it follows that one may not only suppress or disguise truths devoid of all possible utility, but may even be positively deceitful about them by asserting their contraries, without thus committing the sin of lying." Strauss goes on to point out that Rousseau says very little about whether one has an obligation to withhold "dangerous" truths in instances that they could do harm. He surmises that "we are entitled to infer from [Rousseau's] general rule that he would have considered himself obliged to conceal dangerous truths and even to assert their contraries."[10]

Rousseau presents the existence of his children as having been one such truth insofar as he claims that revealing it would have only distracted the general public from the good contained in his *First* and *Second Discourse* and, later, in *The Social Contract* and in *Émile* by destroying his credibility as an authority on education. Additionally, he maintains that his actions risked to be misinterpreted, popularized, and subsequently applied by other young men in similar situations with even more frequency than they already were. Rousseau thereby asserts that he had a duty to shield the secret of his paternity from the public's gaze.[11]

Certainly, we are not obliged to take these claims at face value insofar as we need not seriously believe Rousseau when he claims that he hid his paternity only to protect Thérèse and the general public. But we must not overlook the rhetorical strategy that Rousseau here employs and, more specifically, how he utilizes this particular confession to make a greater commentary on appropriate, as opposed to inappropriate, expressions of anger

wherever friendship is concerned. Rousseau invokes the strict contrast between his honesty with his friends and his simultaneous opacity on the issue
before the public to foreground attacks that he in turn levels against those
who have betrayed him. In so doing, he discovers two grounds on which to
condemn his former friends.

The first, Rousseau claims, is that he was not the only one who potentially stood to lose something on account of the revelation; the public did
as well.[12] Rousseau maintains that he kept both his children and his reasons
for abandoning them from the public for fear that others might emulate
his behavior: "If I stated my reasons, I would be saying too much about
them. Since they were able to seduce me they would seduce many others:
I do not want to expose the young people who might read me to allowing
themselves to be deceived by the same error" (5:299; 1:357; Si je disois mes
raisons, j'en dirois trop. Puisqu'elles ont pu me séduire elles en séduiroient
bien d'autres: je ne veux pas exposer les jeunes gens qui pourroient me lire
à se laisser abuser par la même erreur). The language and argumentation
that Rousseau employs is more than just vaguely reminiscent of the *Letter
to d'Alembert*. Indeed, if one effaces the words "of Geneva" from the following phrase, one can easily imagine Rousseau inserting it into the confession
regarding his children: "With what avidity will the young of Geneva, swept
away by so weighty an authority, give themselves up to ideas for which they
already have but too great a penchant?" (10:254; 5:5; Avec quelle avidité la
jeunesse de Genève, entraînée par une autorité d'un si grand poids, ne se
livrera-t-elle à des idées auxquelles elle n'a déjà que trop de penchant?). One
of Rousseau's central concerns regarding the theater was that he believed
it was difficult—if not impossible—to control what the public takes away
from the examples they are provided with, and this is particularly true when
the goal is to please the public, as is the case with theater. Rousseau therefore maintained that the spectacles presented to the public must contain an
unambiguous moral message.[13]

Along similar lines, in the name of the public good, Rousseau prudently
decided not to reveal his paternity at the time: given his stature in the public's eye on account of his *First Discourse* and his opera at the time he abandoned his children, he risked to be emulated. If he recounts the fate of his
children in the *Confessions*, it is only because the clamor of the public and
the risk of miscomprehension had rendered it one of those "essential narratives" (récits essenciels). Appropriately, Rousseau introduces the story by
saying that he cannot recount it with "too much simplicity" (trop de sim-
plicité) lest it be mistaken for an example to be followed (1:343).

But Rousseau goes even further in exploiting this story to articulate yet another critique of his former friends. The disclosure by his former confidants that Rousseau had fathered and subsequently abandoned his five children made him painfully aware of how the perspectives and judgments of individuals on his past actions were dependent on how said individuals came to figure into his life. This is, of course, a recurring theme in his autobiographical works.[14] Rousseau suggests that those friends in whom he had confided did not judge him harshly at the time of the initial confession. It was only after they had ruptured with him that they publicized the fact that he had fathered these five unfortunate children, presumably to bring ridicule upon him and highlight his supposed hypocrisy for having spoken on the duties of man and, later, composed a treatise on education (on this point, see *Émile* 4:262–63). And it is for this reason and this reason alone that Rousseau believes that he has the right to judge his former friends, and this harshly: they violated the sacred pact of friendship and the trust that such friendship necessarily entails when they publicized Rousseau's paternity.

> I neglected my duties, but the desire to harm did not enter my heart. . . . But to betray the confidence of friendship, to violate the most holy of all compacts, to publish secrets poured into our bosom, wantonly to dishonor the friend one has deceived, and who still respects us when he leaves us, those are not faults; they are acts of baseness of soul and of heinousness.

> (5:301; 1:359; J'ai négligé mes devoirs, mais le désir de nuire n'est pas entré dans mon coeur. . . . Mais trahir la confiance de l'amitié, violer le plus saint de tous les pactes, publier les secrets versés dans notre sein, deshonorer à plaisir l'ami qu'on a trompé, et qui nous respecte encore en nous quittant, ce ne sont pas là des fautes; ce sont des bassesses d'ame et des noirceurs.)

Where his former friends wished to bring further calamity upon Rousseau following their rupture with him, Rousseau maintained respect for them and thus practiced discretion.

For our purposes, what is relevant in the way that Rousseau recounts this story is that he suggests that there need be bounds on one's expressions of anger in the wake of rupture. Further, he maintains that such expressions must not go so far as to seek retribution for personal slight within the public realm. It is telling that, in the letter to Madame d'Epinay dated November

23, 1757, where Rousseau ends his friendship with her in no uncertain terms, he underscores his enduring respect for what the friendship once meant to him: "If one could die from pain, I would no longer be alive. But I have finally made my decision. Friendship has been extinguished between us, Madame, but that which is no more maintains certain rights, which I know how to respect" (*Correspondance*, vol. 4, no. 580; Si l'on mouroit de douleur, je ne serois pas en vie. Mais enfin j'ai pris mon parti. L'amitié est eteinte entre nous, Madame, mais celle qui n'est plus garde encore des droits que je sais respecter). Rousseau regards himself as still bound by the same discretion that he had practiced toward Epinay during their friendship regarding, we may assume, her relationship with Grimm. Implicit within this letter is the suggestion that she would do well to extend to him the same courtesy.

This point is reiterated in his discussion of Epinay and her entourage in the *Confessions*: it is perhaps an error to abandon one's duties to one's chil dren, but it is base to render public what was confided in intimacy, and this regardless of whether such intimacy continues. "By this fact alone" (5:301; Par ce seul fait), Rousseau writes of his friends in the *Confessions*, "they have been judged" (1:359; ils sont jugés). This statement is derived from a recurring theme in Rousseau's oeuvre: more often than not, one's judgment of another man's worth has a tendency to become distorted when it comes into contact with the influence of *le public*, the latter of which has an unfortunate tendency to judge others through prejudice and self-interest. Only in certain intimate relationships are fair and disinterested judgments possible. At times, as Rousseau had repeatedly learned, such relationships come to an end. But the former, more favorable judgments that were formed in strict intimacy should either endure or be silenced forever. To reverse such judgments and render them public is to be insincere: such, again, was Saint-Lambert's advice regarding Rousseau's rupture with Diderot. Whereas Rousseau seems to be willing to accept that the unforgivable may occur in friendships, thereby bringing such relationships to an end, one nevertheless owes to one's former friends the same degree of mutual delicacy and discretion that both parties had enjoyed prior to the rupture.

The fact that, out of anger and envy, Rousseau's friends would reverse their stance on his paternity and render it public imparts onto Rousseau the right to judge them, not so much because they betrayed him personally but rather because they betrayed the most sacred dictates of friendship. Rousseau therefore exploits his own anger at the exposure of his secret to make a subtle commentary as to how the duties of friendship and intimacy must continue even in the wake of rupture. This story also illustrates the pointlessness and potentially detrimental effects of gossip, which is essentially what Rousseau reduces this story to. In this manner Rousseau contrasts the petty anger of his former friends with his own righteous indignation at the violation of the enduring demands and obligations of friendship. That he uses the more impersonal, passive formulation of "they have been judged" (ils sont jugés), as opposed to "I have judged them" (je les ai jugés) is not therefore an insignificant detail.

Such an attitude toward anger is part and parcel of what, as discussed earlier, Coleman has observed to be Rousseau's tendency to depersonalize anger so as to claim greater authority in observing ethical life. With regard to the revelation of his abandoned children, Rousseau's anger would not qualify as sufficiently depersonalized if he were to judge his former friends on account of an isolated incident that had no greater significance than the pain and embarrassment it caused to Rousseau. If that were his only complaint, then his anger would be rooted in inflamed amour propre, and that would hardly be laudable. Accordingly, Rousseau must not cast the anger that he feels because his confidence has been betrayed as an automatic, passionate, or self-interested response to personal slight if he is to maintain any credibility.[15] On the contrary, his anger must be presented as principled, generalized, and symbolic of something greater. Arguably, it must also have pedagogical attributes that a spectatorial third party can be reasonably expected to grasp. Basically, now that his friends have let the proverbial cat out of the bag, he must experience and express through the written word a citizen's anger.

If we read the story of the foundling hospital as a commentary on the enduring claims of friendship, then the story represents a forceful statement that these claims endure even in the wake of rupture and slight. Anger, whatever its cause and no matter how justified, must not lead an individual to renounce these greater general claims, even if the particular individual to whom they are attached no longer figures favorably into our life. There are therefore limits that need be placed on the expression of personalized anger, as the expression thereof must not betray the dictates of a former bond of intimacy. In keeping with both his predecessors and contemporaries, expressions of anger—if they are to win Rousseau's approval—must not be detrimental to the greater good. The result is that Rousseau ends up asserting that only righteous indignation may be and, indeed, need be publicized, as only it is potentially instructive to those who witness it. Rousseau, therefore, avoids having to tackle the question as to whether he need forgive his former friends for having exposed his secret for the simple reason that expressions of indignation—because depersonalized—can never be excessive and thus need no remedy. Much to the contrary, were Rousseau to forgive his former friends out of vestigial traces of affection, he would undermine the principle from which his indignation springs forth and, as a result, reduce the impact of the valuable lesson that is to be learned from the story he recounts. We recall that, in *The Social Contract*, Rousseau maintained that the sovereign should rarely bestow grace for precisely this reason.

By recounting the story in such a way, Rousseau renders the actions of Epinay and her entourage unforgivable—both from a social, public perspective, as well as from a personalized one. Because his former friends have rendered their anger public by making a very public accusation regarding his paternity, Rousseau can no longer forgive them in the name of any personal qualities that they may possess or out of any affection he may still experience toward them. This, again, is because once personal anger or, in this case, disdain is rendered public, the emotion can only be resolved in a similar manner, which is to say publicly and in accordance with the general will (or, at least, public opinion).

I would also suggest that, by making a larger commentary about the enduring claims of friendship and expressing his indignation that such claims have been violated, Rousseau casts his complaint against his former friends in a manner intended to appeal to public opinion. The social contract maintains its integrity and is bearable only if men are allowed an intimate sphere where their authentic selves can be realized and rendered visible to other individuals acting and relating to one another as such. The state of nature and the independence that one enjoys there cannot be recovered. But some vestigial traces of this absolute freedom from social constraints can still be experienced and enjoyed in certain scenarios. Friendship was, for Rousseau, one such example. As Alessandro Ferrara has observed, "Contrary to the primitivist interpretation, this lack of concern for approval is to be attained, according to Rousseau, not by keeping others at greater distance but by reducing social distance. Intimate relations, for instance, bring the actors closer together and yet reduce their concern for the other's valuation of their appearances." Ferrara points out that this does not mean Rousseau's vision of an emancipated society meant that the social bond must coincide with intimate bonds. Rather, it means that one of the measures of emancipation is "the extent to which a society does not prevent or distort relations in which the awareness of others is somehow independent of the concern for one's status."[16] Ideally, Rousseau would have been able to relish his individuality and his freedom in the company of intimate friends.

Unfortunately, he rarely found (and never succeeding in maintaining amicable relations with) any worthy candidates, as the story of the foundling hospital demonstrates. This left Rousseau no choice but to withdraw absolutely into himself and to live out the end of his life in solitude.

Rousseau's unfortunate fate renders the betrayal of Epinay and her entourage even crueler, as by publicizing what had transpired in the intimate realm, she undermined the grounds on which Rousseau could feel secure in those relationships in which he had experienced freedom from the demands of the state and the alienation that attends to them. Further, the story of the foundling hospital also illustrates yet another important tenet of Rousseau's political theory: the public realm should not be littered with distractions that have no bearing on the public's greater good, as particular interests have no place on the public's stage.

Rousseau had no choice but to defend himself as a citizen and thus to express his indignation once the secret of his paternity had been rendered public. This is one of the primary reasons why he must address the issue in the *Confessions*. His former friends—once individuals in his eyes who merited his individuated consideration and utter discretion—opted to relate to him not as individuals but rather as mere citizens (and mediocre ones at that). They exposed his secret in the hopes of publicly gaining ascendancy, and this to the detriment to the greater good. Rousseau thus had no other option but to do the same in his turn. He therefore invites the reader and posterity to judge his former friends—and refuse them forgiveness—in the name of and in accordance with what he claims must be the general will. In the end, his friends chose the playing field. Rousseau merely drew attention to the fact that they had crossed the foul line that was always already there.

The events in the *Confessions* that we have just examined are by no means exceptions within Rousseau's oeuvre. Rather, they constitute an application and further development of many of the ideas regarding reconciliation within private, interpersonal relationships (as exposed to public or political ones) that Rousseau had already explored in at least two of his literary contributions. In fact, the peculiar demands of friendship and, it follows, the apolitical nature of forgiveness as practiced in Rousseau's relationship with Sophie and Saint-Lambert has its antecedent in both *Julie* and *Émile and Sophie*, to which I now turn. In both of these texts, Rousseau confronts the subject of reconciliation head-on and, in so doing, addresses the question as to what paradigmatic forgiveness entails within the intimate realm.

7

FORGIVENESS AMONG MEN AND CITIZENS

In a letter to Julie, Saint-Preux details his reconciliation with Edouard following the latter's public insinuation that Julie was somehow less than perfectly chaste (which, indeed, was the case). Saint-Preux recounts to Julie how, following the incident, Edouard arrived at his door accompanied by three individuals, got down on his knees, and offered the following apology:

> I come, Monsieur, to retract formally the abusive remarks drunkenness caused me to utter in your presence: their injustice makes them more offensive to me than to you, and I owe myself formal disavowal of them. I submit to whatever punishment you may wish to impose, and will not consider my honor restored until my fault is repaired. Whatever the price, grant me the forgiveness I ask of you, and restore me your friendship.

> (Je viens, monsieur, rétracter hautement les discours injurieux que l'ivresse m'a fait tenir en votre présence: leur injustice les rend plus offensant pour moi que pour vous, et je m'en dois l'authentique désaveu. Je me soumets à toute la punition que vous voudrez m'imposer, et je ne croirai mon honneur rétabli que quand ma faute sera réparée. A quelque prix que ce soit, accordez-moi le pardon que je vous demande, et me rendez votre amitié.)[1]

After hearing the apology, Saint-Preux replies, "I can surely distinguish between remarks dictated by the heart and those you utter when you are not yourself; may they be forever forgotten" (133; 2:164; je sais bien distinguer en vous les discours que le coeur dicte de ceux que vous tenez quand vous n'êtes pas à vous même; qu'ils soient à jamais oubliés). Saint-Preux then offers his hand to Edouard and lifts him up. At this point, Edouard thanks the men who had accompanied him and advises them to remember that "he who thus rights his wrongs will suffer wrongs from no one" (celui qui répare ainsi ses torts, n'en sait endurer de personne), presumably cautioning them about the risk they run if they continue to spread any further the rumor that he had himself initially started. Edouard concludes his apology with the phrase: "You may publish what you have seen" (133; 2:164; Vous pouvez publier ce que vous avez vu). The three men who had accompanied Edouard to the scene suddenly retire, and just as soon as Edouard and Saint-Preux are alone, they embrace in the most tender and amicable manner.

When Julie hears of Edouard's actions, she is overcome with joy and admiration. "Bring Milord Edouard tomorrow," she writes to Saint Preux,

> so I can throw myself at his feet as he did at yours. What magnanimity! What generosity! Oh how little we are beside him! Preserve this precious friend like the apple of your eye. Perhaps he would be less worthy if he were more temperate; did ever a man without flaws have great virtues?

> (137; 2:167; amène demain milord Edouard, que je me jette à ses pieds comme il s'est mis au tiens. Quelle grandeur! quelle générosité! O que nous sommes petits devant lui! Conserve ce précieux ami comme la prunelle de ton oeil. Peut-être vaudroit-il moins s'il étoit plus tempérant: jamais homme sans défauts eut-il de grandes vertus?)

It is hard to understate how admirable, yes, but also how odd Edouard's apology appeared to Saint-Preux, to all those who witnessed it, and, we may assume, to the eighteenth-century reader given, again, the prevailing semantic practices of the time. Saint-Preux describes how "surprised" (surpris) he was by Edouard's behavior and how, even in spite of his blind rage at the initial affront, he was moved to lift Edouard up after seeing him prostrate himself (133; 2:163). This he did not only out of affection but also out of extreme discomfort at what he was witnessing. By eighteenth-century standards, the fact that Edouard—a nobleman—got down on his knees in public in front of a much younger roturier with neither family nor fortune to beg for forgiveness was a rather bold move indeed. Even hours later, Saint-Preux could not help but to express to Edouard his surprise at "such a public and immoderate gesture" (136; 2:166; un procéde si authentique et si peu mesuré). Edouard in turn explains that he was moved to such a grandiose apology on the grounds that anything less would have been unworthy of his courage and, further, would have served to discredit him without necessarily repairing the evil he had committed. Besides, he claims, "my reputation is made; I can be just without being suspected of cowardice; but you who are young and starting out in the world must come out of your first affair so clean that it will tempt no one to involve you in a second" (136; 2:166; Ma réputation est faite, je puis être juste sans soupçon de lâcheté; mais vous, qui êtes jeune et débutez dans le monde, il faut que vous sortiez si net de la première affaire, qu'elle ne tente personne de vous en susciter une seconde).

This one example, perhaps more than any other in Rousseau's oeuvre, demonstrates just how critical Rousseau was of the magnanimous model of forgiveness so prevalent in his day. It also shows how eager he was to sketch a more intimate model of forgiveness that could be exchanged in the private, interpersonal realm. To be sure, this particular scene violates that model on almost every level, turning it on its head. There is, first and foremost, the reversal of rank—at least as far as any external observers are concerned. In his publicly performed apology, Edouard essentially asks for forgiveness from someone who is beneath him in every respect. Saint-Preux is, again, younger, of lower social rank, and financially dependent on the charity of others. Further, as Julie herself points out, Saint-Preux would be sure to lose in a duel with Edouard were one to take place—and one very nearly did (130; 2:158). Edouard was thus in position not only of social superiority but of tactical superiority as well. What is more, Edouard had empirical truth on his side: indeed, his allegations about an affair existing between Julie and Saint-Preux were correct, a fact that Julie herself confirmed in letter 58 of part 1. Nevertheless, touched by Julie's love for Saint-Preux and her willingness to sacrifice herself to save her lover's life, Edouard decided to essentially exchange roles with Saint-Preux and assume that of the guilty party.

If, as discussed earlier, for Diderot one must have "much modesty, meticulousness, and art to wrest forgiveness from those to whom one is superior," this is certainly not the case in Rousseau's literary imagination.

Indeed, Saint-Preux was anything but modest prior to this in his dealings with Edouard. He refused to suppress his anger at the moment of the initial affront, a fact that was duly noted by all who were present.[2] And, as Patrick Coleman notes, although he is rarely moved to anger, one of Saint-Preux's definitive characteristics is that he "never retracts his bold claim to possess a sensibility as refined as any nobleman."[3]

Even Julie's letter, the one that ultimately inspired Edouard to renounce his anger, can hardly be considered either cunning or modest. Although she essentially throws herself at Edouard's mercy and appeals to the latter's reputation for being generous and fair, she does not hesitate to end her letter in a somewhat saucy manner. She closes the letter by underscoring—not without a fair dose of sarcasm—the incongruity between having a "beautiful soul" (l'ame belle) and "sensible heart" (le coeur sensible) and taking pleasure in vengeance. She then intuits that the actions Edouard has resolved to take betray the fact that, for all his discoursing on humanity, he appears to take pleasure in rendering other people miserable (131; 2:161). Put simply, what brings about Edouard's performative apology is not Julie's timidity but rather her incomparable boldness in pointing to the incongruities in his behavior.

If, as argued in part 1, Rousseau believed that forgiveness as exchanged among citizens relating to one another as such had to be granted in accord with and in the interest of preserving social norms, customs, and, most important, the law, in *Julie* he does not hesitate to present forgiveness as exchanged among individuals qua individuals as consisting in something entirely different. Far from serving as an affirmation of the social system in which they reside, Saint-Preux and Edouard's reconciliation attacks it at its roots, in much the same way that Saint-Lambert and Rousseau's did. Immediately following their reconciliation, Edouard not only pleads Julie and Saint-Preux's case to the Baron d'Etange but also encourages the couple to elope and thus essentially renounce the ties that bind them to the society in which they reside. Just as Rousseau had accorded special consideration to Saint-Lambert and Sophie on account of their love for each other, Edouard is ready to do the same in Julie and Saint-Preux's case—and this at his own expense. Saint-Preux's reconciliation with Edouard thus inaugurates a friendship that exists at the fringes of society and in contradistinction to generalized codes of conduct. That Saint-Preux feels awkward about accepting it is yet another example of what Donald R. Wehrs has observed to be a basic tension in Saint-Preux's character: he is simultaneously driven to both destroy the social order and uphold it through subordination. Wehrs writes, "[Saint-Preux] identifies himself with his passion. . . . At the same time, he defines his moral being through subordination to the social order. . . . Saint-Preux defines himself simultaneously through impulses which threaten the social order and through principles which require subordination to it."[4]

The apolitical nature of Saint-Preux and Edouard's reconciliation (and the friendship it creates) is reaffirmed by the fact that, in the larger public sphere Edouard's attempts at damage control fail miserably: neither the rumor he had started nor his publicized anger can be retracted so easily as he had believed, as Edouard's and Saint-Preux's drunken antics take on a life of their own and eventually lead to the discovery of the affair.[5] Indeed, the scandal continues and is amplified out in the world just as it is resolved in the hearts of both Edouard and Saint-Preux. In the end, Edouard's very public and ceremonial request for forgiveness proves irrelevant to those individuals who had previously witnessed Edouard's indignation, made it their own, and taken his side. This is very likely because Edouard's apology could not be fully grasped by the external observers who had been called on to ratify it on account of the fact that they had not read Julie's heartfelt pleas and thus could not share Edouard's newfound love and affection for the star-crossed lovers. But this does not render Saint-Preux and Edouard's reconciliation any less authentic or the friendship it inaugurates any less sincere. Much to the contrary, it marks the beginning of mutual and unwavering dedication on the part of both men.

Whereas publicly, Saint-Preux accepted Edouard's grandiose apology, I want to suggest that it was not at that moment that they truly forgave each other. The moment of forgiveness occurs when Edouard embraces Saint-Preux and explains the true motivations behind his actions. Their indebtedness to each other and their mutual affection and devotion throughout the remainder of the novel proves that, even if forgiveness fails to be ratified by the world, it is nevertheless an effective vehicle for renewing private, interpersonal attachments. The fact that this scene can occur only once all the witnesses have left seems to suggest that genuine forgiveness as exchanged among friends cannot sustain the garish light of the public sphere without becoming corrupt with self-interest.

It is therefore worth noting that Edouard admits that his public apology was not performed without concern for his own reputation entirely. Instead, it was carried out by Edouard's public persona in the hopes of advancing a very personal and heartfelt desire. Of Edouard's explanation for his actions, Saint-Preux writes,

But, beyond the reason he had already given me, he added that partial satisfaction was unworthy of a man of courage; that one had to leave it full or nil, for fear of abasing oneself without obtaining any reparation, and seeing a deed accomplished ungraciously and against one's will attributed to fear.

(136; 2:166; Mais, outre la raison qu'il m'en avoit déjà donnée, il a ajoûté qu'une demi-satisfaction étoit indigne d'un homme de courage; qu'il la faloit complette ou nulle; de peur qu'on ne s'avilit sans rien réparer, et qu'on ne fît attribuer à la crainte une démarche faite à contrecoeur et de mauvaise grace.)

Notice here how Saint-Preux recounts how Edouard referred to his already-established reputation in explaining to Saint-Preux the reasoning behind his public and performative apology. In so doing, Eduourd revealed that he had already done a fair amount of calculating as to the ramifications that his public apology would have on his public image out in the world. He knew that this forgiveness ceremony would constitute a debit in his account wherein social prestige is currency. However, he was confident that he had enough credit to offset it.[6] But all this is largely immaterial as far as Saint-Preux is concerned, as, again, it is not this ceremonious variety of forgiveness wherein Edouard more or less nominated Saint-Preux his "superior" and the arbiter of his fate that henceforth bonds the two men. It is, rather, that higher form of forgiveness that occurs once all witnesses have left. The lesson that Saint-Preux (and, for that matter, the reader) is supposed to take away from this is that appropriate behaviors necessarily vary depending on whether one is acting in his capacity as a public or private individual.

Throughout the novel, in fact, forgiveness—at least as exchanged among those characters who eventually find their way to the idyllic and decidedly isolated Clarens community—is consistently presented as a means of bucking the system in the name of love and friendship. In all these instances forgiveness proves antithetical to fixed hierarchies, social calculation, and the desire for domination. We can, for example, consider Julie's forgiveness of Saint-Preux upon learning of the latter's infidelity, forgiveness that she bestows immediately. It is revealing that she claims that his confession causes her more pain than anger (244; 2:297). She refuses to see herself as a betrayed lover who feels shame and anger on account of having been displaced by another. According to Julie, Saint-Preux's infidelity serves as proof that he is losing himself in his hopes to gain the approval of others. In her mind, it is not an injury to her amour propre that needs to be forgiven. Rather it is the evil that Saint-Preux has done to himself that she must reconcile herself to. She therefore calls him out in what can perhaps best be described as Saint-Preux's voyeuristic tendency to look on the wretchedness of others with what is, by all accounts, some degree of pleasure (246; 2:302). Finally, and worst of all, Saint-Preux fails to realize that his predilection for the company of "people of condition" (gens de condition) amounts essentially to approbation of the very same system that keeps them apart.

> Is it moreover not odd that you should give in to the same flaw with which you reproach modern comic authors . . . as if you had not paid dearly enough for the vain prejudices of the nobility to despise them, and you thought you would be degraded by frequenting the honest bourgeoisie, who are perhaps the most respectable order in the Country where you are?

> (248; 2:305; N'est-il pas singulier encore que vous donniez vous-même dans le défaut que vous reprochez aux modernes auteurs comiques . . . comme si les vains préjugés de la noblesse ne vous coûtoient pas assez cher pour les haïr, et que vous crussiez vous dégrader en fréquantant d'honnêtes bourgeois, qui sont peut-être l'ordre le plus respectable du Pays où vous êtes?)

It is Saint-Preux's failure to be true to himself that, for Julie, is what needs to be forgiven.

Julie's critique of Saint-Preux is meant to be a stinging one. After all, Edouard and Saint-Preux's forgiveness was ultimately brokered on the grounds that Edouard cared little for the privileges and entitlements of rank wherever the value of individuals qua individuals are concerned. Certainly, Edouard recognizes the privileges that his rank affords him and, at times, uses them to his advantage. Nevertheless, throughout the novel it is clear that he does not see them as having any intrinsic value. Much to the contrary: it is on account of this perspective that he is able to extend his respect to all of humankind and ultimately debase himself in front of witnesses by begging for Saint-Preux's forgiveness before men of high rank.[7]

The fact that, after his reconciliation with Edouard, Saint-Preux opts to chase after illusions in the name of winning the public's accolades renders him, in Julie's eyes, unworthy of both the friend he has made and the love that she has for him. Thus, whereas Saint-Preux's remorse about his infidelity and his "sincere confession" wins for him Julie's pardon, she maintains that he must now render himself worthy of it by revising his perspective and becoming true to himself once again: "An involuntary error is easily forgiven and forgotten. As far as the future is concerned, remember this maxim from which I shall not deviate: Whosoever can twice deceive himself in such a case was not deceived even the first time" (250; 2:305; Une erreur involontaire se pardonne et s'oublie aisément. Quant à l'avenir retenez bien cette maxime dont je ne me départirai point: Qui peut s'abuser deux fois en pareil cas ne s'est pas même abusé la première). In short, Julie's forgiveness consists in adopting a perspective of Saint-Preux that brackets the misdeed. The challenge, then, with which Saint-Preux is confronted is to prove to both Julie and to himself that he desires to create for himself to the greatest extent possible an entourage where his actions and his emotions, his deeds and his principles, may better coincide. Only by making efforts to attain such an existence will his ailing conscience be quieted.[8]

Such a unified existence may be impossible in society such as it is, but it can be found in true friendship and, we may assume, in a variety of love that has been voided of both its passion and its jealousy, such as the variety of love that both Julie and Saint-Preux come to share. This desire must maintain its force to such an extent that Saint-Preux will shun in his heart the appearances on which society is based, refusing to lend them any credence in his actions or sentiments. He must resist the urge to participate in the licentious behaviors that are all too often accepted and, at times, lauded within a corrupt social sphere. He must overcome inflamed amour propre in all things that directly or indirectly concern Edouard or Julie. The approval of like-minded, virtuous individuals is the only thing that he should try to win in a sphere of exteriority. In this way, Saint-Preux will render himself worthy of the forgiveness that Julie has preemptively bestowed. Julie's forgiveness thus concerns itself and is directed toward who Saint-Preux is or, perhaps more accurately, could once again become rather than what he has done.

The fact that Saint-Preux "confesses" as a crime an action that people from outside of their relationship would unlikely regard as such also proves that he views his relationship with Julie as having a particular and very individualized set of obligations. Much like the author of the *Confessions* had done when he stole a certain ribbon, when Saint-Preux beds another woman he falls victim to external pressures and acts in a manner that does not accord with the enduring self he knows himself to be. Yet the fact that he requests forgiveness from Julie proves that he cannot for this reason automatically transfer the deed into a realm of nonculpability or find solace in the approval that his "infidelity" brought forth among his dinner companions. Overcome by his guilty conscience, he solicits Julie's judgment and rigor and expresses a desire for punishment. He cannot escape his conscience by merely taking a resolution to act differently and pointing to external factors. Rather, he feels the need to be purged through a confession addressed to the one he believes he has wronged. He desires to be seen as he truly is in light of what he has done:

> I have come to the end of this awful narrative; may it never again sully your eyes or my memory. Oh you from whom I await my sentence, I implore you to make it harsh, I deserve it. Whatever my punishment may be, it will seem to me less cruel than the memory of my crime.

> (244; 2:297; J'ai fini ce récit affreux; qu'il ne souille plus tes regards ni ma mémoire. O toi dont j'attends mon jugement, j'implore ta rigueur, je la mérite. Quel que soit mon châtiment, il me sera moins cruel que le souvenir de mon crime.)

The boundary between appropriate and inappropriate behavior in Saint-Preux and Julie's relationship had always been (and remains throughout the novel) drawn not according to social norms but rather according to the extraordinariness of their bond and their circumstances, coupled with the intimate knowledge they have of each other. So too is Julie's forgiveness both requested and granted. Essentially, in having requested forgiveness, Saint-Preux expressed regret for the loss of his true self, the self that Julie is still able to see and still loves. In granting it, Julie voices her desire for Saint-Preux to act in a way consistent with his true self, which—she assures him—was never really lost but merely obscured in his dealings with society and the actions he performed therein.

What is fascinating about this particular example is that, although Julie is a professed Catholic (and is deeply saddened by the fact that Wolmar is not), she does not mention Christ in her dealings with Saint-Preux in this particular instance.[9] What is more, though arguably invoked in a secularized form by Saint-Preux, Julie outrightly rejects the Christian notion of confession and absolution. Indeed, she appears somewhat annoyed that Saint-Preux would feel the need to confess to her *and* think that so doing would constitute the righting of a wrong. Appropriately, the tone of this particular letter often borders on chiding.

Later in the novel and after Julie has married Wolmar, the tables are turned. Julie, in pressuring Saint-Preux to give his consent to the marriage, had betrayed her promise to remain always faithful to Saint-Preux. Somewhat paradoxically, as Saint-Preux himself notes, her betrayal was itself the result of precisely those character traits in her that he most admired, namely virtue and courage: "That feat of courage that restores you to the fullness of your virtue only makes you even more like yourself. No, no, whatever torture I experience in feeling and saying this, you were never more my Julie than at the moment you renounce me" (Cet effort de courage qui vous ramene à toute votre vertu ne vous rend que plus semblable à vous-même. Non, non, quelque supplice que j'éprouve à le sentir et le dire, jamais vous ne fûtes mieux ma Julie qu'au moment que vous renoncez à moi). Saint-Preux admits to feeling a certain degree of humiliation on account of the fact that others regarded him as unworthy of Julie's hand. When they were together, Saint-Preux was able to overcome such sentiments of social inequity on account of their love for each other and what they experienced when they withdrew from the world and thus their socially ascribed roles: "Why count the differences that love effaced? It raised me, put me on a plane with you, its flame sustained me" (Pourquoi compter des différences que l'amour fit disparoitre? Il m'élevoit, il m'égaloit à vous, sa flamme me soutenait). But on account of Julie's consent to the marriage and the end of their affair, Saint-Preux claims that he feels that he has returned to his "lowly status" (bassesse) and again feels the full force of its sting. At least initially, he struggles with anger and rage to such an extent that his language breaks down: "She is bringing happiness to someone else? . . . O fury! O hellish torment! . . . Unfaithful woman!" (301; 2:366; Elle fait le bonheur d'un autre? . . . ô rage! ô tourment de l'enfer! . . . Infidelle!). This anger and his aphasia are the result of the trauma of being forced out of his inner retreat and back into his identity as a (lowly) man among men.

Saint-Preux is ultimately able to overcome these feelings of anger and rage—both of which are aroused on account of inflamed amour propre—on account of the transparency of Julie's heart and the fidelity thereof, even if her actions bare no visible trace of this. True, he may no longer physically possess her, but the window to her soul is still open to him. As a result, they are able to withdraw together once again, but this time on different terms. He writes, "by engaging yourself otherwise you have committed a crime that love nor perhaps honor cannot forgive, and it is for me

alone to claim the property that Monseiur de Wolmar has stolen from me"
(302; 3:367; vous avez fait en formant d'autres noeuds un crime que l'amour
ni l'honneur peut-être ne pardonne point, et c'est à moi seul de réclamer
le bien que M. de Wolmar m'a ravi). Honor and romantic love—and that
appears to be the variety of love to which he is referring—may not be able
to forgive a betrayal such as Julie's, as both are associated with mastery
and possession of the other and therefore with concern for how one perceives oneself (and one's possessions) in relation to others. Accordingly,
both honor and romantic love are presented as inextricably bound up with
inflamed amour propre. Fortunately, Saint-Preux's intimate knowledge of
Julie's character, her true motivations, and his faith in her enduring attachment to him enable him to see her infidelity in a different light. He is able
to forgive her at the moment that he ceases to regard himself as the betrayed lover and recalls to mind the impossibility of the situation she found
herself in and the unassailability of both her affection and her virtue: "Let
us forget each other . . . forget me, in any case. I have so resolved, I swear
it; I shall speak to you no more of myself" (302; 2:366; Oublions-nous . . .
oubliez-moi, du moins. Je l'ai résolu, je le jure; je ne vous parlerai plus de
moi). Saint-Preux in turn recognizes that Julie's happiness is more important to him than the pride he once had in possessing her. He also realizes
that there is a certain joy to be found in the fact that she has recovered her
virtue. It is this that enables him to see beyond the empirical fact of her
betrayal and, in turn, to partake pleasure in the domestic happiness she has
found. In this letter, Saint-Preux asserts that the woman he still loves and
only briefly possessed entitles her to special consideration. Such consideration enables him to forgive her even in the wake of what was technically
the gravest of misdeeds, namely the breaking of a promise that resulted in
an infidelity.

In a quite touching manner, Saint-Preux closes the letter by advising Julie
to refrain from admitting their affair to Wolmar.

> Keep a dangerous secret which nothing obligates you to reveal, the
> communication of which can undo you and is of no use to your hus-
> band. If he is worthy of this confession, his soul will be saddened by
> it, and you will have distressed him for no reason; if he is not worthy,
> why would you wish to give him a pretext for his betrayals of you?

> (Gardez un secret dangereux que rien ne vous oblige à réveler, dont
> la communication peut vous perdre et n'est d'aucun usage à votre

époux. S'il est digne de cet aveu, son âme en sera contristée, et vous l'aurez affligé sans raison: s'il n'en est pas digne, pourquoi voulez-vous donner un prétexte à ses torts envers vous?)

To his own ability to see Julie through a lens unobstructed by amour pro-pre and generalized standards of conduct, Saint-Preux makes a hypothetical comparison to Wolmar. If Wolmar is worthy of Julie, which is to say, if he appreciates her individuated distinctness, he will be saddened by her past errors and forgive them (just as Julie was saddened by Saint-Preux's earlier infidelity), as he will recognize that they do not reflect her true character. If he is unworthy of her, then he will judge her according to social norms, and her crime will be for him irreparable. He will in turn render domestic life unbearable for her and perhaps drive her back into temptation once again. Saint-Preux therefore advises Julie to wait until she has "a more perfect acquaintance [of her husband]" (une connoissance plus fairfaite de votre époux) and until Wolmar is better acquainted with her character before making such an avowal (303; 2:368). Julie's crime is forgivable only for those who know her intimately and refuse to judge her according to the dictates of public opinion and generalized codes of conduct. Whether Wolmar is capable of this remains to be seen at this point in the novel.

Wolmar and Saint-Preux's mutual forgiveness is granted along similarly extraordinary lines. Indeed, viewed from the exterior, their entire relation-ship has a certain improbability to it given their mutual claims against each other within the social sphere. From Saint-Preux's angle, Wolmar stole Julie from him and, as we learn later in the novel, he did so knowingly. From Wolmar's angle, Saint-Preux deflowered the woman whose hand he had been promised.

At first glance Wolmar's actions toward Saint-Preux and, in particular, the invitation that he extends to Saint-Preux to live at Clarens appear to strongly resemble the magnanimous pardon. To be sure, Wolmar has a cer-tain degree of tactical superiority insofar as he ultimately won the prize. He is also of higher social standing, the master of the house, and universally admired for his wisdom. What is more, and as we learn later, he was fully apprised of the situation when he married Julie (405; 2:488). Finally, and most important, Julie and Saint-Preux's "criminal" affair would undoubt-edly be universally condemned were it to be publicized. If Wolmar were to broadcast the fact that he had forgiven the former lovers he could therefore expect that the external observer would respect him all the more for having been able to overcome his jealousy and anger in accepting both into the fold and, in the process, of having saved Julie from certain ruin. In short, Rousseau sets the perfect stage for a magnanimous pardon à la Corneille.

But this is not the model that Rousseau ultimately portrays. In letter 7 of part 4 Julie recounts to Claire Wolmar's estimation of Saint-Preux. She quotes Wolmar as having said,

> We shall not leave such an honorable man in doubt about himself; we shall teach him to rely more on his virtue, and perhaps one day we shall enjoy with more advantage than you think the fruit of the attentions we are undertaking. As for now, I can already tell you that his character pleases me, and I have high regard for him above all for something he hardly suspects, that is to say his coolness with regard to me.

> (353; 2:428–29; Nous ne laisserons point un si honnête home en doute sur lui-même; nous lui apprendrons à mieux compter sur sa vertu; et peut-être un jour jouirons-nous avec plus d'avantage que vous ne pensez du fruit des soins que nous allons prendre. Quant à présent, je commence déja par vous dire que son caractère me plait, et que je l'estime surtout par un côté dont il ne se doute guère, savoir la froideur qu'il a vis-à-vis moi.)

What I want to bring attention to here is Wolmar's focus on who Saint-Preux is and his concern for how Saint-Preux regards himself. Wolmar wants Saint-Preux to move beyond self-doubt and to have faith in his own moral integrity. He does not wish to dominate Saint-Preux absolutely in either ethical or domestic matters. Rather, he wants Saint-Preux to master himself and his passions and, in so doing, recover his freedom.

This point is stressed further when Wolmar describes Saint-Preux's "coolness" (froideur) toward him not with disdain but with approbation. For him, Saint-Preux's iciness serves as proof of the latter's good character: were Saint-Preux to caress Wolmar because social decorum demanded it, he would be a hypocrite. Saint-Preux's more reserved behavior, on the other hand, proves his respect for the ideal of true friendship. Saint-Preux does not demonstrate marks of affection that he does not genuinely experience, not even toward the man so generously hosting him. And, whereas out in the world this could be taken as a lack of gratitude and respect, Wolmar makes it clear that this is not how he views Saint-Preux, who, despite his many failings, is incapable of compromising his own sincerity. For Wolmar,

Saint-Preux's coolness is more indicative of the latter's exceptional moral character than any outpouring of socially appropriate gratitude could ever be.[10]

Wolmar's extraordinary character is again emphasized later on in the same letter. Julie recounts how, in conversation, Wolmar had drawn a comparison between himself and the Baron d'Etange. In so doing, Wolmar had expressed his desire to place himself on equal footing to Saint-Preux, at least as far as their respective virtue was concerned.

> Between your father and him there is a natural antipathy based on their contrary maxims. As for me who has neither systems nor prejudices, I am sure that he does not hate me naturally. No man hates me; a passionless man can inspire aversion in no one. But I have robbed him of his property, he will not so soon forgive me. He will only love me the more tenderly for it, once he is perfectly convinced that the harm I have done him does not prevent my looking on him favorably. If he flattered me at this point he would be a knave; if he never did he would be a monster.
>
> (353; 2:429; Il y a entre votre pere et lui une antipathie naturelle fondée sur l'opposition de leurs maximes. Quant à moi, qui n'ai ni sistèmes ni préjugés, je suis sûr qu'il ne me hait point naturellement. Aucun homme ne me hait; un homme sans passion ne peut inspirer d'aversion à personne: Mais je lui ai ravi son bien, il ne me le pardonera pas sitôt. Il ne m'en aimera que plus tendrement, quand il sera parfaitement convaincu que le mal que je lui ai fait ne m'empêche pas de le voir de bon oeil. Si'il me caressoit à présent, il feroit un fourbe; s'il ne me caressait jamais, il seroit un monstre.)

With these words, Wolmar reveals his willingness to view not only himself but also others independently of social norms, even when said norms reaffirm his own rectitude and superiority. We can, once again, detect Wolmar's expressed desire to avoid a quid pro quo wherein, in exchange for his magnanimity, Wolmar would be within his rights to demand outward expressions of gratitude from Saint-Preux.[11]

What is more, by admitting that he committed an "evil" toward Saint-Preux, Wolmar accords legitimacy to the latter's enduring feelings of rancor that, he assumes, must still remain, even if Saint-Preux's actions bare no trace of this. By this I mean that Wolmar admits that Julie had "belonged" to Saint-Preux in some metaphysical sense and that it was in fact he who had stolen her. Regardless of the degree to which social custom and local mores approve of his claim to Julie, Wolmar is nevertheless willing to admit a certain degree of culpability and, for this reason, a certain amount of vulnerability vis-à-vis Saint-Preux. Wolmar therefore claims that he will not genuinely be forgiven until Saint-Preux knows that Wolmar is aware of the pain that he has caused and that he experiences a degree of remorse on account of it. Once Saint-Preux recognizes that Wolmar views him favorably and genuinely trusts him in spite of the former's crimes, Saint-Preux will understand that Wolmar's strength of character consists in his disdain for the arbitrariness of rank that led to Saint-Preux's undoing, even if Wolmar himself profited from it. Unlike the Baron d'Etange, Wolmar is free from prejudices and inflexible maxims. He can therefore find little comfort in them. Having observed men closely from a young age, Wolmar knows that a man's true worth is not determined by public opinion, rank, or wealth.[12] The challenge before him is to prove this to Saint-Preux. It on account of the individuated perspective they have of each other that, in spite of the harm Wolmar has done to Saint-Preux (and Saint-Preux had done to him), the two men are able to genuinely forgive each other in the most intimate of ways. In so doing, they reform their estimation of each other in such a way that enables both men to see their similarities instead of their differences, their mutual affection instead of their fear, and their shared preference for sincerity over social decorum. This shared perspective ultimately (and only after some time has passed) inaugurates an authentic friendship, one that hinders the men's respective claims from resonating in their relations with each other.

Wolmar's reconciliation with Saint-Preux serves as a fascinating contrast to the Baron d'Etange's reconciliation with the same. Whereas Saint-Preux claims that his reconciliation with the baron is sincere, the two men never quite manage to see eye to eye. Indeed, Saint-Preux overcomes his fear of the baron only on account of the fact that the damage has already been done. Because he has nothing left to lose, Saint-Preux has nothing left to fear from the prejudices that, we may assume, the baron still maintains. Similarly, the baron no longer has anything to fear from Saint-Preux: Julie has married Wolmar, and both Julie's and Saint-Preux's passion for each other has, so far as the baron can surmise, been extinguished. The baron and Saint-Preux can therefore finally spend agreeable moments together hunting, and need not be on their guard. The changed set of circumstances have essentially rendered their former rivalry moot.

But, and this Saint-Preux assures Edouard he cannot forgive, the baron periodically makes reference to Saint-Preux and Julie's affair in a mocking tone whenever they find themselves alone together. The baron may pity Saint-Preux for the evil he has done to him, but he does not apologize for it. Further, he never ceases to lord his victory over Saint-Preux: Julie has married the socially appropriate and handpicked suitor over the lowly Saint-Preux. The baron may very well be frank, generous, and respectable, but he has not abandoned his old prejudices. He still finds solace in the rights and duties that his rank affords him. Accordingly, the baron does not truly regret his decision. Or, if he does regret it, he lacks the moral vocabulary that would enable him to articulate as much.

Recognizing the baron's failure to truly evolve morally and sincerely share in the values that pervade Clarens, Saint-Preux fancies himself at least partially avenged on account of the fact that the baron dare not mock Julie and Saint-Preux's love affair in front of others (2:605). The baron's existence within the Clarens community consists in a constant suppression of his desire to flout his victory over Saint-Preux. Peaceful though it may be, his existence entails a certain degree of frustration and alienation: the members of the community in which the baron resides do not share the values that he still clings to. His identity at Clarens is therefore largely performative. He acts like a good citizen, without truly loving the laws, virtues, and equality that reign there. Saint-Preux takes a certain amount of pleasure in knowing this: the baron's alienation constitutes Saint-Preux's revenge. As Wehrs has observed, Clarens strongly resembles the idyllic society recommended in *The Social Contract*, insofar as "individual desires are subordinated to the interests of the community as a whole and tight control is maintained by an all-powerful Legislator (Wolmar)."[13] Because of his incapacity to abandon his former prejudices, the baron, we may assume, lives with a certain degree of fear that his feigned civic virtue may someday be revealed to be insincere.[14] Every time he lords his "victory" over Saint-Preux, he makes an unwitting confession of sorts, of which Saint-Preux is the depository: he is not who he pretends to be.[15] The baron and Saint-Preux have thus been reconciled only as far as the world that surrounds them is concerned, and their conduct toward each other (at least when they are in Julie's and Wolmar's presence) reflects this. But they do not see each other as equal in the way that Wolmar and Saint-Preux have come to. They are not truly friends, and the bitterness remains palpable between them, occasionally rearing its ugly head whenever they find themselves tête-à-tête. Saint-Preux and the baron's forgiveness of each other is in essence nothing more than an extension of their allegiance to the wishes of the community at Clarens and, it follows, their adherence to the codes of conduct that reign there. In this respect, their reconciliation is fundamentally political insofar as it loses much of its force and all its laudable qualities just as soon as the men find themselves alone. On account of the baron's incapacity to abandon the prejudices and maxims with which his rank inculcated him, the baron and Saint-Preux never get beyond relating to each other as citizens of the Clarens community, itself a microcosm of a larger society. That is, they never succeed in relating to each other as individuals qua individuals. The baron and Saint-Preux's forgiveness of each other is perhaps admirable, but it is a far cry from sublime insofar as it is merely performative. In this respect Rousseau illustrates that there are limits to what the more political variety of forgiveness can achieve: it may very well bring about peace, but it fails to create a space where love and affection can truly flourish.

8

TO FORGIVE OR NOT TO FORGIVE?
THAT IS THE QUESTION

The unfinished sequel to *Émile*, *Émile and Sophie*, has long been a source of confusion, frustration, and outright consternation among critics. Being the product of a meticulous education, Émile's and Sophie's enduring happiness seems all but secured at the end of the fifth book, with the conclusion of their marriage and the announcement that a child is on its way. Yet, much to the reader's surprise, in the sequel, things do not go quite as planned. The two young lovers find themselves in the depths of despair, the victims of a corrupt society, certainly, but also of their own poor decision making. The result: Sophie is pregnant with another man's child, and Émile is lost and indecisive as to what course of action he should take. He is desperate and, quite frankly, miserable.

The protagonists' respective fates were so unexpected, and so very antithetical to Rousseau's expressed aims in *Émile*, that Bernardin de Saint-Pierre, a close friend and admirer of Rousseau, could not help but wonder what must have been going through Rousseau's mind when he composed the text. Upon reading *Émile and Sophie*, he admonished Rousseau, "do you not fear that, in seeing Sophie become culpable, one might ask you what the use of so many refinements, and of so many efforts might be? Is this really the fruit of nature's education?" (ne craignez-vous qu'en voyant Sophie coupable, on ne vous demande à quoi servent tant d'apprêts, tant de soins? est-ce donc là le fruit de l'éducation de la nature?).[1] Even the briefest overview of more recent critical literature on the topic reveals that Bernardin de Saint-Pierre's question still resonates widely in our own time, as whether

Émile and Sophie represents the failure or success of Rousseau's educational system is still very much open up for debate. What are we to make of Sophie's apparent infidelity? Further, how are we to understand Émile's flagrant incapacity to decide what to do in response to it without the careful guidance (and manipulation) of his tutor?

In the pages that follow, I explore these very questions. Unlike many of those who have already done so, however, my point of focus is the role that conflict plays in assessing the quality of both Émile's and Sophie's respective educations. My view is that *Émile and Sophie* represents not so much a failure of the educative principles that Rousseau propounds in *Émile* but rather a further development on them. Further, I do not read this text as simply another instantiation of Rousseau's pessimism, whereby history always leads to catastrophe and degeneration, as is the case in the *Discourse on Inequality*. Instead, I see the conflict and the tragedy with which both Émile and Sophie are confronted as a necessary step in their acquisition of independence from corrupting societal norms and, most important, of a more self-conscious perspective that enables both protagonists to articulate and, to an extent, anyway, reconcile their split identities as individuals and as citizens. An analysis of Émile's deliberations concerning the appropriateness of forgiveness in the case of Sophie's infidelity (and her own response to them) demonstrates that the very sophistication of these two star-crossed lovers' reflections reveal their keen awareness as to the complications and alienation that inevitably results from the social contract and, for that matter, from all contracts derived therefrom (particularly that of marriage). In this manner the text picks up on a very similar theme to that which we find in the *Dialogues*, as discussed earlier. Specifically, whereas Émile and, to a lesser extent, Sophie had been raised to be somewhat resistant to such alienation, they were not educated in a manner that would have prepared them to actually observe or rectify it were it to appear in their own behavior.

The problems and self-doubt on the part of the protagonists that arise on account of Sophie's infidelity are what must eventually lead them, after many trials and tribulations, to the discovery of way to reconcile their own bifurcated identities. I demonstrate how the views on anger and reconciliation expressed in *Émile and Sophie* relate to Rousseau's thoughts on subjectivity and, especially, the radically dissimilar psychological experiences of the individual-acting-as-such and that of the citizen qua citizen that underpin his philosophical system. Émile's contemplations concerning the appropriateness of forgiveness in the case of Sophie hinge on a decision as to whether he wishes to respond to her infidelity as a citizen or as an individual. The letters that constitute *Émile and Sophie* thus grapple not only with the question as to whether forgiveness is possible following grievous personal slight but, more important, with the question as to how deliberations regarding the appropriateness of reconciliation can and should be carried out. As the text advances, it becomes clear that even the product of a meticulously orchestrated moral education cannot help but struggle to answer these questions and, in so doing, experience the sublime terror that inevitably results when the individual within battles against the citizen in which it is housed. Interrogating the larger implications of what transpires in *Émile and Sophie* sheds new light on the problem of subjective identity under the rubric of Rousseau's philosophical system.

It is worth stating explicitly that what follows is a response and a challenge to those who have interpreted *Émile and Sophie* as an admission of failure on Rousseau's part as to the natural education outlined in *Émile* or as an instantiation of the decay that invariably follows every golden age. Indeed, more recent critics have been no less flabbergasted by what befalls Émile and Sophie after the tutor has passed away than Bernardin de Saint-Pierre had been shortly after the composition of *Émile and Sophie*. Critical analyses of the text often begin with a similar question as to whether the text was intended to indicate either the failure or the success of Émile and Sophie's respective educations. Nancy Senior, for example, suggests that Émile's education undoubtedly fails, as "in the first crises he must face, he runs away from all responsibility." According to Senior's reading, Sophie fairs only slightly better. Although her behavior ends up being unsatisfactory, she ultimately performs in a manner that was inevitable given the (faulty) education that she had received: "She carries on in difficult circumstances in a way which could not have been predicted, for which she was not prepared, and which is the opposite of the result aimed at in her formation. Thus there are in her case two kinds of failure: first, where education determines her conduct, the result is unsatisfactory; and second, where her conduct is admirable, it is not determined by her education." According to Senior, if Sophie behaves admirably at times, this is an accident rather than the predicted and intended outcome of the education she was provided with.[2] Luck, spontaneity, and confusion—not skills honed by Rousseau's pedagogical techniques—are ultimately posited in her reading as Sophie's saving graces.

In contrast to Senior, Denise Schaeffer provides a much more positive assessment of what exactly occurs in *Émile*, at least with regard to Sophie. She challenges the notion that Sophie does not possess the wholeness of a unified soul devoid of internal conflict and thus that she does not achieve the ideal that Rousseau presents as being the means to achieving freedom and happiness. Instead, she suggests that Sophie's dividedness does not represent a failure but rather "a more complex model of the human soul than does that of Émile," which is both self-possessed and consciously maintained. Schaeffer does so, first, by stressing that utter self-sufficiency and wholeness are presented as impossible to maintain—even for meticulously educated individuals—beyond the arrival of puberty, which gives birth to the passions that "will take [Émile] outside of himself for the first time; he needs another human being." She in turn notes Émile's dependence on Sophie for sexual gratification and the like. Finally, Schaeffer underscores the moral independence and the capacity to reason that Sophie must exercise (in contradistinction to Émile). In so doing, she draws the reader's attention to the following (and often-overlooked) passage from *Émile*: "She becomes the judge of her judges; she decides when she ought to submit herself to them and when she ought to take exception to them. . . . As soon as she depends on both her own conscience and the opinions of others, she has to learn to compare these two rules, to reconcile them, and to prefer the former only when the two are in contradiction" (4:383). Through a variety of examples from *Émile*, Schaeffer convincingly demonstrates that Sophie is neither as effaced nor dependent as she is often seen to be: she freely chooses the books she reads, the lessons she takes from them, and the lover she eventually marries. Most important, she decides "when to submit and when to lead," which, as Schaeffer points out, is "hardly the mark of an individual deprived of moral or intellectual autonomy." Schaeffer thus lauds Sophie for her self-awareness of the fact that she must exist "both inside and outside the whole" that she must willfully maintain. This leads Schaeffer, first, to the conclusion that Sophie's education "must not merely compliment Émile's; it must comprehend it and transcend it" and, second, that "her imperfection, in the form of her divided soul, is both inevitable and necessary. It is what allows her to accept imperfection in turn; she chooses the real over the ideal."[3]

I do not take issue with Schaeffer's very carefully nuanced reading of Sophie's character. Further, I find her observation that the recognition of her "imperfection in the form of her divided soul" is a source of accepting imperfections in others (and, in particular, in Émile) quite compelling. I do, however, think that her assessment of the character of Émile, particularly in her discussion of *Émile and Sophie*, is perhaps overly polarized. That is, I suggest that Émile *does* become aware, albeit somewhat tardily, of the "tension in human existence that makes the family, understood as an unstable and imperfect whole, both possible and necessary." Whereas Schaeffer reads Émile as capable only of alternately inhabiting his identity as a man and a citizen, and as therefore incapable of avoiding the extremes of either engulfment or detachment from his role at the head of the family, my view is that Émile acquires the capacity to better negotiate the tensions inherent to his own existence over the course of the text.[4] *Émile and Sophie* does not represent the eternal separation of two very different perspectives and thus approaches to the problem of subjective identity. Rather, the text narrates the gradual convergence of two views that were largely independent from each other (if not in outright opposition) in *Émile* into a more self-conscious perspective that both Émile and Sophie are eventually able to share. This perspective is gleaned from deliberations on the meaning and possibility of reconciliation in the wake of grievous personal slight.

The first letter of *Émile and Sophie*, written by Émile and addressed to his perhaps already-deceased mentor (Émile is unsure), begins as follows:

> These papers will not reach you; I cannot hope for it. Doubtless they will perish without having been seen by any man, but it does not matter; they have been written, I gather them together, I bind them, I continue them, and it is to you that I address them: it is for you that I want to trace those precious memories that both nourish and distress my heart; it is to you that I wish to give an account of myself, of my feelings, of my conduct, of this heart that you gave me.

> (Ces papiers ne vous parviendront pas, je ne puis l'espérer. Sans doute ils périront sans avoir été vus d'aucun homme: mais n'importe, ils sont écrits, je les rassemble, je les lie, je les continue, et c'est à vous que je les addresse: c'est à vous que je veux tracer ces précieux souvenirs qui nourrissent et navrent mon coeur; c'est à vous que je veux rendre compte de moi, de mes sentimens, de ma conduite, de ce coeur que vous m'avez donné.)[5]

Published in 1764, approximately six years prior to the completion of the *Confessions*, Émile's address already bears the stamp of Rousseau's post-*Confessions* period, as both his *Rousseau, Judge of Jean-Jacques* and the *Reveries* (or so he maintained) were written not for another, not for posterity, but rather for the author himself. What is more, in a manner quite similar to the Rousseau who wrote the opening lines of the *Reveries*, the writer of these letters composes them in utter solitude: "still young I lost everything—wife, children, friends, in sum everything—even all commerce with my fellows" (13:685–86; 4:881; jeune encore j'ai tout perdu, femme, enfans, amis, tout enfin, jusqu'au commerce de mes semblables). On account of his utter isolation, the letters that Émile composes are expressly written without any concern for a world of witnesses that may either condemn or approve of the story he recounts. Confident that his sincerity attests to his unwavering fidelity to those principles that were the cornerstone of his education, namely independence from social prejudice and arbitrary concerns for rank and reputation, Émile claims that he shall withhold no details about what led to his misfortune: "I shall say everything, the good, the bad, my pains, my pleasures, my faults; but I believe that I have nothing to say that could dishonor your work" (13:686; 4:882; Je dirai tout, le bien, le mal, mes douleurs, mes plaisirs, mes fautes; mais je crois n'avoir rien à dire qui puisse deshonorer vôtre ouvrage).

Émile's confidence in his integrity and sincerity notwithstanding, these letters—and in particular the first one—confront the problem of amour propre and the alienation of the individual that the sentiment is so adept at fostering. Émile's education did not, as we learn, render him or, for that matter, Sophie immune to amour propre or the trappings of a corrupt civil society, as both protagonists fell prey to the Parisian temptations almost immediately upon contact. Yet, and this is what ultimately saves Émile, his education had instilled in him the capacity to recognize when the influence of social commerce had overreached its proper bounds and its effects had become deleterious. What remains to be seen is if and how Émile's education and experience of subjectivity ultimately directed his reflections on whether or not he should forgive Sophie and the extent to which this illustrates the acquisition of moral maturity and self-reliance.

Rousseau, as we have already discussed, had two very distinct notions of forgiveness—one that was directed toward the world and that derived both its authority and efficaciousness from its ability to conform to public opinion and another directed toward and bestowed in the name of its object. The former variety of forgiveness is thus inextricably connected to (albeit a higher form of) amour propre, which motivates agents to strive to bring both their expression of anger and its resolution into agreement with the generalized codes of conduct of the society in which they reside, while the latter variety constitutes a rejection of the very grounds on which such an agreement could be reached.

Émile's contemplations concerning the appropriateness of forgiveness in the case of Sophie hinge on a decision as to which perspective he can and should adopt toward her. In fact, the letters that constitute *Émile and Sophie*

grapple not only with the question as to whether forgiveness is possible following grievous personal slight but also with the question as to which variety of rectificatory action one can and should consider when one is gravely
wronged by the object of one's love in the context of marriage.

Appropriately, the text begins with Émile thanking his already-deceased
teacher for the upbringing he had received. Émile credits Jean-Jacques for
having provided him with the maxim that saved him from certain demise, a
maxim that he could fully appreciate only once in the face of adversity: "In
order to know the universe by means of everything that could concern me,
it was enough for me to know myself; once my place was assigned, everything was found" (13:686; 4:882–83; Pour connoitre l'univers pour tout ce qui
pouvoit m'intéresser il me suffit de me connoitre; ma place assignée, tout
fut trouvé). Émile then begins to narrate the events that led to the dissolution of his marriage and his subsequent choice to abandon his beloved wife.

The loss of a child and an inconsolable mother necessitated a move to
Paris, the seat of all vice. As Émile explains, very quickly following the
death of Jean-Jacques, both he and Sophie became utterly corrupted by both
their surroundings and their grief: they ate and drank in bad company; they
became somewhat lax in fulfilling their domestic duties; they grew apart.
Soon after their arrival in Paris, Sophie's and Émile's affection for each other
began to wane, and for some initially unknown reason, Émile no longer
enjoyed the *droits d' époux* that Sophie had so willingly honored him with
previously. The reason, Sophie finally avowed, is that she was pregnant with
another man's child.[6] What follows this confession is the first-person narrative of the internal struggle Émile underwent in response to such a discovery, a struggle in which he found that both the dictates of his conscience and
his knowledge of Sophie's temperament constantly clashed with traditional
views on both marriage and adultery and with what he took to be the judgment that society would render if it were to be apprised of his situation.

Émile's deliberations begin with the assertion that there is no crime as
vile as that which Sophie committed. Overcome with grief and not above
contemplating vengeance, Émile proclaims, "There is no debasement, no
crime comparable to hers" (13:697; 4:896; Il n'y a point d'abbaissemement,
point de crime pareil au sien). This conclusion is undoubtedly a reference
to the civic education he had received. In *Émile* the narrator defines the role
of the woman as being the sacred vessel of domestic virtue: "She serves as
the link between [the children] and their father; she alone makes him love
them and gives him the confidence to call them his own" (13:535; 4:697; Elle
sert de liaison entre eux et leur pére, elle seule les lui fait aimer et lui donne
la confiance de les appeller siens). Because the woman's role is to act as the

gluc that bonds the family together, her infidelity threatens the security and integrity of the familial unit at its core. A husband's infidelity, however dishonest or pernicious it may be, is in this respect incomparable:

> Doubtless it is not permitted to anyone to violate his faith, and every unfaithful husband who deprives his wife of the only reward of the austere duties of her sex is an unjust and barbarous man. But the unfaithful woman does more; she dissolves the family and breaks all the bonds of nature. In giving the man children which are not his, she betrays both. She joins perfidy to infidelity. . . . What does the family become in such a situation if not a society of secret enemies whom a guilty woman arms against one another in forcing them to feign mutual love?
>
> (*Émile*, 13:535–36; 4:697–98; Sans doute il n'est permis à personne de violer sa foi, et tout mari infidelle qui prive sa femme du seul prix des austéres devoirs de son séxe est un homme injuste et barbare: mais la femme infidelle fait plus, elle dissout la famille et brise tous les liens de la nature; en donnant à l'homme des enfans qui ne sont pas à lui elle trahit les uns et les autres, elle joint la perfidie à l'infidélité. . . . Qu'est-ce que alors que la famille si ce n'est une societé d'ennemis secrets qu'une femme coupable arme l'un contre l'autre en les forçant de feindre de s'entre-aimer?)

It is on account of the woman's responsibility to assure the legitimacy of the children she bears and, it follows, guarantee the affections of their father toward them that Rousseau maintained that, to do honor to her husband, a woman was bound to respect the laws and judgments of society and tradition in a way that a man was not. Because a woman's virtue is what ultimately ensures the cohesion of the family unit and, by extension, that of society, her actions must be directed always to the preservation of her good name. Her virtue must not only be recognized by her husband; it must also be ratified by public opinion:

> It is important, then, not only that woman be faithful, but that she be judged to be faithful by her husband, by those near her, by everyone. It is important that she be modest, attentive, reserved, and that she give evidence of her virtue to the eyes of others as well as to her own conscience. If it is important that a father love his children, it is

important that he esteem their mother. . . . Opinion is the grave of virtue among men and its throne among women.

(13:536, 540; 4:698, 702–3; Il n'importe donc pas seulement que la femme soit fidelle, mais qu'elle soit jugée telle par son mari, par ses proches, par tout le monde; il importe qu'elle soit modeste, attentive, reservée, et qu'elle porte aux yeux d'autrui comme en sa proper conscience le témoignange de sa vertu: s'il importe qu'un pére aime ses enfans, il importe qu'il estime sa mère. . . . L'opinion est le tombeau de la vertu parmi les hommes, et son trône parmi les femmes.)

It is worth pausing here for a moment to consider the conundrum in which Émile found himself when he learned of Sophie's affair: the gravity of her crime is largely derived from social norms and concerns for rank. In a hierarchical society wherein titles and rank and therefore pedigree are of the upmost importance, the crime of infidelity on the part of any woman functions as an attack not just on the cuckold husband but on the fabric of society as a whole. What is more, the woman's infidelity is against nature. Indeed, as Rousseau maintains in *Émile*, the lack of parity between the sexes is not a social construct but rather the result of nature and of the "constitution of sexes" (4:695; constitution des sexes):

The strictness of the relative duties of the two sexes is not and cannot be the same. When woman complains on this score about unjust manmade inequality, she is wrong. This inequality is not a human institution—or, at least, it is the work not of prejudice but of reason. It is up to the sex that nature has charged with the bearing of children to be responsible for them to the other sex.

(13:535; 4:697; La rigidité des devoirs rélatifs des deux sexes n'est ni ne peut être la même. Quand la femme se plaint là-dessus de l'injuste inégalité qu'y met l'homme, elle a tort; cette inégalité n'est point une institution humaine, ou du moins elle n'est point l'ouvrage du préjugé mais de la raison: c'est à celui des deux que la nature a chargé du dépôt des enfans d'en répondre à l'autre.)

According to such logic, Sophie's infidelity was not simply a crime in the eyes of society; there was also something intrinsically evil and unnatural about it.

Such a view of infidelity, however, is complicated in *Émile and Sophie*, and Rousseau seems to have returned—at least in part—to his earlier views on monogamy as a social construct as per the *Second Discourse.*[7] What I mean by this is that, in his deliberations, Émile presents Sophie's crime as evil only insofar as it runs against and, indeed, threatens to undermine decidedly social virtues. But as someone who loves her, knows her intimately, and has witnessed her regret, he desires to overlook her infidelity and forgive her, thereby insinuating that—at least as far as he is concerned—her crime was not evil in any absolute sense. Much of the tension in that first letter is born from the difficulty in deciding which viewpoint to adopt, namely that of a citizen or that of an individual.

Sophie is not merely the wife of Émile. She is his soul mate and, in many respects his double. Not surprisingly, therefore, Émile has somewhat of a hybrid view of her, one born from his own bifurcated identity. As a citizen acting in a society with laws, morals, customs, and rights of succession, he condemns her behavior—and this absolutely. Nevertheless, he maintains just as quickly that, in an absolute sense and as an individual and in relation to others, Sophie's virtue remains intact: she committed an error that resulted from poor judgment on her part. Yet this act was neither the result of an innate tendency toward vice nor evidence of an utter disregard on her part for virtue. Of this he seems fairly certain: "Ah! If Sophie sullied her virtue, what woman will dare to count on hers? . . . She is guilty without being contemptible; she may have committed a crime, but not an act of cowardice" (13:689, 699; 4:887, 898; Si Sophie a souillé sa vertu, quelle femme osera compter sur la sienne? . . . Elle est coupable sans être vile; elle a pu commettre un crime mais non pas une lâcheté). What is more, Émile also recognizes that he is at least in part to blame for what occurred. "Oh Émile!" he rhetorically asks himself, "You lost her, you must hate yourself and feel sorry for her; but what right do you have to scorn her? Did you yourself remain irreproachable? . . . You did not share in her infidelity, but did you not excuse it in ceasing to honor her virtue" (13:698; 4:896–97; Ô Émile! tu l'as perdue, tu dois te haïr et la plaindre; mais quel droit as-tu de la mépriser? Es-tu resté toi-même irréprochable? . . . Tu n'as point partagé son infidélité, mais ne l'as-tu pas excusée, en cessant d'honorer sa vertu?). Such reflections soften Émile's hardened heart. He begins to look on Sophie more favorably; he "excuses her" without "justifying her" and "approves" of her confession, even though he cannot "forgive the crime" (4:898; Sans la justifier je l'excusois; sans pardonner ses outrages, j'approuvois ses bons procédés).

These two contradicting views of Sophie and of her crime dictate two diametrically opposed courses of action for Émile: just as Émile flashes between his identity as an individual and that of a citizen, he wavers between forgiveness and punishment. On account of his reflections on Sophie's enduring purity and what he knows of her true character, he briefly considers preserving the marriage, no matter what effect that may have on public opinion and no matter how foolish he may appear in the eyes of others. Further, he reasons that, in a town such as Paris, infidelity is par for the course. This, he surmises, must diminish at least in part the gravity of Sophie's crime, given their location at the time it was committed. Finally, Émile has been raised to follow his own feelings and moral instincts, and he knows that he must not rely too heavily on the support, judgments, or recommendations of others. In his letter to Jean-Jacques, he thus declares his own personal distaste for the rigidity of the laws and of the criteria by which the actions of men (and, for that matter, women) are necessarily judged. In so doing, he expresses a desire to form a more individualized and holistic judgment of Sophie.

Appropriately, after drawing attention to the corrupt nature of "big cities" and the tolerance for infidelity that pervades them, he attempts to bring reason into accord with what is his heart's desire to forgive Sophie:

> "Does a man's honor," they say, "depend on his wife? Must his misfortune cause his shame, and can he be dishonored by someone else's vices?" The other morality might well be more severe; this one appears more in conformity with reason. "Moreover, whatever judgment people might pass on my behavior by my own principles, wasn't I above public opinion? What did it matter what people might think of me, provided that in my own heart I did not stop being good, just, decent? Was it a crime to be merciful? Was it an act of cowardice to pardon an offense?"
>
> Based on what duties was I going to rule myself, then? Had I disdained the men's prejudices for so long in order to sacrifice my happiness to it in the end?
>
> . . . But the one who is reproached more for a fault than a vice and who expiates it by her regrets is more worthy of pity than of hatred; one can feel sorry for her and pardon her without shame; the unhappiness for which she is reproached is a warrant for her for the future.
>
> (13:700–701; 4:900; L'honneur d'un homme, disent-ils, dépende il de sa femme? Son malheur doit-il faire sa honte, et peut-il être déshonoré des vices d'autrui? L'autre morale a beau être plus sévère, celle-ci paroit plus conforme à la raison.

D'ailleurs, quelque jugement qu'on portât de mes procédés, n'étois-je pas par mes principes au dessus de l'opinion publique? Que m'importoit ce qu'on penseroit de moi, pourvû que dans mon propre cœur je ne cessasse point d'être bon, juste, honnête? Etoit-ce une lâcheté de pardonner une offense? Sur quels devoirs allois-je donc me régler? Avois-je si longtemps dédaigné le préjugé des hommes pour lui sacrifier enfin mon bonheur?

. . . Mais celle à qui l'on reproche plustôt une faute qu'un vice et qui l'expie par ses regrets est plus digne de pitié que de haine; on peut la plaindre et la pardonner sans honte; le malheur même qu'on lui reproche est garant d'elle pour l'avenir.)

Here, we see, Émile recounts how Sophie willingly and voluntarily confessed her crime to him. It was plain to him that the pain she experienced on account of her error was intense: "Did I not see her regrets, her repentance in her eyes? Is it not her sadness that led me back to her feet, is it not her touching pain that gave me back all my tenderness?" (13:698; 4:897; N'ai-je pas vû ses regrets, son repentir dans ses yeux? N'est-ce pas sa tristesse qui m'a ramené moi-même à ses pieds, n'est-ce pas sa touchante douleur qui m'a rendu toute ma tendresse?). Émile recognizes the sincerity and depth of Sophie's remorse, so intimate is his knowledge of her, so deep their connection. Further, on account of the vicar's profession of faith, he has been exposed to the idea that, when one focuses one's attention on the pangs of a guilty conscience, one is automatically redeemed—not in the eyes of man but in the eyes of God. He also appears to ascribe to the notion that our errors in the world are often the result of faulty reasoning, a faculty independent from the conscience, the latter of which can never be fooled, as it is the unadulterated voice of the soul (4:594–95). Émile is thus initially moved to forgive Sophie on account of what he takes to be her true character and, according to a transmundane morality, one that is above and beyond the relative and thus fallible morality practiced in the social realm. The words "they say" (disent-ils) at the beginning of the passage just cited underscore the extent to which Émile has internalized public opinion to a degree that allows him to predict the judgment that it would render were his peculiar situation to be rendered public. The rest of the passage, however, betrays his desire to declare his independence from such a yoke.

But even if Émile's love of Sophie and his desire for utter independence in morally judging the worth of others provides its own justifications for forgiving Sophie, the same cannot be said for his socially conditioned faculty of reason. Again, as per book 5 of *Émile*, the tutor regards the infidelity of a husband as unacceptable, certainly. However, the infidelity of a wife is infinitely worse, as it necessarily calls into question the paternity of any and all children that a woman may bear—not just in the eyes of the father but also in the eyes of the world. It is for precisely this reason that infidelity threatens the family unit at its very core and in turn weakens the very fabric of society. From this it follows that the social significance of adultery is amplified exponentially when committed by a woman. To a large extent, Émile is both able and willing to overlook this basic fact and follow his inclinations, as opposed to the socially accepted course of action. After all, Émile had been taught by the vicar: "All the morality of our actions is in the judgment we ourselves make of them. If it is true that the good is good, it must be so in the depths of our hearts as it is in our works, and the primary reward for justice is to sense that one practices it (13:449; 4:595; Toute la moralité de nos actions est dans le jugement que nous en portons nous-mêmes. S'il est vrai que le bien soit bien il doit l'être au fond de nos coeurs comme dans nos oeuvres, et le prémier prix de la justice est de sentir qu'on la pratique).

As the narrative continues, however, Émile realizes that his decision to forgive Sophie is neither laudable nor entirely void of amour propre. The reason for this is quite simple: Sophie and Émile love each other as individuals. But they are *also* husband and wife and are thus joined by a contractual agreement that derives its force and meaning from social conventions. They relate to each other not only as individuals but also as citizens. Their relationship must therefore straddle, navigate, and eventually reconcile the demands of love and duty, of individuated concern for each other, and of respect for the laws of the society in which they reside. To forgive Sophie in the name of her individuated distinctness would entail, on the flip side, undermining Émile's respect for and adherence to the all-too-often obscured but nevertheless necessarily omnipresent laws that legitimize the state in which they both reside as husband and wife. In a manner similar to the Frenchman, Émile must find the means of being true to the general will and what its decree would be were it to manifest itself in public opinion. Again, Sophie and Émile are in Paris, where adultery is more or less accepted and often approved of. But this fact alone does not render adultery permissible as far as the general will is concerned, as the general will is not merely a "majority rules" scenario. Rather, it is that which arises when the general good becomes the guiding force of the law and that which is articulated only occasionally (and in ideal scenarios) by public opinion. Émile may have overcome his personalized anger toward Sophie. What is more, he may

172 Private, Interpersonal Forgiveness

feel that the intensity of her feelings of guilt redeems her. This does not, however, mean that he can—in good conscience anyway—return to living in *marital* bliss with her. In his capacity as an individual he is above public opinion. In his capacity as a citizen, however, he is obliged to admit that the judgment he knows public opinion would offer were his wife's infidelity to be rendered public would not merely be a "majority rules" judgment but rather an expression of the general will functioning properly. Sophie violated the marital contract. The contract is now thus null and void. It is worth quoting Émile's deliberations at length on this point:

> I would have wanted to be able to return to unfaithful Sophie, and I listened with indulgence to everything that seemed to authorize my cowardice. But try as I might, my reason, less tractable than my heart, could not adopt these follies. I could not dissimulate to myself that I was arguing in order to impose on myself, not in order to enlighten myself. I said to myself sadly but forcefully that the maxims of high society do not constitute a law for someone who wants to live for himself, and that, prejudice for prejudice, those of good morals have an additional one that favors them; that it is with reason that one imputes a wife's disorders to her husband, either for having chosen her badly, or for governing her badly . . . and that if Émile had always been wise Sophie would never have been at fault; that one has the right to presume that the one who does not respect herself at least respects her husband, if he is worthy of it, and if he knows how to preserve his authority; that the wrong of not having prevented the dissoluteness of a wife is aggravated by the infamy of putting up with it . . . and that in such a case this impunity shows an indifference for decent morals in the offended man, and a baseness of soul unworthy of all honor.

> (13:701–2; 4:901; J'aurois voulu pouvoir revenir à Sophie infidelle, et j'écoutois avec complaisance tout ce qui sembloit autoriser ma lâcheté. Mais j'eus beau faire, ma raison moins traitable que mon coeur ne pût adopter ces folies. Je ne pus me dissimuler que je raison-nois pour m'abuser, non pour m'éclairer. Je me disois avec douleur mais avec force que les maximes du monde ne font point loi pour qui veut vivre pour soi-même, et que, prejugés pour préjugés, ceux des bonnes moeurs en ont un de plus qui les favorise; que c'est avec raison qu'on impute à un mari le desordre de sa femme, soit pour l'avoir mal choisie, soit pour la mal gouverner; . . . et que si Émile eut

été toujours sage Sophie n'eut jamais failli; qu'on a droit de presumer que celle qui ne se respecte pas elle-même respecte au moins son mari s'il en est digne et s'il sait conserver son autorité; que le tort de ne pas prévenir le déréglement d'une femme est aggravé par l'infamie de le souffrir . . . et qu'en pareil cas cette impunité marque dans l'offensé une indifférence pour les moeurs honnêtes, et une bassesse d'ame indigne de tout honneur.)

Notice here how Émile's deliberations concerning the forgivability of Sophie's crime have changed course. Initially, it was his very personalized anger and, we may assume, injured pride at the infidelity that prevented him from forgiving her. Once he realized that there was nothing absolutely evil and thus utterly unforgivable in her actions or person, it would seem that there was nothing preventing him from forgiving Sophie out of love and out of knowledge of her remorse. Yet this is not what happens. Ultimately, Émile finds that he must reject his very personal inclination to forgive, something he dismisses in the first letter as passionate and irrational. The reason? To do so would evidence a lack of respect for the contract that binds them and the duties that said contract entails. Further, it would evidence an inability to assume responsibility on his part as a social being among many others within a political system: if Sophie failed him it is in part because he had failed her first insofar as he had failed to regulate her affairs and to pay due homage to her virtue in public. Émile's usage of the words "husband" (mari) and "wife" (femme)—both references to Émile and Sophie's civic status in relation to each other—further affirms that Émile views the decision to withhold forgiveness from Sophie as being rooted in the danger that her crime represents for the institution of marriage and, it follows, the sanctity of the social contract in a more general sense.[8]

The rectitude of Émile's reasoning is confirmed by Sophie's reaction when he attempts to return to her—presumably in a moment of weakness. Sophie would not herself be so quickly forgiven. She refused to renounce the rights and duties that her socially appointed role entails. Émile's love and individuated concern for her were not enough to overcome or reverse the judgment that she had already passed on herself: she had been a bad wife and desired to suffer the consequences. Accordingly, when Émile returned to her, she recoiled in horror. At first Émile interpreted her desire to maintain her distance as proof that she no longer loved him and, even worse, that she had grown to hate him (4:902). But he quickly changed his perspective when he again reflected on her character, her remorse, and their history together. Her refusal to return to him was not the result of indifference on her part but rather a sign of her deep and enduring affection, as well as her profound respect for her husband and concern for his good name. Again, according to Émile's learned tutor, the woman is "virtue's throne," an identity that Sophie was unwilling to abandon. She declined to be reconciled with Émile on account of the fact that, in granting forgiveness, Émile would have rendered himself an inadequate citizen (and, it follows, an inadequate husband). If he had agreed to stay with Sophie and provide for the illegitimate child she was carrying, he would have essentially undermined the familial model on which society rests. What is more, their legally and socially recognized marriage would have constituted a lie and a violation of the very system that had provided their marriage with both meaning and content to begin with. Émile would have in turn been forever alienated from his role as husband, and Sophie from her role as wife.

The gravity of Émile's predicament is perhaps best understood in terms of Rousseau's discussion of general and particular wills within *A Discourse on Political Economy*. Rousseau notes that "every political society is composed of other, smaller societies, of different kinds, each of which has its own interests and maxims" (toute société politique est composée d'autres sociétés plus petites, de différentes espèces, dont chacune a ses intérêts et ses maximes). He continues,

> The will of these particular societies has always two relations; for the members of the association, it is a general will; for the great society, it is a particular will; and it is often right with regard to the first object, and wrong as to the second. . . . A particular resolution may be advantageous to the smaller community, but pernicious to the greater.

> (La volonté de ces sociétés particulières a toûjours deux relations; pour les membres de l'association, c'est une volonté générale; pour la grande société, c'est une volonté particulière, qui très souvent se trouve droite au premier égard, et vicieuse au second. . . . Telle délibération peut être avantageuse à la petite communauté, et très pernicieuse à la grande.)

Here, we see, that the individualized standards of conduct and of justice for a smaller group (i.e., guild, community, family) may very well strike the members of said group as representative of the general will. Indeed, this may even be the case *for that particular group of people*. Nevertheless, the smaller group is not for that reason free to throw off the yoke of the larger society in which it is housed. Much to the contrary, if the members of the smaller group are to be considered good citizens of the state, they must be willing to sacrifice their collective interests to the general will of the larger society. This is because, in Rousseau's political imagination, smaller societies are always subordinate to the larger political body to which they belong.[9]

Émile's realization that his desire to forgive Sophie was indeed a particular will that—if realized—would have been pernicious to the general will obliged him to change his perspective. He rather suddenly abandoned all inquiries into the exterior signs of Sophie's guilt, her moral status in his own eyes, her inherent virtue, and the possibility of a similar fault occurring again. He ceased to consider what an unsolicited confession merits as a response from the victim. He no longer pontificated on the arbitrariness of social prejudice or the inescapable nature of vice that a corrupt society so often condones. Instead, he began to consider what his forgiveness would mean for Sophie given her exceptional virtue and, again, her devotion toward her husband. Less important to him became questions of what he himself was capable of; more important became his understanding of freedom and the precedence freedom must take over one's passions. Like Sophie, Émile eventually realized that his decision as to whether to forgive or not to forgive must take into account not only his own freedom and self-image but also those of Sophie as well. Further, it had to accord due credence to the fact that—as man and wife—Sophie not only injured Émile as an individual (something that, again, he was able to overcome) but also deprived him of his exclusive rights to her in his capacity as her husband.

> The idea of Sophie returned to favor was unbearable to her. She felt that her crime was one of those that cannot be forgotten; she preferred to be punished rather than pardoned: such a pardon was not made for her; to her taste even punishment debased her less. She believed that she could not erase her fault except by expiating it, nor do what justice obliged her to do except by undergoing all the evils she deserved.
>
> . . . Sophie could be a criminal, but the husband that she had chosen for herself must be above an act of cowardice. These refinements of her amour-propre could not suit anyone but her, and perhaps I was the only one capable of penetrating them.

(13:709; 4:910; L'idée de Sophie rentrée en grace lui étoit insupport-able. Elle sentoit que son crime étoit de ceux qui ne peuvent s'oublier; elle aimoit mieux être punie que pardonnée: un tel pardon n'étoit pas fait pour elle; la punition même l'avilissoit moins à son gré. Elle croyoit ne pouvoir effacer sa faute qu'en l'expiant, ni s'acquitter avec la justice qu'en souffrant tous les maux qu'elle avoit mérités.

. . . Sophie pouvoit être criminelle, mais l'époux qu'elle s'étoit choisi devoit être au dessus d'une lâcheté. Ces raffinements de son amour-propre ne pouvoient convenir qu'à elle, et peut-être n'appartenoit-il qu'à moi de les pénétrer.)

Knowing the depths of his wife's soul and of her remorse, Émile asserts how inappropriate the bestowal of forgiveness would have been in this par-ticular case. Sophie recognized the gravity of her error, suffered profoundly on account of it, and was therefore redeemed as an individual—both in the eyes of God and those of Émile. Émile's personalized anger was therefore automatically dissipated.

Alas, in Sophie's mind, nothing could excuse the lack of prudence she demonstrated in having permitted herself to be alone with her neighbor and subsequently having allowed their relationship to be consummated. Whether she ultimately consented or not is, in this case, immaterial. More-over, she remained proud of the virtue that she had once possessed and her strength of character in relation to her moral peers. As a result, she could not accept forgiveness in her capacity as a wife. Upon his realization of this, Émile concluded that, regardless of what he may have felt inclined to do, Sophie would have remained forever incapable of forgiving herself the mis-deed she had committed.[10] Sophie did not want to be forgiven because she would rather be declared a failure in her role as wife than maintain the role at the cost of alienation from that very role. Accordingly, Émile decided that he must leave her and dole out the socially mandated punishment that Sophie felt she deserved and that she longed to suffer. If he truly respected Sophie as his wife prior to the crime, then he had to share in the indigna-tion that she felt toward herself for having violated the sanctity of their marriage. As Émile comes see it, to have done otherwise would have been cowardly.

The use of the words "spouse" (epoux) and "amour propre" in the pas-sage quoted earlier are not immaterial. The first of these terms refers to Émile's socially recognized role in relation to Sophie *as seen by the outside world*. The second refers to that (very often wicked) passion that ceaselessly forces an individual to forge comparisons between oneself and others within the social realm. This is not an insignificant detail. If Sophie and Émile relate to each other not only as friends and lovers but also as husband and wife, then their relationship is as contractual as it is emotional. They are bound to each other not only by love but also by socially assigned duties. They are not merely individuals in each other's eyes but also citizens. Because of this, how the both of them measure up to others who share the same roles of husband and wife is paramount in determining whether Sophie's infidelity may be forgiven.

What I wish to bring my reader's attention to, however, is that Émile did not refuse to forgive Sophie out of a personal desire for vengeance or on account of a refusal to accept responsibility, and Rousseau goes to great lengths to emphasize this point. On the contrary, Émile left Sophie, first, to lessen the pain that she would feel, as his presence would have served only to eternally remind her of the agony and humiliation she had caused another. It would have also debased her, as Sophie wanted to suffer the consequences of the loss of her husband in a sphere of exteriority (i.e., shame, poverty, etc.). In short, she wanted to be punished in accordance with the law. Émile was therefore forced to refuse her forgiveness on account of the righteous indignation that adultery—all adultery—arouses in him in his capacity as a citizen. As discussed in part 1, the capacity to experience such indignation at the sight of any action that violates the laws of the state is a duty of the good citizen. It is such depersonalized and principled anger that Sophie insists that Émile must struggle to maintain toward her if he is to preserve his claims to civic virtue. Émile's conundrum is thus not so different from the Frenchman in the *Dialogues*, except for the fact that the former's indignation *is* legitimate in a way that the Frenchman's was not.[11]

That Émile chose to leave Sophie in possession of the child she loved—even though he would have been legally justified in taking him from her—serves as proof that he did not leave her to cause her any retributive suffering; in his eyes (if not in Sophie's), the guilt she experienced had already redeemed her in a metaphysical sense. Moreover, as further evidence of his pure intentions toward Sophie, Émile took every precaution possible to ensure that she would be well provided for. (That he ultimately failed in this endeavor, we are to assume, was beyond his control.) As Pierre Burgelin remarks in his notes to the Pléiade edition of *Oeuvres complètes*, Émile's decision to never lay eyes on Sophie again does not negate but rather strengthens the bond that they share: "Despite the obstacle that forbids them to seek each other out, they never cease to exist in relation to each other. Marriage is a sort of transcendence in relation to one's doubles" (Malgré l'obstacle qui leur interdit de se chercher, ils n'existent toujours qu'en fonction l'un de l'autre. Le mariage a une sorte de transcendance par rapport à ses avatars).[12] Essentially, Émile sacrificed the pleasures that he could have still shared with Sophie on this earth to remain true to the principles that both he and his wife cherished. He did not forgive her in the traditional sense of the term, as that would have been to punish his wife eternally by obliging both himself and her to pretend that the event had never happened. Further, it would have violated the sanctity of marriage as an ideal. Forgiveness in this instance would have reduced the quality and strength of their relationship by adding an element of mere performativity to it in their capacity as citizens. Rather than debasing their former roles of husband and wife, Sophie and Émile opt to abandon these roles altogether and at the expense of the love they still have for each other.

Appropriately, the first letter closes with a description of the very personal sacrifice that Émile feels he made in leaving his family to be loyal to the principles that both he and Sophie—in their capacity as citizens—shared. Upon leaving, he resolves to always fulfill his duties to humankind, duties that will provide no tangible advantages for him personally, as he will no longer have any. He will not, we may assume, enter into any other contractual relationships with individuals whom he loves and esteems as such, as such contractual relationships necessarily circumscribe the individuals involved into fixed relations vis-à-vis each other wherein generalized codes of conduct must prevail over personal inclinations, desires, and affections. Such contractual relationships thus require the participants to resolve any violations of the contract in accordance with the general will and within the juridical sphere, a sphere beyond the sphere in which love-based forgiveness (such as that which Émile is inclined to grant) can intervene. By its very nature the contract ensures that the future of its participants shall function in relation to each other in a manner consistent with a past agreement and the rights and duties that such an agreement entails, regardless of what one's feelings or desires may be. Émile's misery and his confusion as to how to respond to Sophie's infidelity stem from the fact that she had breeched the marital contract in the worst possible way. The only option that was left to Sophie and Émile was to dissolve this contract completely by abandoning each other.

Rather tellingly, from the moment Émile separates himself from his wife and thus from his past, he resolves to live in a perpetual present. His duties, he claims, will not arise on account of contracts or promises he makes, the purpose of which is to ensure a predictable course of action by means of locking the participants into a fixed set of acceptable behaviors. Instead, Émile's duties will be assigned to him always as they arise and as his humanity dictates. In this respect he becomes a man without a country. He recovers the absolute freedom of the wise man, one who has freed himself from all obligations that may be imposed on him by others:

> The wise man lives from day to day and finds all his daily duties around him. Let us not attempt anything beyond our strength and not carry our existence forward. My duties of today are my sole task; those of tomorrow have not yet come. What I ought to do at present is to distance myself from Sophie, and the path that I ought to choose is the one that takes me away from her most directly. . . .
>
> . . . Among the Peoples where I have lived, on the seas that I have traveled over, in the deserts I have crossed, wandering for so many years, I have regretted only one single thing, and that was the one whom I had to flee. If my heart had left me calm, my body would have lacked nothing.
>
> (13:710; 4:911; Le sage vit au jour la journée et trouve tous ses devoirs quotidiens autour de lui. Ne tentons rien au delà de nos forces et ne nous portons point en avant de nôtre existence. Mes devoirs d'aujourd'hui sont ma seule tâche, ceux de demain ne sont pas encore venus. Ce que je dois faire à présent est de m'éloigner de Sophie, et le chemin que je dois choisir est celui qui m'en éloigne le plus directement.
>
> . . . Chez les Peuples où j'ai vécu, sur les mers que j'ai parcourues, dans les déserts que j'ai traversés, errant durant tant d'années, je n'ai regretté qu'une seule chose, et c'étoit celle que j'avois à fuir. Si mon coeur m'eut laissé tranquille, mon corps n'eut manqué de rien.)

Errant and free from the laws of any particular country, it is only the necessary loss of his love object, Sophie, that Émile regrets.

The facility with which Émile adapts to his physical enslavement in the second letter further evidences the fact that the transition was complete, as his desires never extend beyond his immediate physical needs and those of his fellow slaves. What is more, because he has renounced not just the marital contract but also the social contract, he need not regard his slavery as a violation of his rights, as he has no longer has any. Indeed, he is able to be enslaved largely on account of the fact that he has left his country and is thus no longer bound nor protected by any particular social contract. He may, we can assume, remain capable of rage at his own suffering and pity at the sight of others suffering. Nevertheless, socially ratifiable indignation is no longer within his purview. Émile clings only to his humanity and his own self-possessed principles, on which he will henceforth stand or fall.

At the time he wrote the first letter, the task at hand was to examine his conscience fully, to purge himself of his past once and for all through writing, and then to flee. Having accomplished these tasks, Émile's past had nothing more to demand of him: he had confronted it, and, further, he had fulfilled all his responsibilities that his former civic and decidedly linear existence had imposed on him. He had upheld the sanctity of marriage in renouncing his own. But this came at a cost: Émile could no longer bear to live as a member in the society that had forced him to render himself unhappy. Appropriately, the second letter commences with the words: "I drank the elixir of forgetfulness; the past is erased from my Memory, and the universe is opening before me" (13:711; 4:912; J'ai bu l'eau d'oubli; le passé s'efface de ma Mémoire et l'univers s'ouvre devant moi). Indeed, in the second letter no further mention of the past, or for that matter of Sophie, is ever made.

Unfortunately, Rousseau never finished *Émile and Sophie*, and it is thus difficult to know for sure what would have happened to its protagonists had Rousseau done so. Did Rousseau intend for Sophie to die of her remorse? Was she eventually to be reconciled with Émile? What was to become of Émile after regaining his freedom? It is hard to answer these questions definitively. But the accounts offered by both the Abbé Prévost in his "Lettre sur J. J. Rousseau" from the *Archives littéraires de l'Europe* and Bernardin de Saint-Pierre in the notes that he took during his time with Rousseau that were published by Maurice Souriau in 1907 under the title, *La vie et les ouvrages de Jean-Jacques Rousseau*, do seem to reveal that Rousseau imagined a reconciliation taking place between the two lovers.

According to Prévost's account, Rousseau envisioned Émile finding himself on a deserted island adorned with a temple decorated with fruits and flowers. After some time on the island, Sophie finally reveals herself as the caretaker of this temple to virtue. She is under the mistaken impression that Émile has found another spouse: "Émile learns of the fraud and violence to which she finally succumbed. But, unworthy of being his companion, she wants to be his slave and serve her proper rival" (Émile aprend le tissue de frauds et de violence sous lequel elle a succombé. Mais indigne désormais d'être sa compagne, elle veut être son esclave et server sa proper rivale).[13] Wanting to be with his true love once again, Émile develops a plan to reconcile himself to Sophie: he engages the services of a fake rival for Sophie who pretends to be his wife. Sophie is hurt but goes to great efforts to dissimulate her pain. Eventually, Émile reveals the truth and forgives her.

> This supposed rival had another husband that they present to Sophie. And Sophie finds [her husband] again, who not only forgave her for an involuntary error, one that had been expiated by the cruelest of pains and repaired through repentance, but who also esteemed and honored in her those virtues of which he had only had a faint idea until these virtues had occasion to develop themselves fully.
>
> (4:clxiv; Cette prétendue rivale avait un autre époux qu'on présente à Sophie; et Sophie retrouve le sien, qui non-seulement lui pardonne une faute involontaire, expiée par les plus cruelles peines, et réparée par le repentir, mais qui estime et honore en elle des vertus, dont il n'avait qu'une faible idée avant qu'elles eussent trouvé l'occasion de se developer dans toute leur étendue.)

Bernardin de Saint-Pierre's account differs only slightly from Prévost's. According to him, in the conclusion to *Émile and Sophie*, Émile arrives on a mysterious island with a meticulously maintained statue of the Virgin. He then falls in love with the daughter of the Spanish caretaker. According to this account, after years of searching, Sophie finds Émile on the eve of his marriage: "I have come . . . to expiate my misdeed and serve you for the rest of my life" (4:clxv; Je viens, dit-elle, pour expire ma fautte, vous server le reste de ma vie). Émile's fiancée hears this and prepares for a party following the nuptials between her and Émile, meticulously adorning the conjugal bed. When the moment arrives to consummate the marriage, his new wife cannot help but be moved by compassion for Sophie. She recognizes that Sophie is in fact Émile's true wife: "Sophie," she says, "is your first wife. Her repentance and her rights are more sacred" (Sophie . . . Émile, est votre ire epouse; son repentir et ses droits sont plus sacrés). Émile, "assailed by a tender love for the young Spaniard" and "by Sophie's repentance" and the "dangers [Sophie] undertook," decides that he could not choose between these two women. Diplomatically, therefore, he heroically opts to "imitate the patriarchs" and take both of these women as his wives. Émile never again mentions Sophie's misdeed, and the three live out their lives on a

secluded island away from a society that would surely condemn their polygamous union (4:clxv).

What is fascinating about both Prévost and Bernardin de Saint-Pierre's
accounts is that, in both of them, Émile eventually ends up forgiving Sophie
in a manner that proves irreconcilable to the social mores of the society
from which they hail. It is revealing indeed that they are able to live together
once again as husband and wife only after they have both found their way
to a deserted island, on which the rigid duties and obligations of their for-
mal marital contract no longer hold any sway. Bernardin de Saint-Pierre's
account is even more drastic in this regard, as it entails not only Sophie and
Émile ascribing to a new and individualized marital contract but also to a
polygamous relationship with the Spaniard (!). This is possible only because,
again, they are far from the society that would have commanded Émile
to publicize his indignation at Sophie's infidelity and in turn abandon her.
Émile is able to forgive Sophie and, in so doing, finally satisfy the inclination that his intimate knowledge of her had dictated to him all along once
they are both absolutely free from the social and legal confines that had prevented such reconciliation in the first place. Émile's eventual forgiveness of
Sophie therefore establishes a fundamentally and self-consciously apolitical
and utterly personalized rapport.

As discussed in my introduction, at least since the publication of
Judith Shklar's now canonical text, *Men and Citizens*, and, for that matter,
Jean Starobinski's seminal work, *Jean-Jacques Rousseau: La transparence et
l'obstacle*, Rousseau's philosophical system has customarily been regarded
by both political philosophers and literary critics alike as being primarily
concerned with the alienation that inevitably results within the social milieu on account of the irreconcilable nature of socially imposed duties and
obligations on the one hand and the demands of both emotion and natural
freedom on the other. On account of this metaphysical dualism, it is often
the case that the whole of Rousseau's thought is viewed as containing at
its core the unhappy observation that one must ultimately choose between
self-realization and public acceptance, between self-fulfillment and alienation, between nature and civilization, and between authenticity and a life
consumed by very calculated and insincere social intercourse. Ultimately,
or so it is often argued, one must make the choice—regretful though it is—
between being a wholly integrated man or a virtuous citizen.

Whereas it is true that, in many of Rousseau's works, it appears that a
choice must inevitably be made as to whether to prioritize the individual-
as-such or the emphatic citizen both in education and in one's own person,

it appears that Rousseau also believed that, even once the initial choice was made, it could be, and even needed to be, reaffirmed repeatedly throughout an individual's life. What I have tried to show in my reading of *Émile and Sophie* is that the text demonstrates that the experience of conflict in the form of grievous personal slight necessitates such affirmation. If an individual who becomes aware of personal alienation does not carefully carry out the deliberations in good faith, then one's socially recognized role risks to become merely performative and thus insincere. What is more, the experience of pain as a result of personal slight and the attendant deliberations regarding its resolution are presented in the text as an integral step to developing a mature and self-possessed moral outlook. *Émile and Sophie* thus evidences that the difficulty of resolving conflict was not simply an unrelenting theme within Rousseau's own life but, further, an integral formative experience of at least two of the characters he invented and analyzed in the continuation of one of his major literary and philosophical works.

Although the scenarios we have analyzed differ greatly, some similarities need to be highlighted. As was the case with Saint-Lambert and Rousseau, Julie's forgiveness of Saint-Preux and Saint-Preux's reconciliations with both Edouard and Wolmar and Émile's reconciliation with Sophie are all presented in a manner that constitutes a breaking of rank and a throwing off of social codes. To a large extent this is is not entirely surprising. Rousseau's disdain for fixed hierarchies and social norms based on what he took to be arbitrary and socially assigned rank is well documented. This disdain stemmed from his belief that, whereas hierarchy and inequality may very well be empirically omnipresent in modern society (and impossible to eradicate), neither contained any ontological significance; so went the thrust of the *Second Discourse*. But Rousseau did not for that reason necessarily believe that true egalitarianism was either possible or recommendable given the current state of affairs. Indeed, whereas in *The Social Contract* he states that, in an ideal state, democratic rule is superior to a monarchical system, he just as quickly notes that the possibilities of realizing such a democracy are decidedly slim. He concludes, "Were there a people of gods, their government would be democratic. So perfect a government is not for men" (59; 3:406; S'il y avoit un peuple de Dieux, il se gouverneroit Démocratiquement. Un Gouvernement si parfait ne convient pas à des hommes).

Perfect and lasting equality being an improbability within the political realm, Rousseau thus preferred to envision fruitful, intimate relations as consisting in a constantly shifting and quite fluid hydraulics of power and subjugation, at least within the intimate realm. Elizabeth Rose Wingrove's notion of consensual nonconsensuality is helpful in imagining this, as she sees Rousseau as having endorsed an ethics and a politics wherein individuals will the circumstances of their own domination. Whereas within the political sphere, the citizen's subjugation to the law and the powers that be had to be complete, this was not true for the individual acting as such. In private, interpersonal relationships the subjugation that one agrees to incur toward a particular individual entails, on the flip side, dominating in another dimension or aspect of the relationship. Wingrove sees male-female relationships as both the finest example of such consensual non-sconsensuality and its ultimate source. After all, in *Émile* the tutor advises his pupil to "[b]e a fulfilled but respectful lover. Obtain everything from love without demanding anything from duty, and always regard Sophie's least favors not as your right but as acts of grace." As Wingrove, in my view correctly, points out, "by acknowledging that Sophie remains her own mistress, Émile consents to be ruled: only her desire can authorize the satisfaction of his own."[14] Émile and Sophie's relationship is one of give and take, wherein each dominates and consents to be dominated in his or her turn. As Arthur Melzer observes, "the well-ordered family, like the well-ordered state, will be constituted by a relation of rough equality, an artful balance of powers."[15] Though Émile, as head of the family, may be recognized as Sophie's master and possessor out in the world, he is just as dependent on her good graces and benevolence at home as she is on his.[16] The intimate sphere thus provides a certain degree of freedom for the individual from the constraints of fixed hierarchies and stringently codified behaviors that characterize the public, social realm. Indeed, it is the freedom from these constraints within the private realm that render the individual capable of enduring the hardships and alienation that necessarily attend to the social contract.

With regard to forgiveness, I want to suggest that Rousseau believed that, in its paradigmatic form, it should serve to both preserve and establish power structures of this nature within private, interpersonal relationships. Under the rubric of such a power dynamic, when one forgives another one gains ascendancy over the other only by an act of consent on the part of the guilty party. In requesting this consent, the individual who forgives thus admits to a certain degree of dependency and of vulnerability insofar as the guilty party can always refuse it. This, again, is the lesson that Émile learned when he resolved to return to Sophie, only to be turned away. But if the culpable party consents to be forgiven, the forgiveness enacted establishes a debt of gratitude on both parties and not just on the recipient. The one who grants it must remain grateful for not having been refused. The one who receives it must be grateful for the bracketing of the misdeed on the part of the offended party wherever consideration of the perpetrator's character is concerned. Such gratitude, it must be stressed, is not a compulsory form of obligation that one is compelled to carry out on account of societal pressures. As Rousseau observes, "recognition is a duty that one must perform, but it is not a right that one can demand" (la reconnaissance est bien un devoir qu'il faut rendre, mais pas un droit qu'on puisse exiger).[17] For Rousseau, gratitude was positive only so long as it was sincere. For it to be sincere, it had to be expressed freely and without fear of repercussions should it be withheld. What is more, such gratitude must also be directed to and for its object, and not toward a voyeuristic social realm that is—by definition— always eager to ascribe fixed values to individuals in relation to others.

Forgiveness of the paradigmatic variety is quite similar. In its private, interpersonal form, it entails a large degree of trust. Intimate knowledge of the other's true character, expectations, and affections, as well as good faith and discretion on the part of all those involved, is therefore a necessary precondition for its bestowal. Finally, because forgiveness requires the consent of the guilty party, it must be offered and communicated directly to and for its object. Forgiveness can neither be addressed to third parties nor can it aim for either their approval or their affirmation of the superiority of the one who has forgiven in the way that the magnanimous pardon so often did. As we saw earlier, lording forgiveness over another in the way that the Messieurs do over Jean-Jacques in the *Dialogues* negates the sincerity of the action in Rousseau's eyes, thus eradicating the possibility for consensual nonconsensuality, as well as the more egalitarian grounds on which, according to Rousseau, forgiveness should be granted within private, interpersonal relationships.

Forgiveness as exchanged among friends or, in Sophie and Émile's case, sincere lovers can occur only so long as all parties involved refuse to publicize the anger that they experience in the wake of personal slight (that Émile speaks of Sophie's crime only to a deceased interlocutor is also quite relevant). Such a refusal to publicize anger serves as proof that the victim wishes to continue the relationship in a realm in which generalized standards of contact and social norms hold no sway. Saint-Lambert's discretion and Edouard's (ultimately failed) backtracking drive this point home, as does the fact that Émile opts to leave Sophie to forestall the need for the public to pass judgment on her.

As Rousseau saw it, forgiveness of the more intimate variety can perhaps best be described as a perspective in which the injured individual refuses to see both the fault and the perpetrator through the lens of amour propre, a lens that always references one's standing within society writ large and thus one's concerns with rank, prestige, and domination. What is more, it is a perspective that effectively brackets the perspectives of others who do not actively participate in the friendship or, in the case of Julie and Saint-Preux and of Émile and Sophie, a love relationship that has been voided of its passion. As a result, Rousseau moves beyond merely transferring the misdeed into a realm of nonculpability wherein society ultimately bears responsibility for forcing individuals to commit wrongs against one another. Rather, for him, forgiveness as practiced within authentic, intimate relationships consists in a staunch refusal to measure another's behavior with social metrics, even when culpability is empirically present and verifiable by external observers and would-be judges. Such forgiveness is possible because it entails a perspective in which the true character of the culpable agent—the enduring self—remains the principal point of focus in spite of the misdeed.

Rousseau makes it abundantly clear in the *Discourse on Inequality* that anger loses much of its bite and all its endurance once it is severed from society and the amour propre that pervades it. This is not to say that personal slight does not occur in the intimate realm. Indeed, as this analysis has shown, it most certainly does. Nevertheless, among friends willing to renew their commitment to one another and who refuse to see their relationship as one that exists within a fixed hierarchy defined by domination and subservience, by reputation and public affirmation, by custom and the law, one need not dwell on slight or flaunt one's magnanimity. As a result, forgiveness of an utterly personal variety that addresses the individuated distinctness of its object remains a very real possibility.

CONCLUSION

As I have tried to demonstrate throughout the course of this study, Rousseau had very complex and multifaceted views as to the roles that anger and its antidotes could and should play in both political and private, interpersonal contexts. This was due in large part to his strict distinction between the man and the citizen, and the ethical imperatives that each of these subjective identities entails whenever conflict arises. The result was that Rousseau articulated two very different assessments of anger's significance and the ways in which it could be experienced and articulated and either satisfied or resolved depending on the realm in which it was manifest.

As we have seen, anger's potentially productive capacities in group formation and, in particular, its unparalleled ability to compel the citizen to view the Other as an enemy when necessity demanded it fascinated Rousseau and proved amenable to his political theory. Rousseau, in my view correctly, noted that to eradicate the public's capacity to collectively experience anger and indignation is to eradicate its ability to rise up against those values and ideologies that threaten to undermine the sanctity of the state and the ideals of justice that it espouses, however the latter may be defined.

But, as Rousseau was just as quick to point out, anger is a very dangerous emotion indeed, and it must be very carefully deployed by the powers that be. As we have seen, this was a central premise of *Rousseau, Judge of Jean-Jacques*, as the discovery that the collective anger of a community is misguided or unjust can lead individual citizens into a nearly impossible situation, one that threatens their identity as a member of that community.

This is because the zeal of emphatic citizens simply cannot withstand the revelation of systematic injustice on the part of their compatriots. What is more, the devotion of emphatic citizens equally cannot—without great confusion and consternation, in any case—allow for political forgiveness in instances where culpability has been convincingly demonstrated, as such a pardon undermines the very authority of the law that the citizens have grown to love and thus the very reasons why they identified with the state in the first place.

With regard to private, interpersonal relationships, Rousseau also provided guidelines as to how anger need be expressed and resolved for it to accommodate the ethic of authenticity that he espoused and the ideal of friendship that he embraced. By his lights, forgiveness need not be a public performance when practiced among friends; indeed, it could not be. Further, forgiveness need not and, when paradigmatic, could not result in the subjugation of the offending party. Finally, because generalized codes of conduct hold no sway in friendship, at least not as Rousseau understood it, he found himself obliged to cut out a space for an utterly emotive variety of forgiveness, one based on enduring affections and an individuated perspective more so than on pragmatic concerns, political motives, necessity, or anything of the kind. Such forgiveness, because individuated, need not be ratified or even articulated on the public stage. Discretion, in fact, appears to have been fundamental to its bestowal, as Rousseau's relationships with Saint-Lambert and Sophie d'Houdetot, as well as his depictions of conciliatory action in both *Émile and Sophie* and *Julie*, demonstrate. Because of this, for Rousseau private, interpersonal forgiveness was a very intimate and even unpredictable experience indeed. Such forgiveness was therefore incompatible with notions of duty, pragmatic concerns, and concerns for reputation. For Rousseau, authentic forgiveness, at least as practiced in the intimate sphere, cannot be commanded, it cannot be publicized, and, above all, it must not be based on a felicitous calculation of ends and means.

The contrast between Rousseau's treatment of anger and conciliatory action with those of his contemporaries and immediate intellectual precursors could not be starker. From Francis Bacon, Hobbes and Descartes to Locke, Montesquieu, and Joseph Butler; from *Le dictionnaire de l'Académie Française* to Diderot and d'Alembert's *Encyclopédie*, through Holbach, Helvétius, Morelly, and Voltaire, we consistently find that the primary concern regarding anger (colère) in seventeenth- and eighteenth-century moral theory was how to effectively quell exterior manifestations of the emotion to the extent necessary to maintain peace within civil society. And whereas

Butler and Locke did recognize—somewhat fleetingly—that there may in some instances be a certain degree of metaphysical significance to what we might today refer to as righteous indignation, they did not think it incumbent upon themselves to attend to the effects that the sentiment could have when relegated to the innermost realms of the human heart. Until what could perhaps be most aptly referred to as the Rousseauvean intervention, little attention was paid to the emotional strife that unresolved anger might cause or the alienation that may arise on account of it when left to fester. Much of this had to do with the instrumental rationality and contract theory that the aforementioned thinkers (with the exception of Descartes) espoused and that overwhelmingly permeated the intellectual scene for so much of the seventeenth and eighteenth centuries, both in France and across the Channel. The result was that most secular justifications for renouncing one's anger were rooted in an ethic of selfish sociability and in a proto-utilitarian perspective.

Patrick Coleman sums up quite well the collective approach to anger these early modern thinkers espoused:

> Enlightenment thinkers, such as Morelly or d'Holbach, emphasized the ongoing regulation of behavior by philosophical rulers guided by their knowledge of natural laws. In a well-ordered society as these writers imagined it, there would be little occasion for anger in response to personal offense. Immediate physiological reactions to frustration could not of course be eliminated, but they would be correctible or at the very least containable, originating from the inevitable frictions of the social system rather than from expectations of personal consideration.[1]

It is telling in this respect that even the meaning of resentment (ressentiment) was quite different for the early modern subject than it is for us today. Whereas today we might define resentment as enduring feelings of pain, rancor, or distrust resulting from a perceived or actual misdeed, this was not the case in the seventeenth and eighteenth centuries. Much to the contrary, during this period, resentment was typically regarded as a passion or "disorder of the soul" (desordre de l'âme), one that was rooted in a desire to achieve actual vengeance and thus often led to the (social or physical) demise of its agent. In this regard it was much closer to what we might refer to today as "vengefulness" or "rage" and indeed was by and large used interchangeably with these terms (and their French equivalents). The Chevalier

Louis de Jaucourt's *Encyclopédie* entry "COLÈRE" (ANGER) is a fine—and far from solitary—illustration of just how *active* the sentiment anger was seen to be. He writes, with a little help from Locke,

> ANGER . . . is, in accordance with Locke's definition, that trouble or disorder of the soul that we experience after having received an injury, and that is accompanied with a pressing desire to avenge ourselves; passion that puts us in a state whereby, in searching for the means to repel the evil that threatens us or that has already befallen us, blinds us, and makes pursue vengeance.

> (COLERE . . . c'est suivant la définition de Locke, cette inquiétude ou ce desordre de l'ame que nous ressentons après avoir reçu quelqu'injure, qui est accompagné d'un desir pressant de nous venger: passion qui nous jette hors de nous-mêmes, & qui cherchant le moyen de repousser le mal qui nous menace, ou qui nous a déjà atteints, nous aveugle, & nous fait courir à la vengeance.)[2]

On account of such a view of anger, the goal in both political and moral theory was—if not to obliterate the passion of anger entirely—to create a civil society in which subjects would recognize that more was to be gained than lost by letting bygones be bygones.[3] This belief was to hold equally in both private, interpersonal relationships and on the public stage.

It is indeed prodigiously the case that interrogations into the meaning and value of forgiveness throughout the early modern period were composed primarily with these concerns and goals in mind. Little attention was thus paid to how an agent felt about the malefactor once vengeance had been foresworn and peace restored. Forgiveness in such a context was thus utterly (and, depending on one's assumptions about forgiveness in a transhistorical sense, merely) actional. That anger could and need defend the dictates of justice was only occasionally considered as a possibility and never, to my knowledge, given systematic treatment until Rousseau came along. We recall, for example, that, in Diderot's *Encyclopédie* article "TO FORGIVE" (PARDONNER), as well as in Pierre Corneille's plays and Descartes's *Passions of the Soul*, it was power and tactical superiority—more so than justice—that was stressed when the appropriateness of forgiveness in a particular instance was being discussed. The notion that forgiveness could or should create or restore an affective bond was not even considered.

It is instructive, in this regard, that in *Le Cid*, Rodrigue and Chimène—though they love each other—cannot for that reason overcome the (very public) personal slight that keeps them apart. Indeed, both protagonists find themselves torn between their love for each other and their duties to avenge their fathers' honor. Where forgiveness is concerned, love is not only not enough; it is irrelevant. The lovers can be reconciled only when a publicly legitimized action that restores the disequilibrium and defends the honor of their respective families has been carried out. Though it may strike today's reader as paradoxical, the reconciliation between Rodrigue and Chimène is ultimately produced by a duel.

Even lower on the list of priorities of early modern political theorists, writers, and moral philosophers alike was the need to restore a victim's sense of self-worth in the wake of grievous personal slight. Much to the contrary, an analysis of these earlier discussions of reconciliation reveals that the vast majority believed that highlighting the potentially deleterious effects of vengeance and thus appealing to pragmatic concerns, social and civic obligations, and, often, rank was sufficient to inspire the victims of misdeeds to forswear vengeance, and this was true both in the private and public spheres.[4] *Émile*'s reflections regarding Sophie's fate in *Émile and Sophie*, as well as Wolmar's treatment of Saint-Preux, offer in this sense an unambiguous divergence from such a semantic tendency. Whereas the descriptions of forgiveness in each of these instances differ greatly from each other, they all rest on the same basic premise: how an individual responds to slight and how an individual forgives is both influenced and contributes to one's subjective identity. Similarly, how an individual responds to being forgiven is a direct reflection of one's sense of self. When taken together, forgiveness and the response it elicits inscribe a relationship rather definitively within either a political or private, interpersonal context.

The importance of Rousseau's philosophical and literary contributions to forgiveness discourse is perhaps most aptly seen in the contributions of his immediate intellectual successors and disciples. Of course, concepts do not evolve overnight, and the new and old meanings of a word can co-exist and, at times, even commingle, forcefully reasserting themselves and graciously deferring to one another in their turn. In the French canon, for example, the magnanimous pardon—sullied, weary, and down-trodden though it may have been by the time Rousseau was through with it—still survived as a legitimate and, at times, even laudatory model until well into the nineteenth century. Cardinal Richelieu's pardoning of d'Artagnan in

Alexander Dumas's *The Three Musketeers* (1844) is in this respect a prime example.

But for those who saw themselves as the immediate disciples of Rousseau we can see that their treatment of both anger and forgiveness differs sharply from that of the aforementioned Enlightenment thinkers. For those who believed that it was only through hard-won self-knowledge and absolute candor that one could be purified of social corruption, we find that, like Rousseau, they too were obliged to maintain that forgiveness as exchanged in private, interpersonal relationships must originate within the innermost realms of the human heart to have both validity and force. The conclusion to Madame de Staël's *Corinne* (1807), which I have discussed in detail elsewhere, is a very fine example.[5] In this particular text we very clearly see the distinction between private, interpersonal forgiveness and that variety of forgiveness that objective third parties may either provide or refuse. The notoriously slippery and intrusive narrator, who incidentally has the last word in the text, concludes the discussion of Oswald with the following cryptic lines:

> Lord Nelvil gave the most regular and pure example of domestic life. But did he forgive himself for his past behavior? Did the world that approved of it console him? Was he content with a common lot after all that he had lost? I do not know, and I do not, with regard to this question, either want to blame him or absolve him.

> (Lord Nelvil donna l'exemple de la vie domestique la plus régulière et la plus pure. Mais se pardonna-t-il sa conduite passée? Le monde qui l'approuva le consola-t-il? Se contenta-t-il d'un sort commun, après ce qu'il avait perdu? Je l'ignore, et ne veux, à cet égard, ni le blâmer, ni l'absoudre.)[6]

The narrator's ambivalence, we see, is ultimately rooted in uncertainty as to whether Oswald has truly learned from his mistakes and appropriately repented them. The narrator, who is recounting a story supposed to instruct as much as entertain, essentially alludes to a principle that has been generalized and that the reader will accept. What we see, then, is that the narrator's publicized indignation at the fate of the heroine remains without either remedy or satisfaction on account of the narrator's inability to penetrate Oswald's conscience. The narrator's indignation remains in limbo because an answer as to whether Oswald has fulfilled the criteria necessary to earning forgiveness from third-party spectators cannot be answered. His external behavior—the only thing that either the public or the narrator can judge at this point—neither affirms nor disproves that he has truly become a new man and could thus be integrated into the fold of those who share the narrator's moral ideals. He can therefore neither be forgiven nor condemned, accepted as a like-minded individual or rejected as an Other. The reader's affective response, therefore, culminates in dubiousness rather than certitude.

Corinne, on the other hand, who loved Oswald and, it must be noted, refrained from publicizing her anger at the (eventually mortal) wound that Oswald had inflicted on her, does find a way to forgive. Near death, she spontaneously absolves Oswald of his misdeeds. This is not done on account of rational deliberation on her part but rather out of a sudden movement of love. In fact, her forgiveness of Oswald was as much of a surprise to her as it was to anyone else: "I do not know why I do not have any resentment for you, even though the pain you have caused me makes me tremble with terror. Since I do not feel a movement of hatred, I must love you still" (Je ne sais pas pourquoi je n'ai point de ressentiment contre vous, bien que la douleur que vous m'avez causée me fasse frissonner d'effroi. Il faut que je vous aime encore pour n'avoir aucun mouvement de haine).[7] Whereas Corinne's forgiveness is certainly presented as sincere, it is not presented as having any universal validity—the spectator, lacking a love bond with Oswald, must carry out deliberations as to the sincerity of Oswald's moral evolution along quite different lines. Such deliberations lead only to ambivalence, hence the narrator's inability to pass judgment on Oswald. The ending of the novel therefore suggests that there may indeed exist two modes of forgiving: one for those who have a love bond with their perpetrator and quite another for those who witness and are collectively called on to judge the evils that a third party has committed in their midst.

Benjamin Constant's *Adolphe* (1816) also confronts the problem of public versus private identities and the differing approaches to forgiveness that these identities entail. Throughout the novel, we see the hero (rather desperately) attempting to negotiate the tensions between what society mandates and what his heart, conscience, and lover demand. The result, of course, is that he fails on both fronts, finding himself culpable vis-à-vis both his lover and society for having failed to definitively choose one over the other in a timely manner. When he finally acquires the fortitude to leave Ellenore, he is once again able to enter society and reassume the role that his education and birth entitled him to. His escapades, we may assume, were quickly excused as youthful follies. His previous failures to live up to societal ideals were automatically forgiven on the grounds that he had finally decided to fall back into line. The outside world could once again look at him with tender indifference in place of the disdain and fear they had experienced during the time that he remained beholden to Ellenore.[8]

Ellenore, on the other hand, the only one who had truly loved him, demonstrates the most unwavering tenderness toward him, his cruel words and demeaning treatment of her notwithstanding. Whereas she never says explicitly that she forgives him, her final actions and, in particular, her efforts to shield Adolphe from her written reproaches do, I think, constitute forgiveness. She asks him to bring her papers and begins to burn many of them, presumably those that she had written in anger. She implores Adolphe to burn a final letter addressed to him but that she is unable to find. This final letter, which Adolphe eventually finds and reads despite Ellenore's pleas to the contrary, was clearly written with the intention to pique Adolphe's conscience eternally. What is more, it was written with the hope of rendering the hero utterly dissatisfied with the choice he had made. It was, in short, rather vengeful.

> You shall walk alone in the midst of this crowd that you are so eager to join. You shall know them, these men whose indifference you are so grateful for today. And perhaps one day, wounded by these arid hearts, you will regret the heart that once belonged to you, that lived off of your affection, that had braved a thousand perils in your name, and that you no longer deign to compensate with a single regard.

> (Vous marcherez seul au milieu de cette foule à laquelle vous êtes impatient de vous mêler! Vous les connaîtrez, ces hommes que vous remerciez aujourd'hui dêtre indifférents; et peut-être un jour, froissé par ces cœurs arides, vous regretterez ce cœur dont vous disposiez, qui vivait de votre affection, qui eût bravé mille périls pour votre défense, et que vous ne daignez plus compenser d'un regard).[9]

The letter that Ellenore had written (and that, again, she had implored Adolphe not to read after her death) expressed her hope that Adolphe would suffer profoundly on account of losing her. At the time she composed this letter, she was confident that his sacrifice would someday fill him with regret and that he would fall prey to utter alienation. In this sense, the letter expresses Ellenore's desire that retribution for her suffering be posthumously achieved. The fact that, in the end, she implored Adolphe to burn the letter without reading it is what constituted her forgiveness: prior to dying, she renounced the vengeance she had resolved to pursue by attempting to destroy the vehicle by which it was to be achieved. Adolphe, who accidentally came upon the opened letter and read it shortly after her death, thus became the unwitting agent of his own moral demise and thus of Ellenore's vengeance. Somewhat counterintuitively perhaps, this utterly passive variety of vengeance is what enabled Adolphe to realize that he had indeed been forgiven. The sting of Ellenore's final letter was intense indeed. As the rest of the novel demonstrates, the hero's existence is marked precisely by the alienation that Ellenore had described. The fact that she had tried to save Adolphe from such pain and had decided, albeit somewhat tardily, not to reveal to him the meaninglessness of the choice he had made attests to love's uncanny ability to forgive even the most humiliating and painful of injuries.

Society, having never understood the special bond that existed between Adolphe and Ellenore, could not appreciate the forgiveness that Ellenore had granted. Of course, this is not altogether surprising when one considers that the public was equally incapable of perceiving the gravity of the fault that had been committed. As was the case with Saint-Preux and Julie, Ellenore and Adolphe have established their own criteria by which the moral worth of their actions can and must be judged within the context of their relationship. The knowledge that they have of each other's peculiar capacity for suffering on account of their individuated attachment is what, in both instances, provides the grounds on which they can injure and, in turn, forgive each other. Adolphe can overlook Ellenore's unreasonable behavior and demands on the grounds that both are the proof of her devotion. Ellenore's knowledge that Adolphe will be dissatisfied with the lot he has chosen is what motivates her to withdraw her statements that Adolphe has committed himself to a world that can never have meaning or affection for him. To know how to destroy a culpable individual not just socially and physically but, especially, at the very core of his or her being is to know how to exact the most sublime variety of vengeance. To refrain from doing so, particularly in the wake of grievous personal slight, is to bestow the most transcendent variety of forgiveness.

I do not mean to suggest by this that neither Constant nor Staël had Rousseau's notion of private, interpersonal forgiveness in mind when they composed their novels. As discussed in the introduction, Rousseau was notoriously unforgiving and was hardly considered an authority on the subject, even by those who consciously followed in his philosophical footsteps. Further, German idealism, particularly that of Kant, certainly colored both Constant's and Staël's treatment of right and wrong, and this rather profoundly. Accordingly, if one were to explicate fully their views on forgiveness (and I do not pretend to do so here), one would also have to take that into account. What I do mean to suggest, however, is that it is perhaps inevitable that a bifurcated view of forgiveness will emerge once the public and private realm are no longer conceptually coextensive, as is the case within Rousseau's political theory. In this respect, Rousseau's notion of subjectivity is very likely at play in both Staël's and Constant's respective treatment of conciliatory action in their novels, if somewhat unconsciously.

Again, this represents a rather remarkable divergence from what we find in secular discussions prior to the Rousseauvean intervention. Given their adherence to the notion of selfish sociability, it was widely assumed among the eighteenth-century philosophes (and among the British materialists before them) that if the public sphere functioned properly, the legitimacy of its social codes and laws would extend even into the household. As a result, in an ideal world, the love for the law and the fear of both the legal and social consequences of expressing one's anger within the public sphere were supposed to infiltrate the family unit and the intimate sphere more generally, bringing about a tendency toward reconciliation and acceptance.[10] Otherwise put, these essentially political motivations, born ultimately of self-interest, were supposed to carry over to and direct the course of interpersonal relationships, even in (especially in) the wake of personal slight. The individual, whether acting in the public sphere or at home among friends and family, was supposed to reconcile oneself to others always in a similar fashion and for identical reasons: anger is counterproductive, apolitical, exceedingly dangerous, and utterly pernicious to society as a whole.

But such a view of the meaning and significance of anger and forgiveness is possible if and only if the gulf between man-as-citizen and man-as-individual does not exist conceptually. Once that gulf has been revealed, one has no choice but to contend with the fact that the rights, duties, feelings, and vulnerabilities of the man and of the citizen are rarely one and the same. Personal slight, perhaps particularly when it is visible to third-party spectators, makes this reality all the more palpable, as the decision as to whether to rectify the wrong publicly or privately must be made. Rousseau, in having accorded moral relevance to sentiment and in having propounded the importance of authenticity in our relationships with others stumbled upon what has become a basic truth for the modern subject: like love, the grounds on which forgiveness may be granted or denied in the private, in-terpersonal sphere are increasingly difficult (if not impossible) to articulate to outsiders. As at least two of Rousseau's immediate intellectual successors discovered, for the modern subject, to be the object of anger is to have cer-tainty, whereas to be the object of forgiveness is to have a certain degree of doubt. It is therefore not surprising that the reader is left with the sense that both Oswald and Adolphe remain themselves uncertain as to whether they were truly forgiven by their respective victims and thus remain partially and perpetually beholden to their past mistakes.

To what extent did Rousseau's contributions change the nature of the de-bate regarding the role of forgiveness, in politics and in private, interper-sonal relationships? Is he the long-lost transitional figure between old and new ways of understanding forgiveness? Was he the first to truly posit that there are two modes of forgiveness and that it must thus be practiced differ-ently depending on whether it is circulating in the public or private sphere? Unfortunately, the secular history of the concept has yet to be written, and so it is impossible to answer these questions definitively. Certainly, thanks to the efforts of David Konstan and Donald W. Shriver Jr., we do have at our disposal a fairly comprehensive idea as to how forgiveness (or something akin to it) was viewed throughout antiquity and into the Renaissance. We are, however, still at somewhat of a loss to explain both how and why the ideal of forgiveness may have changed throughout modernity. I have tried to shed some light on some of the prevailing semantic tendencies of the period to which Rousseau was responding to demonstrate the novelty of his thoughts on the subject. Yet there is still much work to be done if we are to understand both how and why the meaning(s) of forgiveness in secu-lar ethics changed over the past three hundred to four hundred years. As I am currently arguing in another, ongoing work, it appears as though early modern political thinkers were confronted with a discursive crisis as they at-tempted to render forgiveness compatible with emerging political thought. By discursive crisis I mean a peculiar situation in which a concept proves to be increasingly incompatible with a specific communicative system's histor-ically determined vocabulary but cannot be abandoned for both ideological and practical reasons. Through an analysis of the philosophical, theological, political, and literary contributions of the most influential political thinkers of the period, I hope in subsequent work to provide a nuanced understand-ing as to why forgiveness became increasingly difficult to speak about dur-ing the early modern period and, in turn, reveal how these difficulties may still influence our understanding of the concept of forgiveness today. In this way, my future contributions, while focused on the premodern period, will work to disclose once again how the past—in this case the European Enlightenment—has a powerful claim on the present.

But even without this history yet at hand, we are still able to at least partially surmise how integral Rousseau must have been to the development of modern notions of forgiveness simply by looking at some contemporary modes of discussing it. As covered in my introduction, today it is fairly common to speak of forgiveness as being an excruciatingly personal experience that must originate in a pure and disinterested love for a person's individuated and distinct essence if it is to be authentic. As mentioned earlier, although they have done so according to quite varied methods, Jean Améry, Jacques Derrida, Julia Kristeva, Simon Wiesenthal, and Charles L. Griswold, among others, have provided us with accounts of forgiveness that—despite their great methodological and ideological differences—would be incomprehensible without a value system that was both subject centered and simultaneously accorded a great deal of importance to the predilections and emotional states of the agent. Indeed, in constructing their accounts of forgiveness, all these thinkers rely heavily on the belief that the wholly psychological I-ness of personality and the emotional state of the agent are the measures by which the success or failure of any bestowal of forgiveness can be assessed. As I have shown throughout this study, such a manner of interpreting forgiveness would have been largely incomprehensible during much of the long eighteenth century and does not appear to have preceded the Rousseauvean intervention. Accordingly, we are somewhat obliged to credit Rousseau as having at least in part laid the conceptual groundwork that made the aforementioned accounts possible.

But Rousseau's influence on contemporary discussions also extends into more straightforwardly political accounts as well. In recent times there have been numerous efforts to counterbalance the more emotive and decidedly apolitical varieties of forgiveness mentioned earlier to maintain or reestablish forgiveness as a political possibility. One approach that has increasingly become popular among historians and political theorists alike is to focus on the possibility of creating shared historical narratives that admit the crime without shaming its perpetrators. Such accounts in turn accentuate the productive and ethical qualities that can attend to political reconciliation if properly executed.

But even these approaches to the problem of forgiveness betray at least the indirect influence of both Rousseau's political thought and literary imagination. And, whereas I do not mean to suggest that Rousseau fully anticipated or even would have agreed with this particular approach to the problem of forgiveness, his contributions to modern subjectivity and to political theory more generally may very well be at play in a large share of them.

We have, in recent years, witnessed the appearance of quite a bit of scholarship devoted to the analysis of truth commissions and reparations mechanisms—be they restorative or retributive—that seek to carve out a space on the historicopolitical stage where reconciliation can occur. The most famous of such truth commissions remains the South African Truth and Reconciliation Commission, which has served as a model for analogous commissions throughout Europe and Africa and which itself took its cue from earlier Latin American ones. The challenge before such commissions and conciliatory mechanisms is to accord due credence to the need for peace and the desire for a renewed sense of community within populations that have been devastated by massive and collective malfeasance. These conciliatory mechanisms must, in the process, protect the dignity of victims by ensuring both them and their suffering a place in public memory and political discourse. These commissions are themselves necessitated by the fact that, as Shriver has observed, "public amnesia about one's publicly imposed suffering is an ultimate indignity."[11] The solution to the predicament of irreversibility in the wake of grievous collective offenses and the indignity they produce is therefore very often to be found in the careful crafting of historical narratives. When successful, these narratives serve to develop understanding and empathy between the involved parties that produce the environment necessary for peace. These narratives are able to do so because they foster new collective identities by bridging political divides and utilizing historical dialogue as an essential tool of political reconciliation. More often than not, these narratives attend to constructing a new "truth" as to what happened, one that proves itself to be compatible with the demands of newly established standards of justice without, simultaneously, requiring those involved to follow the letter of the law by meting out punishments to culpable agents. The contributions of Elazar Barkan, David Engel, Ronald Grigor Suny, James T. Campbell, Robert Enright, and Donald W. Shriver Jr. are noteworthy in this regard.[12] What links the accounts of political forgiveness that these political theorists and historians have offered is that they all explicitly acknowledge the threat to the subjective identity of victims that collective misdeeds and public crimes pose. They in turn stress the utter importance of public acknowledgment of the suffering that victims have experienced to the processes of political reconciliation, even in instances where restitution (financial or otherwise) and punishment are to be set aside. France's increasingly strict laws against denying genocide, such as that which was passed on January 23, 2012, are a fine example of just how integral the construction of shared historical narratives in the wake of grievous offense are perceived to be to the processes of reconciliation and to the construction of collective cultural identity.[13]

The recognition of the threat to subjective and cultural identities that public crimes and misdeeds pose and thus the necessity of constructing shared historical narratives is itself an outgrowth of what today is often viewed as a quality inherent to resentment, namely its unparalleled capacity to alienate the individuals who find themselves in its grip. As Jeffrie G. Murphy has observed, the passion of resentment has a "defensive role," one that is "defensive of the rules of morality and of the social fabric those rules define." In this respect, when justified, both anger and resentment "function primarily in defense, not of all moral values and norms, but rather of certain *values of the self.*" Murphy continues,

> The primary value defended by the passion of resentment is *self-respect*, that proper self-respect is essentially tied to the passion of resentment, and that a person who does not resent moral injuries done to him . . . is almost necessarily a person lacking in self-respect. Thus some of the primary reasons justifying forgiveness will be found, not in general social utility, but in reasons directly tied to an individual's self-respect or self-esteem, his perception of his own worth, of what he is owed.[14]

Here, Murphy highlights what is, at least today, an important connection between how anger or resentment is experienced by an individual and said individual's sense of self-worth. He also stresses how forgiveness must be brokered with this in mind. The crimes and misdeeds to which we fall prey threaten the core of who we know ourselves to be, as they call into question the legitimacy of the rights we claim within the social structures from which we derive our identity. When crimes are committed against us publicly and when justice offers us no redress, they destabilize our position within the civic order or system in which we reside. In extreme instances, the wrongs we suffer may even lead us to consider the duties we owe to our families, friends, colleagues, and to society more generally as illusory. What is more, if we do not accord due credence to our own legitimate feelings of resentment, we ourselves become instruments of the malefactor insofar as we amplify the alienating effects of the initial misdeed. One's dignity can only sustain so many injuries and insults before it finds itself obliged to fight back in its own defense. Forgiveness may put an end to such a fight, but it cannot and must not subsequently mock the initial fight as unjustified if it is to be felicitous and, frankly, healthy.

Such an understanding of the psychological ramifications of resentment has greatly affected how forgiveness may be practiced and exchanged within the private, interpersonal and political spheres. On account of the pervasiveness of an ethic of authenticity in public discourse, both the political and public spheres are increasingly viewed as needing to accommodate, metabolize, and protect the individuated distinctness and sensibilities of its members. As a result, political forgiveness is all the more often called on to cater to the demands that the ethic of authenticity imposes, albeit with significantly less emphasis on affective bonds that may exist between the victim and the perpetrator than its more personalized counterpart. The result for many thinkers is that political forgiveness, if it is to be considered felicitous in a postmodern context, must be enacted in such a way that not only restores a sense of self-worth to the victim at a very personal level but, further, that articulates that worth (and condemns both the crime and the perpetrator that threaten it) in a manner that is visible and memorable on the larger, historicopolitical scene.[15] Such political forgiveness must equally strive to make all those involved not only abide by but also love the ideals of justice that this revised collective identity entails.

As incisive as such statements regarding anger, resentment, and forgiveness may be in a postmodern context, it is unlikely that most eighteenth-century readers would have agreed with, or even understood, such argumentation.[16] They would equally have been perplexed before contemporary models of private, interpersonal forgiveness as discussed earlier, at least until the arrival of Rousseau. This is, again, because the capacity of unresolved anger to alienate its agent had not yet been articulated.

Admittedly, in his discussions of anger and forgiveness as exchanged within the political realm, Rousseau did not go so far as to explicitly suggest that the careful construction of new historical narratives could provide a solution to this predicament.[17] That being said, he most certainly recognized and decried the potentially alienating effects on the citizen of dissatisfied anger and indignation against one's compatriots. In this sense he moved beyond the widespread notion that only external manifestations of anger (vengeance, for example) need be attended to solely by the lawmakers, magistrates, and philosophers. And although we may safely assume that he would be dubious—if not outright appalled—by the widespread insertion of emotivism into contemporary public and political discourse, the sentiment of collective anger, and not just its palpable effects in a sphere of exteriority, was something that he believed needed to be addressed. For Rousseau nothing was more terrifying or ruinous for the emphatic citizen than being forced to relegate legitimate anger to the innermost realms of his heart in the wake of a public humiliation or misdeed. Not only the Frenchman and the character of J.-J. in *Rousseau, Judge of Jean-Jacques* but also Saint-Preux and Rousseau himself had all learned this the hard way. And, although Rousseau may not have provided a model of paradigmatic political forgiveness that attended to these basic truths, he certainly articulated the need to formulate one, and this rather vehemently. It is worth noting that the foundational myth that establishes and legitimizes the society at Clarens at the end of *Julie* is one of what had appeared initially to be an impossible reconciliation but one that, once achieved, enabled all the involved parties to live together in peace. Similarly, *Rousseau, Judge of Jean-Jacques* ends with the Frenchman vowing to be the protector of J.-J.'s writings, presumably with the hope of someday telling the latter's story to a society ready to reconcile itself to the errors of its past and give its victims the homage and the respect they were denied. Rousseau may not have explicitly endorsed the construction of shared historical narratives as a mode by which political forgiveness could be granted. Be that as it may, the bifurcated identity between the man and the citizen and the need for citizens to love the laws to which they are beholden that were at the core of his political theory led him to invoke the shared historical narrative as a means of brokering collective and political reconciliation.

In closing, although there are many who advocate a transcendent, universalizing notion of the concept of forgiveness, as we look to the early modern period's treatment of the concept, it becomes clearer that there is a historicity to the concept of secular forgiveness and that it therefore cannot be interpreted independently of the concept's own historical development. We therefore cannot help but ask how we can relate more recent accounts that pretend to universality to an otherwise predominant tendency to historicize the concept of forgiveness. There are, in fact, numerous early modern discussions of forgiveness from which patterns of continuity emerge, and these discussions not only resonate with but also direct some more contemporary analyses. Rousseau's contributions demonstrate this quite well.

Notes

INTRODUCTION

1. Shriver, *Ethic for Enemies*; Konstan, *Before Forgiveness*.

2. Konstan, *Before Forgiveness*, 152–59.

3. Rousseau, *Émile*, 12.

4. Alberg, *Reinterpretation*; Coleman, *Anger*.

5. Griswold, *Forgiveness*.

6. Arendt, *Human Condition*, 241.

7. The tendency to describe forgiveness in these terms is emphatically true of Derrida's and Jankélévitch's accounts.

8. In articulating what I am referring to as the "ethic of authenticity" and Rousseau's influence thereon, I am very much indebted to Alessandro Ferrara's study, *Modernity* (see, in particular, page 89). Other noteworthy discussions of this development and of Rousseau's influence on it include Taylor, *Ethics*, 27, 47; Stewart, *L'invention*, 179, 200–201; Sennett, *Fall*, passim and, in particular, 108; Weintraub, *Value*, 39; and Ogrodnick, *Instinct*.

9. Taylor, *Sources*, 363–65.

10. In *Before Forgiveness*, Konstan gestures toward a similar point. He notes that the focus on feelings of remorse, affection, and "self-transformation" that pervades contemporary discussions of forgiveness was absent in late antiquity and the Middle Ages. He further observes that something resembling the "modern conception of forgiveness" began to appear systematically in the early nineteenth century and, above all, in the twentieth century (152–59). But he does not discuss in detail how we arrived at this "modern conception" not where and how it developed.

11. It is worth noting that "resentment" (ressentiment) and "anger" (colère) were much more closely related conceptually in the early modern period than they are today. Accordingly, when speaking about the early modern period I at times use these terms interchangeably, while maintaining the distinction between these terms when discussing contemporary ethical discourses.

12. Shklar, *Men and Citizens*, 1.

13. Rousseau, *Rêveries*, 4:1066.

14. I am referring to chapter 4 of Coleman, *Anger*.

15. Ibid., 7.

16. Ibid., 6. Coleman also notes that such expressions were still largely confined to comedy and that the idea that such people had the right to take offense, particularly at offenses leveled by their betters, was still regarded as somewhat absurd (6).

17. Ibid., 97. This is not to say that Rousseau condoned anger everywhere. Coleman points out that there is a tension in Rousseau's oeuvre regarding the emotion; at times Rousseau's style "conveys eloquent indignation and philosophical calm, even as he depicts with equal vividness human beings liberated from emotional disturbance and reacting passionately to insult and injustice." The epigraph to *Émile* is a case in point, as Rousseau recalls the calm of the Stoics when he cites Seneca's *De ira*: "The ills which ail us are curable; we were born to be upright, and nature itself, should we wish to be improved, will help us" (as quoted in Coleman, *Anger*, 95–97). See also Kelly, *Rousseau's Exemplary Life*, 91.

18. Unless otherwise noted, all references are to this edition of Starobinski's *Jean-Jacques Rousseau*, and all translations are my own.

19. Shklar, *Men and Citizens*, 1, 5; Masters, *Political Philosophy*, 89–95.

20. Shklar, *Men and Citizens*, 13–15; Masters, *Political Philosophy*, 10–14 and 89–95.

21. As Masters observes, "To create [civil man], man must be 'denatured' by transforming love of oneself, the first principle of natural man, into selfless patriotism" (*Political Philosophy*, 14).

22. Masters, *Political Philosophy*, 10.

23. Rousseau, *Émile*, 13:399, 4:535. Unless otherwise noted, all other references to *Émile* are from Rousseau, *Oeuvres complètes*, and all translations are from Masters and Kelly, *Collected Writings*, vol. 13. All subsequent citations appear parenthetically in the text with the English translation cited first, followed by the French text.

24. Barth, *Nineteenth-Century Theology*, 207.

25. Even though in the "Profession of Faith," in *Émile*, the vicar claims that his conscience makes him sense that there must be a system of rewards and punishments for those who propagate the injustice that reigns on earth, reasoned reflection makes him doubt even this. Once the body is no longer attached to the soul, the vicar maintains, evil too walks out the door. The vicar's conscience thus recoils before the idea of the Final Judgment, and he even seems to suggest that he is prepared to appeal to God for a doctrine of general amnesty instead (367–70).

26. Masson, *Religion*, 273.

27. All references to the Christian Bible are from *The Holy Bible: King James Version*.

28. Palmer, *Catholics*, 173. See also 43, 98, and 193–94.

29. Ibid., 174.

30. Alberg, *Reinterpretation*, 7, 9.

31. This is especially evident in the tendency to regard Kant's theory of guilt as a redemptive sentiment as the direction to which all seventeenth- and eighteenth-century secular discussions of forgiveness tended, a theory that, according to Ritschl, Barth, and Lehmann, inevitably leads to the diminished importance of God and, ultimately, the view that man may forgive himself ad infinitum. This is part of an overwhelming tendency to consider Kant as exemplary of Enlightenment moral theory, notwithstanding the fact that his opposition to empiricism and utilitarianism was antithetical to the beliefs that a majority of Enlightenment thinkers held dear (Rousseau, of course, excepted). For examples of such a tendency, see the chapter "And Man Forgives Himself" in Lehmann's *Forgiveness*, and Ritschl, *Critical History*, 219, 492–93.

32. Indeed, subsequent studies have been even more dismissive than Ritschl's, as Ritschl appears to have acknowledged that there had at least been attempts on the part of Christian apologists to compose an account of forgiveness compatible with rational humanism. Implicit within such a reading is the supposition that their secular counterparts had also been unwilling to admit the need for forgiveness within moral theory.

33. Barth, as quoted by Jaroslav Pelikan in his introduction to Barth's *Protestant Thought*, 8. See also 18–19, 33–35.

34. Ibid., 151, 181.

35. It is telling indeed that in Barth's (highly favorable) appraisal of Rousseau in *Nineteenth-Century Theology*, justification and reconciliation—two concepts about which Barth had written a great deal—are not discussed. Rousseau, though he was for Barth the figure in whom "eighteenth-century man achieved fulfillment," is not regarded as having done more than repeat the standard view when it came to conciliatory action (174).

36. See Pagani, "Uses and Abuses."

37. Both the meaning of forgiveness and its constitutive processes within a religious context were vigorously attacked by thinkers such as Jonathan Trichard, Hobbes, Voltaire, and Baron d'Holbach, *independently* of their attacks on the rational basis and credibility of Christian revelation. The impetus behind these critiques was most often rooted not in disdain for or indifference

toward the plausibility of forgiveness as a secular ideal. Rather it was rooted, first, in distaste for centuries of Christian abnegation and, second, in a shared desire to do away with the confession-absolution model, an institution regarded by many Enlightenment thinkers as being little more than smoke and mirrors employed by a select few in an effort to control the masses through fear. Almost all the secular Enlightenment thinkers believed that the most deplorable aspect of the Christian models they had inherited was that these models too easily absolved the guilty conscience. Confession and absolution negated the debt that the malefactor viewed himself as owing to his fellow man and replaced it with a debt toward God. The result, in their view, was that a decisive lack of moral responsibility was fostered among believers. It was not simply the traditional justification and authority for the action that Voltaire, Jaucourt, Holbach, and others wished to challenge. Rather, they wished to revise the very processes by which forgiveness was granted, the forces by which it was motivated, and the effects that it achieved. What they sought was a practical account that could allow for the possibility for misdeeds to be forgiven in specific instances *without* leading to a systematic clearing of the conscience, something that they believed was inevitable in cases where moral peers were absent. See Trichard, *Contagion*, 86–87; Holbach, *Christianisme dévoilée*, 38; Voltaire, *Dictionnaire philosophique*, 147–48; Jaucourt's entry for the *Encyclopédie* titled "PARDON"; and the Abbé Claude Yvon's entry for the *Encyclopédie* titled "AMOUR-PROPRE."

38. Barth, *Nineteenth-Century Theology*, 174. This is part, I would argue, of Barth's assertion that at no point did Rousseau become "specifically anti-clerical," even after the condemnation of *Émile* by both Protestant and Catholic authorities (206). Rousseau remained firmly fixed on what he saw as the shortcomings of modern, secular philosophy.

39. Blumenberg, *Legitimacy*, 7, 22, 65.

40. Ibid., 65.

41. Ibid., 15, 110.

42. Caradonna, "Death of Duty," 281, 282.

43. Alberg, *Reinterpretation*, xii.

44. Rousseau, *Confessions*, 1:7. Unless otherwise noted, all references to the *Confessions* have been taken from this edition and all translations are from volume 5 of Rousseau, *Confessions and Correspondence*, in Masters and Kelly, *Collected Writings*. All subsequent quotations are cited parenthetically in the text with the English translation cited first, followed by the French text.

45. Rousseau, *First Discourse*, in Rousseau, *Oeuvres complètes*, 127; 3:3.

46. A fine example is Hearnshaw's essay "Rousseau," in *Social and Political Ideas*, 185–86. Kavanagh's *Writing the Truth* and Babbitt's *Rousseau and Romanticism* are two others. See, in particular, pages 155, 174, and 220–21 of the latter. Starobinski also offers an overview of this literature in *Jean-Jacques Rousseau*, 433–38. With regard to forgiveness, Alberg's study, *Reinterpretation*, also seems to share this approach.

47. Cassirer, *Question*, 39–40; see also 95.

48. Cassirer, quoted in Kelly, *Rousseau's Exemplary Life*, 2. The in-text citation is from Cassirer, *Rousseau, Kant, and Goethe*, 58. See also Masters, *Political Philosophy*, vii–x.

49. Rousseau, *Rousseau juge*, in Rousseau, *Oeuvres complètes*, 1:56, 1:732. See also Rousseau, *Confessions*, 1:458.

50. That Rousseau rejected forgiveness is one of Alberg's conclusions.

51. Kelly, *Rousseau's Exemplary Life*, 36.

52. Dilthey, *Formation*, 220.

53. Coleman, *Anger*, v, 102–3, 106, 122.

54. By "authentic," I mean bestowed not simply for the sake of one's bettering one's reputation or furthering one's selfish, social interests but rather in the name of expressing an individual's still favorable feelings toward the perpetrator of a misdeed. Following Alessandro Ferrara, I understand Rousseauvean authenticity as including other "indispensable ingredients," which

include "empathy, self-knowledge, the capacity to accept the undesired aspects of the self, a sensitivity to the inner needs linked with the essential aspects of an identity, and a nonrepressive attitude towards one's inner nature" (*Modernity*, 27).

55. Readers interested in how I understand the function of anger and forgiveness in the *Reveries* can consult my article "Living Well."

PART I, INTRODUCTION

1. All references to the *Dialogues* are from Rousseau, *Rousseau juge*, in Rousseau, *Oeuvres complètes*, vol. 1. All translations are from Rousseau, *Rousseau, Judge of Jean-Jacques*, in Masters and Kelly, *Collected Writings*, vol. 1. Quotations are cited parenthetically in the text, with the English translation cited first, followed by the French text.

2. Friedlander, *J. J. Rousseau*, 71. See also Lilti, "Writing of Paranoia." Lilti argues that Rousseau's expressions of paranoia were in large part the result of the difficulty in articulating the problems that celebrity posed for writers of his generation.

3. According to Starobinski, the text's only end is the pursuit of innocence at all costs. *Jean-Jacques Rousseau*, 242–44, 251, 277, 285. On the reception history of the book and the facility with which it has been dismissed, see Masters and Kelly's introduction to Rousseau, *Rousseau, Judge of Jean-Jacques*, in Masters and Kelly, *Collected Writings*, xiii.

4. Di Palma, "Self and Agency," 311–13, 323.

5. Rousseau is quite explicit in his disdain for what he takes to be the philosophes' capacity to silence those who hold opposing views: "For the purpose of using their disciples to prevail over public opinion and the reputation of men, they matched their doctrine to their views, they made their followers adopt the principles best suited to keeping them inviolably attached to them. . . . While appearing to disagree with the Jesuits, they aimed for the same goal nonetheless using roundabout routes by making themselves leaders of factions as they do" (*Rousseau juge*, in Rousseau, *Oeuvres complètes*, 1:238, 1:967; Dans l'objet de disposer par leurs disciples de l'opinon publique et de la réputation des hommes, ils ont assorti leur doctrine à leurs vues, ils ont fait adopter à leurs sectateurs les principes les plus propres à se les tenir inviolablement attachés. . . . En paroissant prendre le contrepied des Jesuites ils ont tendu neanmoins au même but par des routes détournées en se faisant comme eux chefs de parti).

6. Melzer, "Origin," 347. See also Shklar, *Men and Citizens*, 97; and Koselleck, *Critique and Crisis*, 120.

7. Di Palma, "Self and Agency," 322.

8. Masters and Kelly, introd. to *Collected Writings*, xvii. Although Masters and Kelly attribute "narrow scholarly importance" to the *Dialogues*, they nevertheless also detect a "broader political significance" in the text (xix). See also Sheringham, *French Autobiography*. Sheringham suggests that the *Dialogues* "build the reader/Other into the textual edifice, and lay on for his benefit a *mise-en-scène* over which Rousseau exercises total control, a 'scène' designed to demonstrate and thus eradicate the possibility of conflicting views on of his character" (57).

9. It may very well be the case that Rousseau was aware of the dangers that the transformation of the Frenchman posed if emulated by the general populace. As Masters and Kelly observe, Rousseau opted *not* to use a more popular and palatable form (such as the novel, the autobiography, the play). Instead, he decided on the much more opaque and inapproachable dialogue, perhaps out of reticence as to what the larger ramifications could be. As Masters and Kelly observe, "Although the *Dialogues* must be understood in part as an attempt to defend Rousseau's character before the public, his choice of a less popular form indicates that his true audience is 'good minds' rather than seekers of pleasure. In sum the *Dialogues* is a philosophic or unpopular dramatization of the need to influence unphilosophic readers" (introd. to *Collected Writings*, 1:xx).

CHAPTER I

1. Act 5, scene 3. All citations from Corneille's tragedies are from Corneille, *Oeuvres complètes*. Quotations are cited parenthetically in the text. All translations are my own unless otherwise noted.

2. Norman, "Pour une approche."

3. In article 161 of *Passions of the Soul*, Descartes writes, "it is nevertheless certain that a good institution serves quite a bit in correcting the defaults of birth, and that if one occupies oneself often in considering that which is free will, and [if one considers] how great are the advantages that come when one takes a firm resolution to use it well and, on the other hand, how vain and useless are all of the cares upon which the ambitious work, one can exercise in himself the passion and then acquire the virtue of generosity" (il est certain néanmoins que la bonne institution sert beaucoup, pour corriger les défauts de la naissance, et que si on s'occupe souvent à considérer ce que c'est que le libre arbitre, & combien sont grands les avantages qui viennent de ce qu'on a une ferme résolution d'en bien user, comme aussi, d'autre costé, combien sont vains & inutiles tous les soins qui travaillent les ambitieux; on peut exciter en soy la Passion, & ensuite acquerir la vertu de Générosité).

4. Admittedly, Descartes's various definitions of pity are—somewhat unfortunately—plagued with inconsistencies. This is true to such an extent that one ultimately has to guess where precisely in *Passions de l'âme* the true definition is to be found. In article 185 he defines pity as a passion bestowed by the generous individual on those he sees suffering *undeservedly*, in much the same way that Aristotle famously began his definition. And, as per article 183, the inclination to feel pity is one of the markers of generosity. We remember that, for Descartes, generosity consists first and foremost in being, among other things, strong-minded and above contempt. Nevertheless, in article 186, he explicitly states that, with regard to pity, those who think themselves weak and prone to misfortune seem to be more disposed to this passion than others. This is so, he claims, because such individuals expect that the same thing may very well happen to them. Thus, at this moment in the text, Descartes essentially asserts that pity arises because of a perceived shared vulnerability. I do not pretend to be able to resolve these tensions, but it is quite possible that Descartes envisioned a higher and lower form of pity: one form being magnanimous and decidedly aristocratic, and the other being more firmly grounded in fear.

5. La Rochefoucauld, *Réflexions*, in Gilbert and Gourdault, *Oeuvres de La Rochefoucauld*, vol. 1.

6. Ibid. This point is reiterated in maxim 82, though tempered slightly by what can best be described as a fair dose of pragmatism. La Rochefoucauld writes, "Reconciliation with our enemies is nothing more than a desire to improve our condition, a lassitude with regard to war, and fear of a bad event" (La réconciliation avec nos ennemis n'est qu'un désir de rendre notre condition meilleure, une lassitude de la guerre, une crainte de quelque mauvais évènement). Here, we see, La Rochefoucauld also highlights the dangers that vengeance poses to the one who pursues it and, frankly, the energy that it demands. But he also posits that reconciliation can "improve our condition," which, given the thrust of the maxims preceding this particular one and of the *Maximes* more generally, seems to imply that this is a reference to domination. We can also see, however, that La Rochefoucauld is picking up on the vitalist thrust that directed those accounts of forgiveness and reconciliation that we find in Great Britain during the same period. As I have argued elsewhere, Joseph Butler and Hobbes (to say nothing of Francis Bacon and John Locke) also stressed the potentially deleterious effects of vengeance on the part of the agent as a motivating factor behind forgiveness. On this point, see Pagani, "Uses and Abuses."

7. *Encyclopédie*, s.v. "Pardon, Excuse," 11:932.

8. As Reddy observes in *Navigation of Feeling*, "By 1700 love fashions its own morality and may be invoked to set aside conventional moral norms. . . . What was distinctive about Masonic

lodges, salons, and new forms of affectionate marriage and friendship after 1700 was that these practices gradually came to draw legitimacy from a developing conception of sentiment—a secular, naturalistic, and political bundle of ideas close to our own notion of emotion" (153–54). See also Stewart, *L'invention*, 1–5, 67, 78; and Coleman, *Anger*, 6–9.

9. *Encyclopédie*, s.v. "Excuse," 6:229: "(*Grammaire*.) raison or prétexte qu'on apporte à celui qu'on a offensé, pour affoiblir à ses yeux la faute qu'on a commise." An approximate translation is in the sentence that this note references.

10. *Encyclopédie*, s.v. "Pardonnable," 11:933.

11. There is one instance in the New Testament that does point to the extenuating circumstance of ignorance as an argument in favor of forgiveness. It occurs when Jesus implores God to "forgive them for they know not what they do" (Luke 23:24). Be that as it may, both Catholic and Protestant interpretations of forgiveness typically insist on the love and benevolence of both God and Jesus as being necessarily constitutive of divine and interpersonal forgiveness. In short, the extenuating circumstance of ignorance is generally downplayed. The decidedly rational nature of forgiveness—one that seeks to rationalize away the evil of the misdeed—as described in this article from the *Encyclopédie* must thus be regarded as being without a Christian precedent.

12. Examples of this view can be found in Barth, *Church*, 18–19, 33–35; Ritschl, *Critical History*, 30, 34, 128, 187–88; Lehmann, *Forgiveness*, 15, 44–45, 57, 61; and, more recently, L. Jones, *Embodying Forgiveness*, 211–12.

13. *Encyclopédie*, s.v. "Pardonnable," 11:933–34.

14. Some notable texts that propound this view include Bacon, "On Revenge" (1597) and "Of Anger" (1625); Hobbes, "On Human Nature" (1650), chap. 16, sec. 9, and *Leviathan* (1651), 1:15, sec. 18, and 1:17, secs. 1–2, pp. 13–15, 20n7; Locke, *Law of Nature*, in Von Leyden, *Political Essays*, and *Second Treatise on Government* (1690), 84, 95; Voltaire's entry for "Tolérance" in his *Dictionnaire philosophique* (1764); and the entries titled "colère" and "ressentiment" from the *Encyclopédie* and the 1694 and 1762 editions of *Le dictionnaire de l'Académie Française*.

15. *Encyclopédie*, s.v. "pardonnable," 11:933–34.

16. It is worth noting that we find a similar (though subtler) connection between the necessity of superiority and subjugation to the practice of forgiveness in Diderot's *Supplément au voyage* (1772). Thus the more simplistic A says to the philosophical and rhetorically sophisticated B, "It seems that it is my lot to do you wrong even in the most insignificant matters. I will have to be very generous in order to forgive you such continued superiority!" (2:546; Il semble que mon lot soit d'avoir tort avec vous jusque dans les moindres choses; il faut que je sois bien bon pour vous pardonner une supériorité aussi continue!). Character A therefore intuits that there does exist a humble variety of forgiveness, although he also admits that it is difficult to practice and that it is perhaps only a great and noble soul who can bring himself to forgive those who put him to shame.

17. Montesquieu, *Lettres persanes*, 238.

18. Bacon, "On Revenge," in *Essays or Counsels*, 17–18.

19. This argument is reiterated in Bacon's essay "Of Anger" (1625), wherein he writes, "Only men must beware, that they carry their anger rather with scorn, than with fear; so that they may seem rather to be above the injury, than below it; which is a thing easily done, if a man will give law to himself" (233). In "Of Goodness and Goodness of Nature" (1612), Bacon again places the emphasis on the superiority of character that the ability to pardon entails: "If [a man] easily pardons and remits offences, it shows that his mind is planted above injuries, so that he cannot be shot" (53). See Bacon, *Essays or Counsels*.

20. That said, in entries for "pardon," "pardonnable," and "pardonner" we do find the insertion of such words as "tolérance," "tolérer," and "indulgence." The entries for these words show that the magnanimous pardon—if not the only available model—did have a semantic field that extended into and encompassed common parlance within educated circles.

CHAPTER 2

1. Rousseau identifies this as the ultimate source of his friends' jealousy in book 8 of the *Confessions*, 387. For an overview of the reception of *The Village Soothsayer* and the transports and controversies it elicited, see Christensen, *Rameau*, and Launay, *Querelle* and *Musiciens français*.

2. Rousseau, *Dialogues*, 1:32; 1:701. All translations are from Rousseau, *Rousseau, Judge of Jean-Jacques*, in Masters and Kelly, *Collected Writings*, vol. 1. Subsequent citations are given parenthetically in the text with the English translation first, followed by the French text.

3. The text itself was also composed largely as a response to Madame d'Epinay, Rousseau's former friend and eventual archnemesis, and her actions against him. Fearful of what Rousseau might reveal in his *Confessions* of her own relationships, she arranged for his public readings of the text to be halted.

4. Rousseau, *Rousseau, Judge of Jean-Jacques*, in Masters and Kelly, *Collected Writings*, 1:702.

5. For a detailed chronological account of how Rousseau's relationship with the philosophes soured, see Hulliung, *Autocritique*, 202–11.

6. Even the character of Rousseau remains impressed by how methodological and careful the Messieurs were in crafting the image of J.-J. that they circulated in public. See Rousseau, *Dialogues*, 1:964–65.

7. The tendency to use these terms interchangeably is evidenced not only by the literature of the period but also by various contemporaneous dictionaries.

8. In the *Third Dialogue*, and after the Frenchman has seen the error of his ways, Rousseau returns to this same argument. He maintains that one way to help J.-J. without compromising themselves too much would be to call the Messieurs out on the hypocrisy of the grace they have bestowed. In his defense, Rousseau writes, "nothing is more unjust and tyrannical than to force a man to be obliged to us despite himself" (1:947; rien n'est plus injuste et plus tiranique que de forcer un homme à nous être obligé malgré lui). Even this, however, proves to be more of a risk than the Frenchman is willing to take. For a more detailed analysis of Rousseau's thoughts on gratitude, see Coleman, *Anger*, 155–90.

9. Hobbes, *Leviathan*, 2:21, sec. 17.

10. Although Rousseau was certainly critical of any kind of obsessive attention to one's reputation with regard to unnecessary and counterproductive goods (wit, beauty, wealth, etc.), he did recognize the importance of concern for one's reputation as a moral being and a good citizen to functioning in society. Both Nicolas Dent's and Frederick Neuhouser's contributions are instructive, as both contest such readings that see amour propre as a wholly negative attribute within Rousseau's system. On this point, see Dent, *Rousseau*, 144, and Neuhouser, *Rousseau's Theodicy*, chap. 7. I discuss Rousseau's views on amour propre in detail in chapter 3.

11. Hobbes, *Leviathan*, 1:10, sec. 2, pp. 5–7; 2:27, sec. 20.

12. See Rousseau, *Rousseau, Judge of Jean-Jacques*, in Masters and Kelly, *Collected Writings*, 1:948.

CHAPTER 3

1. Rousseau, *Second Discourse*, 143; 3:144. All subsequent quotations are cited parenthetically in the text. All French citations are from the Pléiade editions and are preceded by the English translations, all of which were taken from Rousseau, *Other Early Political Writings*.

2. On this point, see also Coleman, *Anger*, 117.

3. Melzer's *Natural Goodness* remains an authoritative text in this respect. See also Shklar, *Men and Citizens*, passim and, in particular, 10.

4. This point has been made by the likes of Nicolas Dent, Frederick Neuhouser, Pierre Force, and, most recently, Christopher Brooke.

5. Force, *Self-Interest*, 37.

6. See Brooke, *Philosophic Pride*, chap. 8. See also Dent, *Rousseau*, 144; and Neuhouser, *Rousseau's Theodicy*, chap. 7.

7. The importance of comparison for evaluating and constructing one's moral character becomes somewhat complicated in the vicar's discussion of conscience. On the one hand, he asserts that one must orient oneself in relation to others, and because he invokes the language of geometry, he also seems to assert that one's moral value is relative to that of others. But he also states that, when functioning properly, the conscience—the ultimate guiding force—is utterly independent of the opinions of others and that it can and does adequately assess the goodness or evil of one's actions. I do not pretend to resolve this tension. It is possible that there is a distinction between absolute goodness and morality that is operative here. I return to this point later.

8. Brooke brings our attention to the following passage from *Émile*: "Our natural passions are very limited. They are the instruments of our freedom; they tend to preserve us. All those which subject and destroy us come from elsewhere. Nature does not give them to us. We appropriate them to the detriment of nature" (quoted in *Philosophic Pride*, 192).

9. Ibid.

10. On the intellectual roots of Rousseau's views on amour propre, see Force's discussion of Mandeville, Smith, Shaftesbury, and others in *Self-Interest*, 41–47.

11. For a more detailed account of how Rousseau's views on alienation and self-fulfillment were influenced by Stoic philosophy, see Brooke, *Philosophic Pride*, chap. 8.

12. This point is reiterated in *The Social Contract*: "This passage from the state of nature to the civil state produces a very remarkable change in man, by substituting justice for instinct, and giving his actions morality they had formerly lacked" (18; 3:364; Ce passage de l'état de nature à l'état civil produit dans l'homme un changement très remarquable, en substituant dans sa conduite la justice à l'instinct, et donnant à ses actions la moralité qui leur manquoit auparavant).

13. Rousseau does admit that there are indeed two different modes by which one could be moral: one absolute and one dependent on the generalized codes of conduct that prevail in the society in which one resides. I return to this point later.

14. Coleman, *Anger*, 105–6, 97. Another example of this is to be found in *Émile*, 4:545–46, as Rousseau presents his pupil's tendency to inquire into the reasons behind discord whenever he witnesses it as a positive effect of the education he has received. From this we can conclude that when anger manifests itself, it is a duty of those who witness it to inquire into its causes and either nominate it as legitimate (and subsequently partake in it) or, alternately, to condemn it. This is not to say that Rousseau everywhere condoned anger. Coleman points out that there is a tension in Rousseau's oeuvre regarding the emotion; at times Rousseau's style "conveys eloquent indignation and philosophical calm, even as he depicts with equal vividness human beings liberated from emotional disturbance and reacting passionately to insult and injustice." The epigraph to *Émile* is a case in point, as Rousseau recalls the calm of the Stoics when he cites Seneca's *De ira*: "The ills which ail us are curable; we were born to be upright, and nature itself, should we wish to be improved, will help us" (Coleman, *Anger*, 95–97). See also Kelly, *Rousseau's Exemplary Life*, 91.

15. Coleman, *Anger*, 14.

16. Coleman's focus is the tendency in the eighteenth century to "pay serious attention to the anger of men who believed their intelligence and sensibility entitled them to social recognition above and beyond what was warranted by their birth" (*Anger*, 7). Accordingly, he does not address in any detail the anger that the ordinary citizen experiences or the potentially constructive aspects of collective indignation. Although he correctly points out that citizens do not feel anger toward the constraints of the social contract by which they are bound, Coleman does not address whether or how the populace can use anger productively to the end of reaffirming their shared political identity (138n45).

17. Rousseau, *Considérations*, in Rousseau, *Oeuvres complètes*, 3:960. The translations of the *Considerations on the Government of Poland* are from Masters and Kelly, *Collected Writings*, vol. 2. The cited translation is from page 174. All subsequent quotations are cited parenthetically in the text, with the English translation cited first, followed by the French text.

18. Cohen, "Reflections on Rousseau," 199.

19. Ngai, *Ugly Feelings*, 7.

20. Rousseau, *Economie politique*, in Rousseau, *Oeuvres complètes*, 3:245; 253. All translations of *Economie politique* are from Rousseau, *Other Early Political Writings*.

21. See the postscript to letter 34 of part 1 of Rousseau's *Julie*, where Saint-Preux describes the incapacity of a brave officer to fight as a mercenary and then goes on to recount the "joy" (bonheur) that this same officer felt when he took down the enemy's flag in the name of France.

22. Rousseau, *Social Contract*, 3:373. All translations are taken from Rousseau, *Social Contract*. The cited translation is from 27–28. Subsequent citations appear parenthetically in the text with the English translation first, followed by the French text.

23. Riley, "Possible Explanation," 167, 171–72, 175.

24. Shklar, *Men and Citizens*, 4, 15–17.

25. On Rousseau's appraisal of Jesus Christ, see Kelly, *Rousseau's Exemplary Life*, 60–61; and Starobinski, *Transparence*, 88–90.

26. Rousseau makes an identical point in the dedication to the *Second Discourse*: "For, regardless of how a government is constituted, if there is a single person in it who is not subject to the law, all the others are necessarily at his discretion" (115; 3:112; s'il s'y trouve un seul homme qui ne soit pas soumis à la loi, tous les autres sont necessairement à la direction de celui-là). It is also worth considering letter 10 of part 4 of *Julie* in this regard, in which Saint-Preux describes how, although the perpetrator of a crime may indeed be forgiven at times, the witness who fails to report such a crime cannot expect forgiveness but rather can expect to be expelled. This is because the criminal commits a crime out of self-interest, an impulse that is common to all men. The witness, on the other hand, has no such stake in the crimes of another. The failure to report such crimes is therefore done out of "cold blood" (du sang froid) and a decisive lack of interest in the well-being of the community (Rousseau, *Julie*, 381; 2:464).

27. On the Christian's inability to be a good citizen within Rousseau's philosophy, see Barth, *Nineteenth-Century Theology*, 194.

28. Butler, quoted in Digeser, *Political Forgiveness*, 310.

29. Natural man, of course, has no need of justice because, as discussed earlier, he acts always in accord with nature and thus is incapable of both justice and injustice. On this point, see the distinction between natural and moral freedom in Melzer, *Natural Goodness*, 101–8, 126–28, and Shklar, *Men and Citizens*, 34–35.

30. In the *Social Contract* Rousseau writes, "Frequent pardons mean that crime will soon need them no longer, and no-one can help seeing whither that leads" (31–32; 3:377; Les fréquentes grâces annoncent que, bientôt, les forfaits n'en auront plus besoin, et chacun voit où cela mène). Rousseau, with a little help from Augustine, makes a similar point in his *Encyclopédie* entry "ECONOMIE POLITIQUE": "But we ought not to confound negligence with moderation, or clemency with weakness. To be just, it is necessary to be severe; to permit vice, when one has the right and the power to suppress it, is to be oneself vicious" (262; 3:254; Mais on ne doit pas confondre la négligence avec la modération, ni la douceur avec la foiblesse. Il faut être sévère pour être juste: souffrir la méchanceté qu'on a le droit et le pouvoir de réprimer, c'est être méchant soi-même).

31. Rousseau may be thinking here of Locke, in particular the latter's assertion that the magistrate cannot know the hearts of his subjects. In the *First Tract on Government*, Locke writes, "Were faith and repentance, the substantial parts of religion, entrusted to his jurisdiction and open to his knowledge we might possibly find his penalties severer in those things than in any other. But God, the judge of hearts, hath reserved both the knowledge and censure of these

internal acts to himself, and removed those actions from the judgement of any tribunal but his own" (in *Political Essays*, 47). There is one moment in the *Dialogues* (which I discuss later) where Rousseau seems to suggest that grace was properly bestowed by the magistrate; this was not done on account of the culpable party's internal sentiments but rather on account of his actions.

32. One wonders whether Rousseau is indeed consciously borrowing from Hobbes here. Hobbes had similar reservations about the sovereign's use of pardon whenever crime is concerned, as did Machiavelli before him.

33. Even in *Julie*, Saint-Preux observes that both Julie and Wolmar are reticent to forgive those who pose a threat to the general good in the idyllic society of Clarens. Julie suppresses her feelings of compassion—something that pains her most profoundly—to make sure that those who threaten the sanctity of her home and the laws that govern there are appropriately punished and permanently expelled. Her anger is thus defensive of what she takes to be the general will at Clarens, even as it goes against her very personal predilections and emotions. She is able to decide what course of action to take in response to such depersonalized anger precisely because she and Wolmar constitute the sovereign power in their mini society. Thus, if an individual should "forget oneself" (s'oublier) during a celebration and violate the generalized codes of conduct within Wolmar and Julie's idyllic society, they are not reprimanded but rather asked to leave Clarens forever the following day (498; 2:609). In violating the laws, the citizens of Clarens become enemies of the community and must thus be purged from it. In short, their drunken antics betray the degree to which they have failed to truly internalize the codes and ideals of Clarens. Nominated as Others, they become the proper object of collective indignation and a useful example as to what not to do and be in Wolmar and Julie's society.

CHAPTER 4

1. Rousseau presents his opera as having achieved the same effects as the open-air spectacle he described in *The Social Contract*, insofar as it created what Starobinski describes as subjective enthusiasm, with which the entire populace participates in the spectacle, and in so doing it reaffirmed the populace's unity within a cohesive, social whole in an unmediated way (*Jean-Jacques Rousseau*, 120–21). That the Messieurs would opt to preserve *The Village Soothsayer* as a cultural product while destroying its author betrays that they perhaps found more wisdom in Rousseau's political philosophy than they would have cared to admit. The festival as a means of fostering unity is also discussed at length in Coleman, *Rousseau's Political Imagination*; Derrida, *De la grammatologie*; and Ellison, "Rousseau."

2. The fact that the public maintains its anger at J.-J. following his pardon serves to exemplify how pernicious clemency can be when publicized, as it puts the citizenry in a confusing position. On the one hand, because J.-J. has been pardoned, the good citizen is required to allow him to circulate freely. On the other, the Frenchman cannot help but feel aversion and horror at the sight of the Other who has been allowed to remain in his midst. What is more, as the Frenchman points out in the *Second Dialogue*, the anger that his fellow citizens are forced to suppress results in the most barbaric behavior. They taunt J.-J. like devilish schoolchildren. Unable to employ their indignation in the interest of defending the state, their anger is transformed into cruelty, in which they all take pleasure (1:882). One wonders whether this is yet another reason why, in *The Social Contract*, Rousseau maintained that grace should be sparingly employed.

3. Rousseau's distinction between the general and particular will draws heavily on Locke's notion of the "Law of Opinion or Reputation" in its descriptions of the psychology of the citizen. For Locke, public opinion consists in a rational agreement among the populace that, when functioning properly, is always both objective and discriminating. Locke, *Essay Concerning Human Understanding*, bk. 2, sec. 28, pp. 10–12.

4. A similar idea is also expressed in the *Dialogues*. Rousseau writes, "The plot was formed in the bosom of that nation, but it did not come from there. The French are its ardent executors" (1:207; 1:927; Le complot s'est formé dans le sein de cette nation, mais il n'est pas venu d'elle. Les François en sont les ardens execteurs).

5. Rousseau even notes that such individuals may very well sell their own votes in exchange for money.

6. On this point, see Shklar, *Men and Citizens*, 16–18.

7. Alberg, *Reinterpretation*, 34. Alberg concludes that the "only possible explanation for this behavior on the part of the public is provided by the Frenchman's honest response that J.-J. is not forgiven for the sin that the other has committed against him" (35). According to Alberg, after the Frenchman reads J.-J.'s work and becomes acquainted with the individual, he is able to overcome his aversion to forgiving J.-J. only by transferring his own error into a realm of nonculpability. He does so by attributing his misjudgment of J.-J. to an "invincible error," in this case the corrupt but omnipotent social order. Alberg underscores the fact that this is itself a theological term, one that designates errors that are unavoidable given a particular set of circumstances and therefore cannot be imputed to an individual as a sin within Christianity (36; Rousseau, *Dialogues*, 1:937). This leads Alberg to conclude that "in judging Rousseau's enemies to be evil and in understanding that one does not need forgiveness . . . one can grasp the principle of natural goodness." Accepting the principle of natural goodness in place of original sin is therefore "dependent on the fact that Rousseau cannot forgive others and that he himself is not forgiven" (36). Again, my objection to such an interpretation is that it does not afford due credence to the numerous semantic possibilities surrounding the concept of forgiveness that circulated in eighteenth-century France.

8. Admittedly, in the *Third Dialogue* of Rousseau's *Rousseau, Judge of Jean-Jacques*, the Frenchman does claim that he always had found something distasteful in the philosophy of his day: "I have never been able to relish our Gentlemen's system" (in Masters and Kelly, *Collected Writings*, 1:928; je n'ai jamais pu goûter le système de nos Messieurs). Notwithstanding this, as long as the Frenchman privileges his identity as a citizen, he vehemently defends the philosophes. This is part and parcel of what Shklar has observed to be the true mark of a citizen: "The political participation that liberty and equality demand is not a matter of self-expression. The citizens are not meant to bring their private interests, hopes, and opinions to bear upon public affairs" (*Men and Citizens*, 18). It is telling in this respect that the Frenchman cannot admit that he finds the philosophy of his day distasteful until after the veil has been lifted on the scandal and he has subsequently undergone conversion. Given the "arbiters of public opinion," there is no reason why the Frenchman's own personal likes and dislikes would be brought to bear in a discussion regarding an enemy of France (*Rousseau, Judge of Jean-Jacques*, 1:964).

9. This is something that the Frenchman realizes fairly early on in the text. See Rousseau, *Dialogues*, 1:741.

10. We can also certainly read the Frenchman's conundrum as the reader's predicament. As an implicit partner in the dialogue, the reader is supposed to be provoked by the rhetoric to recognize the larger significance of J.-J.'s plight and the heroism it would take to fight on his behalf.

11. Rousseau, *Oeuvres complètes*, 1:1659n1.

12. Similar phrases are indeed dispersed throughout Rousseau's *Dialogues*. Consider in this respect the phrases "one sees that recognition of his innocence would serve only to make him still more odious, and to transform the animosity of which he is the object into rage" (174, 1:885; l'on voit que son innocence reconnue ne serviroit qu'à le rendre plus odieux encore) and "he would be forgiven even less for wrongs about which they would reproach themselves" (175, 1:885–86; on lui pardonneroit bien moins les torts qu'on se reprocheroit envers lui). Eigeldinger discusses the occurrence of these phrases in his article, "Ils ne me pardonneront jamais." He does not, however, discuss incidences of such phrases in other works and therefore seems to intuit that this belief was specific to Rousseau.

13. Hobbes, *Leviathan* 1:9, sec. 8; Franklin, quoted in Morgan, *Genuine Article*, 99.

14. After the Baron d'Etange learns of Julie's love of Saint-Preux, he makes a similar statement of Saint-Preux: "Although I have always felt little inclination for him, I hate him now above all for the excesses he caused me to commit, and shall never forgive him my brutality" (Rousseau, *Julie*, 144–45; 2:177; Quoique je me sois toujours senti peu d'inclination pour lui, je le hais, surtout à présent, pour les excès qu'il m'a fait commettre, et ne lui pardonnerai jamais ma brutalité." In the Baron d'Etange's case, he cannot forgive Saint-Preux for causing him to let his anger get the best of him and physically harm his daughter. The Baron d'Etange blames Saint-Preux for having been the reason he failed to live up to the ideal he had set for himself. This point is underscored by Julie's own thoughts about the event: "The heart of a father feels it is made for forgiveness, and not to have need of forgiveness" (144; 2:175; Le coeur d'un père sent qu'il est fait pour pardonner, et non pour avoir besoin de pardon). Saint-Preux, because of what his existence inspired the Baron d'Etange to do, threatens the latter's sense of self, and for this reason he is unforgivable.

15. Kelly's *Rousseau's Exemplary Life* is an exception in this regard, as he reads the *Confessions* as moral fables intended to have pedagogical attributes that accord with Rousseau's political philosophy. According to Kelly, these subtle political commentaries were to be comprehended by the philosophers. The general public, in contrast, was intended to feel inspired by Rousseau's experiences and, in turn, regard his "exemplary life" as an example to be emulated. But it seems fairly safe to assume that Rousseau's unhappy fate was also meant to be a warning about the consequences of straying too far in one's *behavior* from social norms.

16. Locke, *Essay Concerning Human Understanding*, chap. 28, sec. 11, p. 2. On Rousseau's and Locke's respective notions of public opinion, see Habermas, *Transformation*, 91–99.

17. Sennett, *Fall*, 121.

18. Herdt highlights just how perplexing this problem is for Rousseau scholars in *Putting on Virtue*. See, in particular, pages 284 and 302.

19. See Rousseau, *Dialogues*, 1:940–45. Here, both Rousseau and the Frenchman concur that reversing public opinion is essentially impossible, given the magnitude of the plot and the confidence that the public demonstrates toward the philosophes.

20. In *The Social Contract*, Rousseau claims that one need not necessarily love the law but that one need only act in accordance with it. In so doing, such a citizen remains irreproachable. But it seems difficult to deny that in an ideal scenario the citizen generally loves the law, customs, and norms of the society in which he resides. The Frenchman does not want to lose this love, as he senses the alienation that will necessarily result. Again, Shklar's *Men and Citizens* remains an authoritative text on this aspect of Rousseau's political thought.

21. Even that act of reading the work of J.-J. objectively constitutes a revolutionary act for the Frenchman, which is precisely why it must be the Frenchman-as-an-individual who eventually complies with Rousseau's request that he do so. As a mere citizen (and not a legislator), the Frenchman does not have the right to go against either the laws or public opinion. See *Du contrat social*, 3:381–82.

22. Rousseau maintains that the sentiment that the Frenchman experiences still persists in the hearts of citizens. They may, for the moment, be spellbound by the prestige of the Messieurs, but this prestige will some day fade, and, when it does, the conscience of an entire people "shall be returned to itself" (sera rendue à elle-même). The citizens will then demand that justice be served, and they will avenge J.-J. posthumously (241; 1:970).

23. As Rousseau had pointed out earlier, "The plot was formed in the bosom of that nation, but it did not come from there. The French are its ardent executors" (207; 1:927; for the French text, see note 4 above). Later on in the *Third Dialogue*, however, Rousseau expresses a little bit more disdain for the public than he does in the passage just quoted. He says, "Let the public remain in the error that delights it and that it deserves, and let's show only the person who is

its victim that we don't share it" (225; 1:950; Laissons le public dans l'erreur où il se complait et dont il est digne, et montrons seulement à celui qui en est la victime que nous ne la partageons pas). By saying that the public is deserving of its own blindness, the character of Rousseau does seem to imply that he feels contempt and no small degree of condescension toward it. Later, however, he again casts the public as the unwitting victim who shall one day reawaken and throw off the yoke that the Messieurs represent (1:970–71). I do not pretend to be able to resolve this inconsistency as far as the psychology of Rousseau's character is concerned, but, as shall be argued momentarily, it does not appear that the Frenchman shares this ambivalence toward his compatriots.

24. Charvet, *Social Problem*, 105.

25. The Savoyard vicar's conscience, on the other hand, concerns itself with a transcendental, moral order and is thus fundamentally apolitical. We discuss conscience in more detail in part 2.

26. Rousseau was not the only one of his generation to ask the question, what are we to do when the dictates of personal conscience are in direct conflict with our duties as citizens? Indeed, Diderot also poses the question in *Les entretien d'un père avec ses enfants* (1773) and *Supplément au voyage* (1772).

27. Kant, "What Is Enlightenment?," 3.

28. Kant, likely following in the footsteps of Rousseau, also observes that although the "public use of one's reason" is laudable, such public use should be limited to scholarship. Indeed, he maintains that in instances "through which some members of the community must passively conduct themselves with an artificial unanimity, so that the government may direct them to public ends, or at least prevent them from destroying those ends . . . argument is certainly not allowed" (ibid., 5). The Frenchman's more passive approach, coupled with his decision to become the depository (and, likely, eventual editor) of J.-J.'s writings, seems to anticipate such a sentiment.

29. J. Jones, *Rousseau's Dialogues*, 189.

30. On the theme of nonendings in the work of Rousseau, see ibid., the final chapter.

31. Alberg, *Reinterpretation*, 47, 49.

32. For a detailed analysis of the same scenes, see O'Hagan, *Rousseau*, 45–46.

33. Alberg, *Reinterpretation*, 49.

34. Simon suggests that in this episode "the contract engenders wage-dependency, which Rousseau himself elsewhere identifies as a threat to the autonomy for civic virtue" (*Beyond Contractual Morality*, 51). She goes on to conclude that "Émile was not induced to feel compassion for Robert, only to concentrate on his own hurt and loss and the creation of a contract to prevent future harm" (55). The result, according to her reading, is that the "recourse to legal contracts" constitutes a "missed opportunity" on Rousseau's part, as "Émile's freedom and independence are achieved at the expense of moral autonomy and concrete relations to others" (52). But this is problematic, as Robert refuses the proposed arrangement and instead declares that Émile will be the sole and absolute proprietor of the land he cultivates.

35. The vital importance of property in assuring the citizen's engagement is expressed most clearly in Rousseau's *Discourse on Political Economy*. It is worth quoting him at length on this point:

> It is certain that the right of property is the most sacred of all the rights of citizenship, and even more important in some respects than liberty itself; either because it more nearly affects the preservation of life, or because, property being more easily usurped and more difficult to defend than life, the law ought to pay a greater attention to what is most easily taken away; or finally, because property is the true foundation of civil society, and the real guarantee of the undertakings of citizens

(271; 3:262–63; Il est certain que le droit de propriété est plus sacré de tous les droits des citoyens, et plus important à certains égards que la liberté même; soit parce qu'il tient de plus près à la conservation de la vie, soit parce que les biens étant plus facile à usurper et plus pénibles à défendre que la personne, on doit plus respecter ce qui peut se ravir plus aisément; soit enfin parce que la propriété est le vrai fondement de la société civile, et le vrai garant des engagements des citoyens)

36. Rousseau, *Fragments politiques*, in Gagnebin and Raymond, *Oeuvres complètes*, 3:164. All translations from this text are my own.

37. Coleman, "Property," 258.

PART 2, INTRODUCTION

1. As discussed in part 1, Rousseau was dubious as to whether absolute notions of morality could hold much sway in the political sphere. Instead, in *The Social Contract* he propounded an ethics that was shot through with cultural relativism. At the same time, Rousseau does seem to admit the possibility that—if laws are consistently enacted with an eye toward the general will—the law could perhaps prove to be in accord with transmundane moral laws and eventually manifest itself in public opinion. But, because it is the citizen's duty to experience indignation at the violation of the state's laws (no matter how corrupt or off base such laws may be) and take public opinion as a guide, it is clear that the variety of anger and forgiveness that Rousseau condones in *The Social Contract* (and problematizes in *Rousseau, Judge of Jean-Jacques*) is firmly rooted in the necessary preeminence of public opinion and thus the laws and judgments to which the general populace subscribes.

2. By "love," I do not mean amour passion or even romantic love, as for Rousseau and many of his contemporaries, both of these experiences were often characterized by a desire to possess and master the love object. Jealousy was thus to a large extent unavoidable in such relationships on account of the amour propre that inevitably attended them. The love to which I am referring is, rather, a deep affection for the other and an intimate knowledge of another's true character and sentiments. As discussed later, such love is—in its ideal form—utterly devoid of amour propre and entails a more fluid power dynamics. It is this variety of love that Rousseau propounded in both *Émile* and *Julie*. See my discussion of Elizabeth Wingrove's notion of consensual non-consensuality in *Rousseau's Republican Romance*, as well as my analysis of *Émile* and *Sophie*.

3. Kavanagh, *Writing the Truth*, 30.

CHAPTER 5

1. This is the point of departure for Alberg's interpretation in *Reinterpretation*.

2. Rousseau, *Les Confessions*, in Rousseau, *Oeuvres complètes*, 1:5. Unless otherwise noted, all references to the *Confessions* have been taken from this edition and all translations are from volume 5 of Rousseau, *Confessions and Correspondence*, in Masters and Kelly, *Collected Writings*. All subsequent quotations are cited parenthetically in the text with the English translation cited first, followed by the French text.

3. Alberg argues this point with admirable clarity. See, in particular, *Reinterpretation*, 6–9. Just as was the case with many of his contemporaries, Rousseau seems to have found the idea that God would have created corporeal and therefore fallible creatures only to punish them eternally for falling prey to their own weaknesses fundamentally distasteful. This is expressed most emphatically in the "Profession of Faith." Here, the vicar maintains that he is not sure if a system

of rewards and punishments exists. But he surmises that, if such a system does exist, then God would have no need to punish us in the afterlife, as our conscience would have already made us suffer for our sins sufficiently on earth (4:589–91; 4:595–602).

4. Kavanagh's *Writing the Truth* is another noteworthy contribution in this respect. Starobinski's *Oeil vivant* is yet another.

5. Ogrodnick, *Instinct*, 5; see also 7. Both Starobinski and Strong see the oscillation that pervades Rousseau's autobiographical works as an admission on his part that we have no true nature and thus no true self. Rather than constructing a comprehensible self, Strong reads Rousseau's oscillating nature and conflicting desires as, in point of fact, a rejection of the possibility of fixity or definition and therefore of comprehensibility (Starobinski, *Jean-Jacques Rousseau*, 68–76; Strong, *Jean-Jacques*, 143–44). Jonathan Marks, on the other hand, reads Rousseau as endorsing oscillation and as struggling to incorporate "apparent contradictions into a single way of life." "Our happiness is made of certain disharmonious goods, solitary and social ones, for example," Marks continues. "[Rousseau's] problem is to find a place in a life for those goods without setting himself in contradiction, like the bourgeois, who by seeking both sorts of goods attains neither" ("Who Lost Nature?," 501). As will become clearer later, my own interpretation leans more toward Marks's insofar as I suggest that Rousseau's understanding of forgiveness depends on a certain degree of fixity in character (or at least the belief that such fixity exists and can be rendered visible to the true friend).

6. Unlike other children, Rousseau maintains that he was treated as a "cherished child" (enfant chéri) and never as a "spoiled child" (enfant gâté): "never did they have to repress in me or satisfy any of those fantastic moods that are attributed to nature, and that are all born from education alone" (*Confessions*, 5:9; 1:10; jamais on n'eut à réprimer en moi ni à satisfaire aucune de ces fantasques humeurs qu'on impute à la nature, et qui naissent toutes de la seule education). See also 1:13 and his discussion of his friendship with Bernard. So convinced is Rousseau that the portraits he paints of his family and entourage are flawless that he presents them as further proof of his good character. It is telling in this respect that, rhetorically and with much confidence, he asks, "How could I have become wicked, since under my eyes I had examples only of gentleness, and around me only the best people in the world?" (5:9; 1:10; Comment serois-je devenu méchant, quand je n'avois sous les yeux que des exemples de douceur, et autour de moi que les meilleures gens du monde?).

7. Jean Lacroix is one among many scholars who have noted the purgative qualities of the text. He describes the *Confessions* as the means by which Rousseau attempts to confront his conscience and, in so doing, to redeem himself: "When he affirms that his first duty is to show his conscience, he simply wants to say that one should appear as one is. It is an aphorism in him that whoever has the courage to appear as he is will become, sooner or later, that which he must be" ("Conscience selon Rousseau," 90; Quand il affirme que le premier devoir est de montrer sa conscience, il veut simplement dire qu'il faut paraître ce qu l'on est. C'est un aphorisme chez lui que quiconque a le courage de paraître ce qu'il est deviendra tôt ou tard ce qu'il doit être). Translation mine.

8. Starobinski writes, "Evil is produced by history and society, without altering the essence of the individual. . . . Evil is exterior; it is the passion for the exterior. If man lets himself be seduced entirely by foreign goods, he will be entirely controlled by evil. But, to return into the self for oneself at every moment is the source of salvation" (*Jean-Jacques Rousseau*, 34; Le mal est extérieur et il est la passion de l'extérieur: si l'homme se livre tout entier à la séduction des biens étrangers, il sera tout entier soumis à l'empire du mal. Mais rentrer en soi pour lui, en tout temps, est la ressource du salut). Translation mine. See also Melzer, *Natural Goodness*, chap. 2.

9. Starobinski, *Jean-Jacques Rousseau*, 235.

10. Ogrodnick points out that it is unclear how confident Rousseau was in his abilities to "fix his true character" within his autobiographical works. On the one hand, Rousseau's desire

for self-vindication obliges him to ensure the accuracy of his self-knowledge in both the *Dialogues* and the *Confessions* (*Instinct*, 32). On the other, he seems ready to admit in the *Reveries* that "if there is any consistency, it is an ongoing principle of inconsistency" (Rousseau, *Oeuvres complètes*, 31). Ogrodnick attributes this to Rousseau's pessimism that he could ever be judged equitably and thus reads the *Reveries* as a text in which the desire for self-vindication has been extinguished (*Instinct*, 33). As is argued in my discussion of the *Reveries*, once the desire for self-vindication was extinguished, Rousseau became bolder in asserting the rights and privileges that he believed he was entitled to on account of his utter singularity. Among these rights and privileges was that of taking pride in the peculiar variety of vengeance.

11. Koselleck, *Critique and Crisis*, 120. See also Melzer, "Origin," 344–45, and Kavanagh, *Writing the Truth*, x.

12. Starobinski, *Jean-Jacques Rousseau*, 239.

13. Kelly, *Rousseau's Exemplary Life*, 30–31, 36.

14. Saint-Lambert's exhortation is confirmed in his letter to Rousseau from October 11, 1757 (*Correspondance*, vol. 4, no. 534), which is discussed in greater detail later. All of Rousseau's correspondence is from *Correspondance complète* and was accessed through the Electronic Enlightenment database. Throughout the remainder of this work I will be referring to the letters by their date in the body of the text and by their volume and number in the parenthetical notation. Unless otherwise noted, all translations from the *Correspondance* are my own.

15. Kelly, *Rousseau's Exemplary Life*, 208.

16. This raises interesting questions about whether guilt and, for that matter, compassion, function similarly in all types of relationships within Rousseau's oeuvre. Boyd argues convincingly that pity and compassion "are fueled by an aversion to suffering" and therefore are more prone to cause one to flee than to act on a victim's behalf ("Pity's Pathologies Portrayed," 519). In the citation regarding Rousseau's thoughts on how to proceed with Sophie, however, Rousseau equates compassion with guilt and action, which he in turn contrasts to the more socially directed notion of "shame" (honte) and inaction. It therefore seems possible that, in certain types of relationships, guilt may function differently than it does in others, drawing us, at times, toward those with whom we have a deep and intimate bond in the hopes of making reparations and easing our conscience and, at others, driving us away from those we have wronged but with whom we have no individuated attachment. Saint-Preux's confession to Julie, which is discussed in more detail later, seems to reaffirm this.

17. On Rousseau's refusal to accompany Madame d'Epinay to Geneva and the reaction from Rousseau's entourage, see also Coleman, *Anger*, 124–25.

18. Following these events, Rousseau's paternity was probably one of the worst-kept secrets among the philosophes and those who were close to them. Rousseau's paternity was officially revealed to the general public in 1764 by Voltaire in his anonymous pamphlet "Le sentiment des citoyens," in which Voltaire essentially accused Rousseau of being a hypocrite for having published a treatise on education. But in book 7 of the *Confessions*, wherein Rousseau discusses the abandonment of his children and the betrayal he felt when it was revealed, he does not mention Voltaire. Instead, he mentions Diderot, Grimm, Madame de Epinay, Madame de Luxembourg, Madame Dupin, Madame de Chenonceau, and Madame de Francueil as having been privy to the information and thus responsible for rendering his paternity public, thus leading one to believe that—at least as far as Rousseau was concerned—many people from outside his circle had become apprised of the situation long before Voltaire's pamphlet (357). I discuss this episode in more detail in the next chapter.

19. Rousseau acknowledges this cooling-off explicitly in his letter to Saint-Lambert from September 15, 1757 (*Correspondance*, vol. 4, no. 527).

20. Saint-Lambert himself admits he was the brainchild in a letter to Rousseau dated October 11, 1757, which we will discuss in more detail momentarily.

21. Gagnebin and Raymond write that although Rousseau initially admits to being culpable, he quickly shifts the blame onto others (Rousseau, *Confessions*, 462n3). Gagnebin and Raymond cite Henri Guillemin, *Les affaires de l'ermitage, annales J.-J. R.*, 29:72, and Ernest Seillière, *J.-J. Rousseau*, 211.

22. Rousseau, *Oeuvres complètes*, 1:462n3. All translations from this text are my own.

23. The event involving the ribbon and Rousseau's passing on the blame to others (and even to the devil himself) and to the failings of both language and society has been examined by many scholars. Some noteworthy discussions include Starobinski, *Jean-Jacques Rousseau*, 151; Raymond, *Jean-Jacques Rousseau*, 18 and 107–8; and Clément, *Jean-Jacques Rousseau*, 132–33. In "The Purloined Ribbon," Paul de Man reads the ribbon as a pure signifier in the Lacanian sense. The ribbon thus represents Rousseau's desire to possess Marion and the revelation of his theft as a result of his exhibitionistic desire to reveal himself.

24. Rousseau claims that Sophie hid the correspondence, correspondence that would have exonerated her while inculpating Rousseau (Rousseau, *Confessions*, 1:449). According to Charles Briffaut's research, these letters were preserved until the death of Sophie d'Houdetot, at which point her niece burned them (1:462n3).

25. There is in this episode the suggestion that anger, when privately experienced, may itself need to continue in its unhindered course for a while until such time that it exhausts itself and is replaced by other, more favorable sentiments. Unlike more contemporary understandings of forgiveness (such as those offered by Derrida and Jankélévitch), Rousseau does not characterize forgiveness as a spontaneous and automatic event. Rather, it is a change in perspective that arrives on account of a healing process, one that the heart must carry out at its own pace and in contradistinction to generalized norms of conduct and judgment.

26. Saint-Lambert, aware of Rousseau's thinking about his own character even prior to the composition of the *Confessions*, points to Rousseau's extreme sensibility as yet another reason why he should expect to be easily reconciled with his friends. He characterizes their friendship as being one in which their respective weaknesses are recognized and even loved. One of their shared weaknesses, according to Saint-Lambert, is that they both have "the misfortune to have been born too sensitive to that which happens around us" (*Correspondance*, vol. 4, no. 579; le Malheur d'etre né trop sensible a ce qui se passe autour de nous). This would, of course, prove to be a cornerstone of Rousseau's project of self-vindication in his autobiographical works.

27. This letter is from October 10, 1758, approximately one year after the "affair" between Sophie and Rousseau had been discovered.

28. Charvet, *Social Problem*, 111–12. See also Ferrara, *Modernity*, 37.

29. On their final rupture, see Rousseau's correspondence with Sophie d'Houdetot from March through May 6, 1758. From the correspondence it is clear that the rupture must be blamed on Rousseau's paranoia and hypersensitivity, which is likely another reason why he opted not to go into detail.

CHAPTER 6

1. Ogrodnick, *Instinct*, 153–55.

2. Williams's *Shame and Necessity* remains one of the more eloquent articulations of this tendency. Williams highlights the potentially detrimental effects for the victims that result when the understanding of guilt has reached a certain level of refinement. He claims that although in more primitive understandings of guilt the feelings of the victims remain figured in the construction of guilt, they have become increasingly absent throughout modernity. "When the conception of guilt," he writes, "is refined beyond a certain point and forgets its primitive materials of anger and fear, guilt comes to be represented simply as the attitude of respect for

an abstract law, and it then no longer has any special connection with victims." Williams thus concludes that "the refinement of guilt in this direction can conceal one of its virtues" (*Shame and Necessity*, 22).

3. Rousseau, *Oeuvres complètes*, 1:358n1.

4. Ogrodnick clearly disapproves, as, again, she notes that there was no "remedial effect on Rousseau's moral judgment," thus implying his moral judgment was faulty (*Instinct*, 155).

5. Rousseau, *Correspondance*, vol. 2, no. 757. See editorial note 3 to Rousseau's letter to Madame de Francueil.

6. I am here relying on Williams's distinction between shame and guilt (*Shame and Necessity*, 92–95). The fact that Rousseau recounts that he abandoned his children upon their suggestion and that they had applauded it implies that comparison and thus amour propre founded his initial decision. Subsequently, he "philosophized" on the duties of man and so became entirely self-possessed of his decision. As discussed later, this is one of the rare confessions where interiority and exteriority were perfectly accorded.

7. Admittedly, in *Émile* Rousseau makes an implicit reference to the feelings of guilt that abandoning one's children can inspire: "He who cannot fulfill the duties of a father has no right to become one. Neither poverty nor labors nor concern for public opinion exempts him from feeding his children and from raising them himself. Readers, you can believe me. I predict that to whoever has vitals and neglects such holy duties that he will long shed bitter tears for his offense and will never find consolation for it" (13:175; 4:262–63; Celui qui ne peut remplir les devoirs de père n'a point droit de le devenir. Il n'y a ni pauvreté ni travaux ni respect humain qui le dispensent de nourrir ses enfants, et de les elever lui-même. Lecteurs, vous pouvez m'en croire. Je prédis à quiconque a des entrailles et néglige de si saints devoirs qu'il versera longtemps sur sa faute des larmes améres, et n'en sera jamais consolé). But, as will be discussed momentarily, more relevant to our purposes is how Rousseau rhetorically deals with his paternity in the *Confessions* and, most important, the lesson that the reader is supposed to come away with.

8. Rousseau's discussion in the *Confessions* of what transpired after Claude Anet's death is instructive. Rousseau claims that, upon the death of the latter, he realized that he would inherit—among other things—Anet's black coat. He said as much to Madame de Warens. Seeing the pain he had caused her, he immediately felt remorse: "Nothing made her feel the loss she had suffered more than this craven and odious statement, disinterestedness and nobility of soul being the qualities that the deceased had eminently possessed" (5:172; 1:205; Rien ne lui fit mieux sentir la perte qu'elle avoit faite que ce lâche et odieux mot, le desinteressement et la noblesse d'ame étant des qualités que le défunt avoit éminemment possédées). Rousseau goes on to note that the pain he saw in de Warens's eyes struck him so forcefully that he never committed a similar error again. It is worth noting that this story concerning the coat is the prologue to the story of de Warens's demise and her eventual rupture with Rousseau. Throughout this confession, Rousseau constantly draws comparisons between Anet's abilities to take care of de Warens and his own incapacity to do the same, all of which were duly noted by de Warens (hence the reason she eventually found a replacement for Rousseau). The moment at which Rousseau expressed his desire for the coat he revealed a part of his character that de Warens had never seen before. She was unable to ever fully see past it, hence the cooling between her and Rousseau that occurs from that moment forward. It is not so much the crime that is cast as unforgivable but the lack of sincerity that it revealed in Rousseau's expressed sentiments toward both de Warens and Anet: at least to a degree, Rousseau had always seen the latter instrumentally and as an obstacle to his own full enjoyment of de Warens. This constituted a betrayal of the friendship that the three had shared. Even if Rousseau made and kept a resolution to never utter such a cruel phrase again, he could not win back de Warens's full affection, esteem, and trust.

9. On this point, see Rousseau's reading of Herodotus and the ancient historians in *Émile*. He writes, "The ancient historians are filled with views which one could use even if the facts

which present them were false. But we do not know how to get any true advantage from history. Critical erudition absorbs everything, as if it were very important whether a fact is true, provided that a useful teaching can be drawn from it. Sensible men ought to regard history as a tissue of fables whose moral is very appropriate to the human heart" (Rousseau, quoted in Kelly, *Rousseau's Exemplary Life*, 15).

10. Strauss, "Intention of Rousseau," 470–71. See also Kelly's interpretation of book 4 of the *Rêveries* (*Rousseau's Exemplary Life*, 15–16); and Rousseau, *Julie*, 303; 2:317. In the latter example, Saint-Preux invokes similar argumentation in an effort to persuade Julie that she has no obligation to confess their affair to Wolmar.

11. We can also take as an example what Rousseau says about Madame de Houdetot hiding the letters she exchanged with Rousseau during Saint-Lambert's absence in book 9. He describes this as a "lie assuredly full of honesty, fidelity, generosity, when the truth would only have been a perfidious act" (5:378; 1:449; mensonge assurément plein d'honnêteté, de fidélité, de générosité, tandis que la vérité n'eut été qu'une perfidie).

12. We can also consider in this respect the opening pages of the section of *Émile* titled "Profession of Faith," in which the knowledge that the philosophes wish to impart is critiqued by Rousseau as testimony to their vanity and their desire for ascendancy, not over their reading public but over one another (4:346–50). See also Orwin's discussion of Rousseau's revalorization of ignorance in the *First Discourse* and his liberal interpretation of the Socrates of the *Apology* ("Rousseau's Socratism").

13. Rousseau's discussion of Voltaire's *Zaïre* in the *Lettre à d'Alembert* makes this point with admirable clarity: "When Orosmane sacrifices Zaïre to his jealousy, a sensible woman looks on the transports of the passion without terror; for it is a lesser misfortune to perish by the hand of her lover than to be poorly loved by him" (10:291; 5:51; Qu'Orosmane immole Zaïre à sa jalousie, une femme sensible y voit sans effroi le transport de la passion: car c'est un moindre malheur de périr par la main de son amant que d'en être médiocrement aimée).

14. This theme is especially prevalent in the *Dialogues*.

15. This is in large part due to prevailing understandings of *colère*, *ressentiment*, and *vengeance* in the eighteenth century. Colère was considered a passion and, as such, was seen as an almost visceral response to slight. Colère inspires the passion of ressentiment. In contrast to our own times, wherein resentment is considered to be more of an enduring feeling of animosity or disdain, in the eighteenth century resentment was a much more active passion, and this in the Cartesian sense. Both colère and ressentiment were therefore regarded as moving us to seek out vengeance immediately following slight, and they are often portrayed as linked to self-preservation. Anger of this variety was thus frequently cast as a vestigial trace of the natural state of man. The variety of anger that Rousseau condones resembles what today we would most aptly describe as "righteous indignation." On this point, see the *Encyclopédie* articles titled "COLÈRE," "RESSENTIMENT," and "VENGEANCE," as well as the entries for these same terms in *Le dictionnaire de l'Académie Française*. See also Pagani, "Uses and Abuses."

16. Ferrara, *Modernity*, 37.

CHAPTER 7

1. Rousseau, *Julie*, 132; 2:163. All references to this work are from the Pléiade edition. Unless otherwise noted, all translations are from Rousseau, *Julie, or the New Heloise*. All subsequent quotations are cited parenthetically in the text. The English translation is cited first, followed by the original French text.

2. Claire recounts the event in part 1, letter 56.

3. Coleman, *Anger*, 22.

4. Wehrs, "Desire and Duty," 80. For an alternate reading of Saint-Preux's allegiance to the status quo, see Braun, "Souveraineté populaire." Braun argues that *Julie* is fundamentally anti-revolutionary and instead aims to maintain the existing hierarchical system at the expense of freedom, popular sovereignty, and legal protections. He suggests that Rousseau's thought is based on a general sense of disdain and mistrust of the populace, and that this is reflected in the character of Saint-Preux, who ultimately acquiesces to the existent political structure. See pages 34–38. My own reading more closely approximates that of Wehrs's.

5. As we learn in part 1, letter 62, Edouard is indeed a bit naive and overconfident in his ability to sway public opinion and thus overconfident in the privileges that his own reputation as an upstanding man affords him. It is worth mentioning that this is yet another example wherein Rousseau cautions his readers against the public displays of anger. Once publicized, the demands of anger are such that they can only be resolved publicly—in one way or another.

6. Of course, all of this is offset by another peculiarity in Edouard's character. He is often "impulsive and impetuous" (vif et emporté), frequently attempting to put a rational twist or "stoic veneer" (vernis stoïque) on those decisions that he makes with his heart (103; 2:126).

7. Rousseau, *Julie*, part 1, letter 65. Edouard's disdain for social ascendancy extends even to aesthetic judgments: instead of bolstering his own judgments about art on the more prestigious and lauded faculty of reason, he bases his claims on his own sensitivity (151; 2:131; sensibilité).

8. Given the overall thrust of the novel and of Rousseau's corpus more generally, one can assume that there is bound to be at least some degree of failure in this endeavor. But the effort must nonetheless be carried out. Wehrs's article is again instructive here, as he argues that the text illustrates "not the achievement of an idealized passion but a constant alternation between self-abandon and renunciation" ("Desire and Duty," 81; see also 79 and 82).

9. Julie's and Wolmar's opposing religious views are a fine example of what Hall has observed to be a "general disjunction within the text as to what counts for virtue" ("Concept of Virtue," 22). I would argue that this extends not just to individual characters but is at times encapsulated in one and the same character. Despite Julie's professed Christianity, it is indeed odd that she does not invoke the Christian notion of forgiveness (and, arguably, denounces the confessional model in her dealings with Saint-Preux). This certainly raises the question as to how Christian her notion of virtue truly is, at least where conciliatory action is concerned. As Hall observes, although Rousseau tended to stress virtuous feeling over virtuous actions throughout his corpus and, in particular, when speaking about religion, Julie's Christianity is much more focused on beneficent action than on religious feeling (24). Further, as discussed earlier, Julie and Wolmar are both decidedly unforgiving of the inhabitants at Clarens. When wrongs are discovered, the individuals are asked to leave the next day. The society they create therefore flies in the face of a religious ethic where people are bound to one another through the sacrifice of Jesus Christ and the notion that all human beings are in need of forgiveness, and that it is the job of a good Christian to forgive trespassers. Finally, rather than yielding to her desire she prefers to die. Although this is ostensibly done in the name of maternal love, her final words betray both relief and pleasure at her impending death. On this point, see Blum, "Styles of Cognition," 291.

10. This is another fine example of what Coleman has observed to be Rousseau's quarrel with gratitude. Coleman writes, "[Rousseau's] revolt against the burden of gratitude may have stemmed in part from a sense of his own entitlement, but it was also a principled protest against the whole system of benefaction that governed the life of anyone without enough status or income to give them a margin of independence" (*Anger*, 17).

11. Rousseau was notoriously critical of compulsory expressions of gratitude. See, for example, *Émile*, 4:521. For an in-depth analysis of Rousseau's views on gratitude, see Coleman, "Rousseau's Quarrel with Gratitude," in *Anger*.

12. This is reiterated later when Wolmar recounts how he had spent his youth mingling and working with the lower classes.

13. Wehrs, "Desire and Duty," 79.

14. Breiner sums up the most important task of the citizen admirably well when he states that Rousseau envisages a state in which the citizens are "steadily at work asking what the general will (or the common good) demands" ("Democratic Autonomy," 559). The baron's behavior betrays the fact that he his placing his own amour propre and thus his particular interests ahead of those of the community. That Saint-Preux and Julie's transgression and their subsequent return to virtue constitute the foundational myth for the entire Clarens community renders the baron's behavior utterly treasonous.

15. In this sense, the baron is an exception of sorts within *Julie*. As Blum has observed, all the characters who make their way to Clarens represent what Starobinski so aptly deemed "transparency" or, rather, that quality of presenting oneself to the world in a manner that all obstacles to being totally comprehended are removed. "The characters in *La Nouvelle Héloïse*," writes Blum, "had to be open to one another, free from the taint of hidden motives, secret reactions, or even the white lies of convention" ("Styles of Cognition," 291). The baron, however, presents a stark contrast to these other characters. His true thoughts and feelings remain obstructed, and he is therefore further alienated from the community to which he purports to belong.

CHAPTER 8

1. Bernardin de Saint-Pierre, *Essai sur J. J. Rousseau*, 12:108.

2. Senior, "*Solitaires*," 528. As an example, Senior points out that Sophie was raised to exist not for herself "but through the eyes of others, particularly her husband. She receives her moral and intellectual standards from his, and needs his attention, approval, and affection" (530). She notes that in *Émile*, Rousseau writes, "the first and most important quality of a woman is gentleness" (2:710, quoted on 534; la première et la plus importante qualité d'une femme est la douceur). Nevertheless, Senior also notes that after her initial fall, Sophie displays little of this quality, insofar as she is described as "proud" (fière) and "intrepid and barbaric" in her frankness (intrepide et barbare). Senior contends that this is just one example among many where Sophie's admirable qualities are portrayed as being traits that she possesses in spite of her education rather than on account of it (534).

3. Schaeffer, "Reconsidering," 607, 611, 613, 618, 624.

4. Ibid., 625, 623.

5. Rousseau, *Émile and Sophie*, 13:686; 4:882. Unless otherwise noted, all other references to *Émile and Sophie* are from Rousseau, *Oeuvres complètes*, and all translations are from Masters and Kelly, *Collected Writings*. All subsequent citations appear parenthetically in the text, with the English translation cited first, followed by the French text.

6. There is good reason to believe—and many critics do—that Sophie was in fact raped and thus did not willingly commit adultery. Émile, however, is not aware of this, and so the possibility that Sophie wronged him unwillingly does not figure into his own contemplations concerning forgiveness that we here analyze.

7. On monogamy as a social construct, see, in particular, 3:157–60. Here Rousseau discusses sexual desire. He distinguishes between the occasional physical need for sex and the "moral" need for it, the latter of which arises only in society and is rooted in amour propre. According to Rousseau, for Natural Man, all women are comparable in their capacity to satisfy man's sexual desires, whenever they accidentally come upon one. But because Natural Man is solitary, he is only rarely aroused. On those occasions, he satisfies this desire with the first female he encounters, and, once the need is satisfied, all desire is snuffed out. The two participants in the sexual act then go their separate ways.

8. In French, "femme" means either "wife" or "woman," depending on the context. But the juxtaposition of the word "femme" with "mari" (again, husband) in this passage is clearly

intended to underscore Émile's and Sophie's socially recognized roles as husband and wife, respectively, and thereby draws attention to the civic duties that their relationship entails.

9. Rousseau, *Discourse on Political Economy*, 253, 3:245, 13:254; 3:245–46.

10. Émile writes, "It is for this reason that, intrepid and barbarous in her frankness, she told her crime to you, to my whole family, at the same time remaining silent about what excused her, what perhaps justified her; hiding it, I say, with such obstinacy she never told me a word about it, and which I did not know until after her death" (13:709; 4:910; C'est pour cela qu'intrépide et barbare dans sa franchise elle dit son crime à vous, à toute ma famille, taisant en même tems ce qui l'excusoit, ce qui la justifioit peut-être, le cachant, dis-je, avec une telle obstination, qu'elle ne m'en a jamais dit un mot à moi-même, et que je ne l'ai su qu'après sa mort). As Burgelin wrote in the introduction to *Oeuvres complètes*, the question as to whether or not Sophie was raped is deliberately left open by Rousseau (and hidden from Émile). Accordingly, it remains unclear whether it is the excuse to which Émile is here referring. Even if it is, however, the fact that Émile did not become aware of this until after their separation means that such an excuse did not enter into his deliberations concerning forgiveness (*Émile*, 4:965nn a–f).

11. Again, the fact that Sophie was quite possibly raped complicates this reading. It would perhaps be more correct to say that, had the reasons for which Émile condemned Sophie been factual, his anger would have been legitimate. An oddity about *Émile and Sophie* is that Sophie doesn't ever say in her defense that she was raped, thus leading one to believe that, even if she had been raped, Rousseau means to convey that she was to an extent responsible for it.

12. Burgelin, introd. to *Émile and Sophie*, 4:910n1. All translations from this text are my own.

13. Burgelin, introd. to Rousseau, *Oeuvres complètes*, 4:clxiii. All subsequent quotations are cited parenthetically in the text. All translations of Burgelin's introduction are my own.

14. Wingrove, *Rousseau's Republican Romance*, 5, 87 (*Émile* quotation is on page 87).

15. Melzer, *Natural Goodness*, 245–49.

16. There have been some noteworthy challenges to such interpretations, particularly by those scholars who draw on a feminist perspective. Weiss, for example, has challenged the notion that Rousseau's model of the family fosters any degree of equality between the sexes and thus denies that it can provide any sense of wholeness to women. Instead, she observes that Rousseau's gender-oriented educational system was constructed with the aim of habituating women to work toward providing their male counterparts the capacity to experience wholeness and an undivided subjectivity, at the woman's expense. She notes that Rousseau "justifies intolerance toward a woman's assertion of a demanding 'I,' yet fails to cultivate her sense of community to a point where this 'I' is not a source of conflict for her" (*Gendered Community*, 104). For another interpretation more along the lines of Wingrove's, see Schaeffer, "Reconsidering," 624, and Strong, *Jean-Jacques Rousseau*, 135.

17. Rousseau, *Second Discourse*, 3:182, quoted in Coleman, *Anger*, 163. For a more detailed account of gratitude in Rousseau, please see Coleman, *Anger*, in particular chap. 5.

1. Coleman, *Anger*, 14. In a footnote to this passage, Coleman notes that Montesquieu deviated slightly from the party line insofar as he anticipated the nineteenth-century's "reconceptualization of informal bonds in sociological rather than moral terms." But Coleman also notes that—even in spite of Montesquieu's desire to ensure harmony between positive law and various natural and circumstantial laws—he still maintained that "patterns of angry or grateful behavior" had to be "integrated into a complex whole rather than eliminated entirely."

2. *Encyclopédie*, s.v. "COLÈRE," 3:614. All translations are my own. Jaucourt is likely referring to book 2, chap. 20, sec. 13, of Locke's *Essay Concerning Human Understanding* (1690). See also the *Encyclopédie* entry for "COLERE" (medicine).

3. Indeed, the distinction between political and moral theory was less pronounced (and at times absent entirely) in early modern discourse. This was largely on account of the ethic of selfish sociability that dominated philosophy at the time and the attendant notion that private, interpersonal relationships (particularly the family) were and should be regarded as a microcosm of the political order.

4. This was true presuming that the legitimacy of their indignation was adequately acknowledged by an external third party and, in many instances, the perpetrator. This is one of Coleman's key points, and one that I shall return to momentarily.

5. Pagani, "Judging Oswald."

6. Staël-Holstein, *Corinne*, 587. All translations from this text are my own.

7. Ibid., 571.

8. Constant, *Adolphe*, 110. All translations of this text are my own.

9. Ibid., 106, 112.

10. Voltaire's article titled "Patrie" is a fine example of this mode of thinking. He writes, "A fatherland is composed of many families; and, just as one communally sustains his family because of self-interest [amour propre] in as much as one does not have a contrary interest, one will sustain his city or village, that which one calls his fatherland, by this same self-interest" (*Dictionnaire philosophique*, 335; Une patrie est un composé de plusieurs familles; et, comme on soutient communément sa famille par amour-propre, lorsqu'on n'a pas un intérêt contraire, on soutient par le même amour-propre sa ville ou son village, qu'on appelle sa patrie). Translation mine.

11. Shriver, "Forgiveness," 159. The U.S. Institute of Peace has played a seminal role in sponsoring research into these truth commissions. The institute keeps lists of commissions at http://www.usip.org/library/truth.html. Some noteworthy scholarly works that have looked at such conciliatory mechanisms and the narratives they generate include Rotberg and Thompson, *Truth v. Justice*; Minow, *Vengeance*; Thompson, *Taking Responsibility*; Roht-Arriaza and Mariezcurrena, *Transitional Justice*; Enright and North, *Exploring Forgiveness*; and Helmick and Petersen, *Forgiveness and Reconciliation*. For a partial but by no means exhaustive list of other contributions, see Barkan, "Historians."

12. See Barkan, *Guilt of Nations*; Barkan, "Historians"; Engel, "Reconciling"; Suny, "Truth in Telling"; and Campbell, "Settling Accounts?" See also Shriver, "Is There Forgiveness?," and North, "'Ideal' of Forgiveness."

13. As the current state of Franco-Turkish relations demonstrates, the response to these laws also shows how difficult it is to maintain fruitful political relations when one nation refuses to ratify and share in the historical narratives created by another.

14. Murphy and Hampton, *Forgiveness and Mercy*, 15–16.

15. The account offered by Digeser in *Political Forgiveness* is an important exception in this respect. Seeking a "more rigorous political conceptualization" of forgiveness and lamenting that many contemporary accounts are "burdened with psychological and religious assumptions," Digeser understands political forgiveness as "a state of reconciliation such that the released debt can no longer serve as the basis for future claims" (2–5; see also 199). As even he admits, though, his account of political forgiveness is applicable only if one views politics as being "more about the content of our actions than the character of our motivations" (208; see also 17). He thus maintains that political forgiveness, as he understands it, is possible only if its success "does not depend on the emotional or internal states of the forgiver," as its private, interpersonal counterpart does (4; see also 35). Digeser continues, "If forgiveness requires a change of heart or the removal of resentment, then it is incompatible with that conception of politics" (208). As compelling as Digeser's account of political forgiveness is, it presupposes that the (decidedly grim) assessments of political life in the postmodern world that have been offered by Lionel Trilling, Richard Sennett, Hannah Arendt, Alasdair MacIntyre, and Charles Taylor, among others, simply do not stand. One cannot help but wonder whether Digeser's account must be considered

somewhat archaic for these reasons, as he frequently invokes the philosophy of Locke and, in particular, Hobbes in constructing his account.

16. Montesquieu is perhaps a noteworthy exception in this regard, insofar as he alludes to the potentially alienating effects of unsatisfied anger. In letter 166 of the *Lettres persanes* (1721), Usbek describes how a generous and righteous people (the French) were transformed into a mass of unprincipled lawbreakers on account of an unjust minister. He observes that he saw "the most virtuous men commit unworthy acts and violate the first principles of justice upon the vain pretext that someone had violated [their rights]" (241; les hommes les plus vertueux faire des choses indignes et violer les premiers principes de la justice, sur ce vain prétexte qu'on la leur avait violée). Yet the view that anger could lead one to dismiss the laws when one's own rights had been violated and in turn victimize others was not one that had widespread influence among French intellectuals, writers, or, for that matter, the philosophes. In England the situation was much different indeed. Hobbes, for example, does raise these concerns (and discusses them at some length) in the chapter titled "Of Crimes, Extenuations, and Excuses" of the *Leviathan*.

17. The fact that the Frenchman becomes a depository for J.-J.'s work in anticipation of a day when J.-J.'s true story may be recounted does at least allude to this possibility. At the end of the *Dialogues*, the reader is left with a sense of hope that J.-J. will be reconciled with France, just as soon as the country returns to its true self, of course. This reconciliation will occur when J.-J.'s true story is brought to light.

Bibliography

Alberg, Jeremiah. *A Reinterpretation of Rousseau: A Religious System*. New York: Palgrave Macmillan, 2007.

Arendt, Hannah. *The Human Condition*. Chicago: University of Chicago Press, 1998.

Babbitt, Irving. *Rousseau and Romanticism*. Boston: Houghton Mifflin, 1947.

Bacon, Francis. *The Essays or Counsels, Civil and Moral, 1597–1625*. In *Essays and New Atlantis*, 3–242. Roslyn, N.Y.: Black, 1942.

Barkan, Elazar. *The Guilt of Nations*. Baltimore: Johns Hopkins University Press, 2001.

———. "Historians and Historical Reconciliation." *American Historical Review* 114, no. 4 (2009): 899–913.

Barth, Karl. *The Church and the Political Problem of Today*. New York: Scribner, 1939.

———. *Nineteenth-Century Theology*. London: SGM Press, 1972.

———. *Protestant Theology in the Nineteenth Century: Its Background and History*. London: SCM Press, 1972.

———. *Protestant Thought: From Rousseau to Ritschl*. Translated by Brian Cozens. New York: Harper and Brothers, 1959.

Bernardin de Saint-Pierre, Jacques-Henri. *Essai sur J. J. Rousseau*. In Rousseau, *Oeuvres complètes*. Paris: Méquignon-Marvis, 1818.

Blum, Carol. "Styles of Cognition as Moral Options in *La Nouvelle Héloïse* and *Les Liaisons dangereuses*." *PMLA* 88, no. 2 (1973): 289–98.

Blumenberg, Hans. *The Legitimacy of the Modern Age*. Translated by Robert M. Wallace. Cambridge: MIT Press, 1983.

Boyd, Richard. "Pity's Pathologies Portrayed: Rousseau and the Limits of Democratic Compassion." *Political Theory* 32, no. 4 (2004): 519–46.

Braun, Theodore E. D. "La souveraineté populaire, la volonté générale, et l'autocratie dans *Jacques le Fataliste* et *La Nouvelle Héloïse*." *Diderot Studies* 25 (1993): 27–39.

Breiner, Peter. "Democratic Autonomy, Political Ethics, and Moral Luck." *Political Theory* 17 (1989): 550–74.

Brooke, Christopher. *Philosophic Pride: Stoicism and Political Thought from Lipsius to Rousseau*. Princeton: Princeton University Press, 2012.

Butler, Joseph. *Fifteen Sermons Preached at the Rolls Chapel and a Dissertation upon the Nature of Virtue*. London: Bell and Sons, 1953.

Campbell, James T. "Settling Accounts? An Americanist Perspective on Historical Reconciliation." *American Historical Review* 114, no. 4 (2009): 963–77.

Caradonna, Jeremy L. "The Death of Duty: The Transformation of Political Identity from the Old Regime to the French Revolution." *Historical Reflections/Réflexions Historiques* 32, no. 2 (2006): 273–307.

———. "'The Monarchy of Virtue': The 'Prix de Vertu' and the Economy of Emulation in France, 1777–1791." *Eighteenth-Century Studies* 41, no. 4 (2008): 443–58.

Cassirer, Ernst. *The Question of Jean-Jacques Rousseau*. New York: Columbia University Press, 1954.

———. *Rousseau, Kant, and Goethe: Two Essays*. New York: Harper and Row, 1963.

Charvet, John. *The Social Problem in the Philosophy of Rousseau*. Cambridge: Cambridge University Press, 1973.

Christensen, Thomas. *Rameau and Musical Thought in the Enlightenment*. Cambridge: Cambridge University Press, 1993.

Clément, Pierre-Paul. *Jean-Jacques Rousseau: De l'éros coupable à l'éros glorieux*. Neuchâtel: Baconnière, 1976.

Coby, Patrick. "The Law of Nature in Locke's *Second Treatise*: Is Locke a Hobbesian?" *Review of Politics* 49, no. 1 (1987): 3–28.

Cohen, Joshua. "Reflections on Rousseau: Autonomy and Democracy." In *The Social Contract Theorists: Critical Essays on Hobbes, Locke, and Rousseau*, edited by Christopher W. Morris, 191–204. New York: Rowman and Littlefield, 1999.

Coleman, Patrick. *Anger, Gratitude, and the Enlightenment Writer*. Oxford: Oxford University Press, 2011.

———. "Property, Politics, and Personality in Rousseau." In *Early Modern Conceptions of Property*, edited by John Brewer and Susan Staves, 254–74. New York: Routledge, 1995.

———. *Rousseau's Political Imagination: Rule and Representation in the "Lettre à d'Alembert."* Geneva: Droz, 1984.

Constant, Benjamin. *Adolphe*. Edited by William Morton Dey. New York: Oxford University Press, 1918.

Corneille, Pierre. *Oeuvres complètes*. Edited by André Stegmann. Paris: Éditions du Seuil, 1963.

Davis, Michael. *The Autobiography of Philosophy: Rousseau's "Reveries of the Solitary Walker."* Lanham, Md.: Rowman and Littlefield, 1999.

De Man, Paul. "The Purloined Ribbon." *Glyph* 1 (1977): 28–49.

Dent, N. J. H. *Rousseau: An Introduction to His Psychological, Social, and Political Theory*. Oxford: Blackwell, 1988.

Derrida, Jacques. *De la grammatologie*. Paris: Minuit, 1967.

———. "Le siècle et le pardon: Entretien avec Michel Wieviorka." In *Foi et savoir, suivi de "Le siècle et le pardon."* Paris: Éditions du Seuil, 2001.

Descartes, René. *Les Passions de l'âme*. Paris: Vrin, 1970.

d'Holbach, Paul Henri Thiry. *Le Christianisme dévoilée: Ou examen des principes et des effets de la religion chrétienne*. London, 1756.

Le Dictionnaire de l'Académie Française. 4th ed. Paris, 1762. American Research Treasury for the French Language (ARTFL). Edited by Robert Morrissey. University of Chicago. Accessed August 24, 2014. http://artfl-project.uchicago.edu.ezproxy.lib.utexas.edu /content/dictionnaires-dautrefois.

Diderot, Denis. *L'Encyclopédie*. Edited by Denis Diderot and Jean Le Rond d'Alembert. 1751–72. American Research Treasury for the French Language (ARTFL). Edited by Robert Morrissey. University of Chicago. Accessed August 24, 2014. http://encyclopedie.uchicago .edu.ezproxy.lib.utexas.edu/.

———. *Supplément au voyage de Bougainville*. In *Oeuvres*. Vol. 2, *Contes*, edited by Laurent Versini, 461–578. Paris: Laffont, 1994.

Digeser, Peter E. *Political Forgiveness*. Ithaca: Cornell University Press, 2001.

Dilthey, Wilhelm. *The Formation of the Historical World in the Human Sciences*. In *Selected Works*, edited by Rudolf A. Makkreel and Frithjof Rodi, 3:344–68. Princeton: Princeton University Press, 2002.

Di Palma, Marco. "Self and Agency: A Prolegomenon to Rousseau's Dialogues." *Modern Language Review* 98, no. 2 (2003): 311–26.

Eigeldinger, Fréderic S. "Ils ne me pardonneront jamais le mal qu'ils m'ont fait." *Etudes Jean-Jacques Rousseau* 10 (1998): 77–89.

Ellison, Charles. "Rousseau and the Modern City: The Politics of Speech and Dress." *Political Theory* 13 (1985): 497–533.

Engel, David. "On Reconciling the Histories of Two Chosen Peoples." *American Historical Review* 114, no. 4 (2009): 914–29.

Enright, Robert D., and Joanna North, eds. *Exploring Forgiveness*. Madison: University of Wisconsin Press, 1998.

Ferrara, Alessandro. *Modernity and Authenticity: A Study of the Social and Ethical Thought of Jean-Jacques Rousseau*. New York: State University of New York Press, 1993.

Force, Pierre. *Self-Interest Before Adam Smith: A Genealogy of Economic Science*. New York: Cambridge University Press, 2006.

Friedlander, Eli. *J. J. Rousseau: An Afterlife of Words*. Cambridge: Harvard University Press, 2004.

Griswold, Charles L. *Forgiveness: A Philosophical Exploration*. Cambridge: Cambridge University Press, 2007.

Habermas, Jürgen. *The Structural Transformation of the Public Sphere: An Inquiry into a Category of Bourgeois Society*. Translated by Thomas Burger. Cambridge: MIT Press, 1991.

Hall, H. Gaston. "The Concept of Virtue in *La Nouvelle Héloïse*." *Yale French Studies* 28 (1961): 20–33.

Hearnshaw, F. J. C., ed. *The Social and Political Ideas of Some Great French Thinkers of the Age of Reason*. London: Harrap, 1930.

Helmick, Raymond G., SJ. "Does Religion Fuel or Heal in Conflicts?" In Helmick and Petersen, *Forgiveness and Reconciliation*, 81–96.

Helmick, Raymond G., SJ, and Rodney L. Petersen, eds. *Forgiveness and Reconciliation: Religion, Public Policy, and Conflict Transformation*. Philadelphia: Templeton Foundation Press, 2001.

Herdt, Jennifer A. *Putting on Virtue: The Legacy of the Splendid Vices*. Chicago: University of Chicago Press, 2008.

Hobbes, Thomas. *The Leviathan*. Indianapolis: Hackett, 1994.

———. "On Human Nature." 1650. In *The Elements of Law, Natural and Politic*, 1–108. Oxford: Oxford University Press, 1999.

The Holy Bible: King James Version. New York: Meridian Group, 1974.

Hulliung, Mark. *The Autocritique of Enlightenment: Rousseau and the Philosophes*. Cambridge: Harvard University Press, 1994.

Jankélévitch, Vladimir. *Le Pardon*. In *La philosophie morale*, 991–1149. Paris: Flammarion, 1998.

Jones, James F. *Rousseau's Dialogues: An Interpretive Essay*. Geneva: Librairie Droz, 1991.

Jones, L. Gregory. *Embodying Forgiveness: A Theological Analysis*. Grand Rapids: Eerdmans, 1995.

Kant, Immanuel. "What Is Enlightenment?" In *On History*. Upper Saddle River, N.J.: Pearson, 2001.

Kavanagh, Thomas M. *Writing the Truth: Authority and Desire in Rousseau*. Berkeley: University of California Press, 1987.

Kelly, Christopher. *Rousseau's Exemplary Life: The "Confessions" as Political Philosophy*. Ithaca: Cornell University Press, 1987.

Konstan, David. *Before Forgiveness: The Origins of a Moral Idea*. Cambridge: Cambridge University Press, 2010.

Koselleck, Reinhart. *Critique and Crisis: Enlightenment and the Pathogenesis of Modern Society*. Cambridge: MIT Press, 1988.

Lacroix, Jean. "La conscience selon Rousseau." In *Jean-Jacques Rousseau et la crise contemporaine de la conscience*, edited by Jean-Louis Leuba, 81–96. Paris: Beauchesne, 1980. Colloque international du deuxième centenaire de la mort de J.-J. Rousseau, Chantilly, September 5–8, 1978.

La Rochefoucauld, François, duc de. *Réflexions ou sentences et maximes morales*. In *Oeuvres de La Rochefoucauld*, edited by Jean Désiré Louis Gilbert and Jules Gourdault. Paris, 1868.

Launay, Denise. *Les Musiciens français itinérants au XVIIe siècle*. Paris: CNRS, 1980.

———. *La Querelle des Bouffons et ses incidences sur la musique*. Kassel, Germany: Bärenreiter, 1981.

Lehmann, Paul. *Forgiveness: Decisive Issue in Protestant Thought.* New York: Harper and Brothers, 1940.

Lilti, Antoine. "The Writing of Paranoia: Jean-Jacques Rousseau and the Paradoxes of Celebrity." *Representations* 103, no. 1 (2008): 53–83.

Locke, John. *An Essay Concerning Human Understanding.* Edited by Alexander Campbell Fraser. 2 vols. Oxford: Clarendon Press, 1994.

———. *Essays on the Law of Nature.* In Von Leyden, *Locke.*

———. *First Tract on Government.* In Von Leyden, *Locke.*

———. *The Second Treatise on Government.* 1690. Indianapolis: Hackett, 1980.

Marks, Jonathan. "Who Lost Nature? Rousseau and Rousseauism." *Polity* 34, no. 4 (2002): 479–502.

Masson, Pierre-Maurice. *La Religion de Jean-Jacques Rousseau.* Vol. 1. Paris: Hachette et Cie, 1916.

Masters, Roger D. *The Political Philosophy of Rousseau.* Princeton: Princeton University Press, 1968.

Masters, Roger D., and Christopher Kelly. *The Collected Writings of Rousseau.* 14 vols. Hanover: Dartmouth College, 1990.

Melzer, Arthur. *The Natural Goodness of Man: On the System of Rousseau's Thought.* Chicago: University of Chicago Press, 1990.

———. "The Origin of the Counter-Enlightenment: Rousseau and the New Religion of Sincerity." *American Political Science Review* 90, no. 2 (1996): 344–60.

Minow, Martha. *Between Vengeance and Forgiveness: Facing History After Genocide and Mass Violence.* Boston: Beacon Press, 1998.

Montesquieu, Charles de Secondat, Baron de. *Lettres persanes.* Paris: Garnier Flammarion, 1964.

Morgan, Edmund S. *The Genuine Article: A Historian Looks at Early America.* London: Norton, 2004.

Murphy, Jeffrie G., and Jean Hampton. *Forgiveness and Mercy.* Cambridge: Cambridge University Press, 1988.

Neuhouser, Frederick. *Rousseau's Theodicy of Self-Love.* Oxford: Oxford University Press, 2008.

Ngai, Sianne. *Ugly Feelings.* Cambridge: Harvard University Press, 2005.

Norman, Larry F. "Pour une approche dynamique de la magnanimité chez Corneille." *Romanic Review* 87, no. 2 (1996): 177–95.

North, Joanna. "The 'Ideal' of Forgiveness: A Philosopher's Exploration." In Enright and North, *Exploring Forgiveness,* 15–34.

Ogrodnick, Margaret. *Instinct and Intimacy: Political Philosophy and Autobiography in Rousseau.* Toronto: University of Toronto Press, 1999.

O'Hagan, Timothy. *Rousseau: The Arguments of the Philosophers.* New York: Routledge, 1999.

Orwin, Clifford. "Rousseau's Socratism." *Journal of Politics* 60, no. 1 (1980): 174–87.

Pagani, Karen. "Judging Oswald Within the Limits of Reason Alone in Madame de Staël's *Corinne.*" *European Romantic Review* 23, no. 2 (2012): 141–56.

———. "Living Well Is the Best Revenge: Rousseau's *Reveries* and the (Non)Problem of Forgiveness." *Eighteenth-Century Studies* 47, no. 4 (2014): 407–23.

———. "The Uses and Abuses of Joseph Butler's Account of Forgiveness: Between the Passions and the Interests." *South Central Review* 27, no. 3 (2010): 12–33.

Palmer, Robert Roswell. *Catholics and Unbelievers in Eighteenth-Century France.* New York: Cooper Square, 1961.

Porter, Dennis. *Rousseau's Legacy: Emergence and Eclipse of the Writer in France.* Oxford: Oxford University Press, 1995.

Raymond, Marcel. *Jean-Jacques Rousseau: La quête de soi et la reverie.* Paris: Librairie Corti, 1962.

Reddy, William M. *The Navigation of Feeling: A Framework for the History of Emotions.* Cambridge: Cambridge University Press, 2001.

Rétif de la Bretonne. *Les nuits de Paris, ou l'observateur nocturne.* Parts 1–6. London, 1789.

Riley, Patrick. "A Possible Explanation of Rousseau's General Will." In *The Social Contract The-orists: Critical Essays on Hobbes, Locke, and Rousseau*, edited by Christopher W. Morris, 167–89. New York: Rowman and Littlefield, 1999.

Ritschl, Albrecht. *A Critical History of the Christian Doctrine of Justification and Reconciliation*. Translated by John S. Black. Edinburgh: Edmonston and Douglas, 1872.

Roht-Arriaza, Naomi, and Javier Mariezcurrena, eds. *Transitional Justice in the Twenty-First Century: Beyond Truth Versus Justice*. Cambridge: Cambridge University Press, 2006.

Rotberg, Robert I., and Dennis Thompson, eds. *Truth v. Justice: The Morality of Truth Commissions*. Princeton: Princeton University Press, 2000.

Rousseau, Jean-Jacques. *Considérations sur le gouvernement de Pologne et sur sa réformation projettée*. In Rousseau, *Oeuvres complètes*.

———. *Correspondance complète de Jean Jacques Rousseau: 1756–1757*. Edited by R. A. Leigh. 53 vols. Geneva: Institut et Musée Voltaire, 1965–98.

———. *A Discourse on Political Economy*. In *The Social Contract*, translated by G. D. H. Cole, 247–87. London: Dent and Sons, 1941.

———. *The Discourses and Other Early Political Writings*. Edited and translated by Victor Gourevitch. Cambridge: Cambridge University Press, 2006.

———. *Émile; or, On Education*. Translated by Alan Bloom. N.Y.: Basic Books, 1979.

———. *Julie, or the New Heloise: Letters of Two Lovers Who Live in a Small Town at the Foot of the Alps*. Edited by Jean-Jacques Vaché and Philip Stewart. Hanover: Dartmouth College, 1997.

———. *Oeuvres complètes de Jean-Jacques Rousseau*. Edited by Bernard Gagnebin and Marcel Raymond. 4 vols. Paris: Pléiade, 1959.

———. *Les Rêveries du promeneur solitaire*. Edited by Michèle Crogiez. Paris: Librairie Générale Française, 2001.

———. *Rousseau, Judge of Jean-Jacques*. In Masters and Kelly, *Collected Writings*.

———. *The Social Contract*. Translated by G. D. H. Cole. London: Dent and Sons, 1941.

Schaeffer, Denise. "Reconsidering the Role of Sophie in Rousseau's *Émile*." *Polity* 30, no. 4 (1998): 607–26.

Seillière, Ernest. *J.-J. Rousseau*. Paris: Garnier Frères, 1921.

Senior, Nancy. "*Les Solitaires* as a Test for Émile and Sophie." *French Review* 49, no. 4 (1976): 528–35.

Sennett, Richard. *The Fall of Public Man*. New York: Vintage Books, 1978.

Sheringham, Michael. *French Autobiography: Devices and Desires; Rousseau to Perec*. Oxford: Clarendon Press, 1993.

Shklar, Judith. *Men and Citizens: A Study of Rousseau's Social Theory*. Cambridge: Cambridge University Press, 1969.

Shriver, Donald W., Jr. *An Ethic for Enemies*. Oxford: Oxford University Press, 1998.

———. "Forgiveness: A Bridge Across the Abysses of Revenge." In Helmick and Petersen, *Forgiveness and Reconciliation*, 151–70.

———. "Is There Forgiveness in Politics? Germany, Vietnam, and America." In Enright and North, *Exploring Forgiveness*, 131–49.

Simon, Julia. *Beyond Contractual Morality: Ethics, Law, and Literature in Eighteenth-Century France*. Rochester: University of Rochester Press, 2001.

———. *Mass Enlightenment: Critical Studies in Rousseau and Diderot*. Albany: State University of New York Press, 1995.

Staël-Holstein, Anne Louise Germaine de. *Corinne ou l'Italie*. 1807. Edited by Simone Balayé. Paris: Folio Classiques, 1985.

Starobinski, Jean. *Jean-Jacques Rousseau: La transparence et l'obstacle*. Paris: Gallimard, 1971.

———. *L'Oeil vivant*. 1961. Paris: Gallimard, 1999.

Stewart, Philip. *L'Invention du sentiment: Roman et économie affective au XVIII siècle*. Oxford: Voltaire Foundation, 2010.

Strauss, Leo. "On the Intention of Rousseau." *Social Research* 14, no. 4 (1947): 455–87.

Strong, Tracy. *Jean-Jacques Rousseau: The Politics of the Ordinary*. Thousand Oaks, Calif.: Sage, 1994.

Suny, Ronald Grigor. "Truth in Telling: Reconciling Realities in the Genocide of the Ottoman Armenians." *American Historical Review* 114, no. 4 (2009): 930–46.

Taylor, Charles. *The Ethics of Authenticity*. Cambridge: Harvard University Press, 1992.

———. *Sources of the Self: The Making of the Modern Identity*. Cambridge: Harvard University Press, 1989.

Thompson, Janna. *Taking Responsibility for the Past: Reparation and Historical Injustice*. Cambridge: Wiley-Blackwell, 2002.

Thorne, Christian. *The Dialectic of Counter-Enlightenment*. Cambridge: Harvard University Press, 2010.

Trichard, Jonathan. *La Contagion sacrée ou histoire naturelle de la superstition*. Translated by Baron d'Holbach. London, 1768.

U.S. Institute of Peace. Margarita S. Studemeister Digital Collections in International Conflict Management. Accessed September 5, 2014. www.usip.org/library/truth.html.

Voltaire. *Dictionnaire philosophique*. Paris: Garnier Frères, 1967.

———. *Sentiment des citoyens*. Edited by Frédéric S. Eigeldinger. Paris: Honoré Champion, 2000.

Von Leyden, Wolfgang, ed. *Locke: Political Essays*. By John Locke. Cambridge: Cambridge University Press, 2006.

Weber, Max. "Politics as Vocation." In *From Max Weber: Essays in Sociology*, edited by H. H. Gerth and C. Wright Mills. New York: Oxford University Press, 1958.

Wehrs, Donald R. "Desire and Duty in *La Nouvelle Héloïse*." *Modern Language Studies* 18, no. 2 (1988): 79–88.

Weintraub, Joachim. *The Value of the Individual: Self and Circumstance in Autobiography*. Chicago: University of Chicago Press, 1958.

Weiss, Penny A. *Gendered Community: Rousseau, Sex, and Politics*. New York: New York University Press, 1993.

Williams, Bernard. *Shame and Necessity*. Berkeley: University of California Press, 1993.

Wingrove, Elizabeth Rose. *Rousseau's Republican Romance*. Princeton: Princeton University Press, 2000.

Index

absolute justice, 73–74

absolution
confession-absolution model of forgiveness, 205 n. 37
last-minute, 79–80
Rousseau's rejection of, 17, 19

absolutism, and Rousseau's reconceptualization of duty, 21

Adolphe (Constant), 193–95, 197

Alberg, Jeremiah, 16–17, 83–84, 98, 213 n. 7

alienation
of baron in *Julie*, 223 n. 15
of Émile, 163–64
within social milieu, 11–15, 182
and unsatisfied anger, 226 n. 16

Améry, Jean, 198

amour de soi (soy), 55–56, 130

amour propre
and alienation of Émile, 164
awakening and inflaming of, 58
comparison and, 56–58
distinction between amour de soi and, 55–56
in Émile's forgiveness of Sophie, 171–72
forgiveness connected to, 164
honor and romantic love bound up with, 151–52
as inextricably linked with anger, 3
and susceptibility of Social Man to anger, 58–59

ancient historians, 220–21 n. 9

Anet, Claude, 220 n. 8

anger
Bacon on, 208 n. 19
of Christians, 71
of citizens against outside enemy, 66–67
collective, 68–70, 94, 187–88, 202, 210 n. 16
democratization of, 9–10
depersonalized, 60–61, 84–86, 123, 139
early modern thinkers' concern regarding, 40
eighteenth-century understanding of, 221 n. 15
and ethic of authenticity, 7–8

exhaustion of, 219 n. 25
expression of, 26–27
following pardon, 212 n. 2
and forgiveness in intimate relationships, 26–27
and forgiveness in *Rousseau, Judge of Jean-Jacques*, 44–45
as inextricably linked with amour propre, 3
in intimate relationships, 104–6, 122–26, 188
justified, in *Émile*, 97–101
laudability of, 103–4
Montesquieu on, 224 n. 1
of Natural Man, 53–55
personalized, of Émile in *Émile and Sophie*, 171–73, 176
publicized, 96–97, 122–25, 128, 185, 222 n. 5
resentment and, 200–201, 203 n. 11
resolution of, 52, 75
Rousseau's abandonment of children and, in intimate relationships, 133–41
Rousseau's condoning of, 203 n. 17, 210 n. 14, 216 n. 1
in Rousseau's political theory, 8–9, 25–26
Rousseau's successors' treatment of, 191–97
Rousseau's views on, 187–88, 201–2
Rousseauvean versus Rousseau's, 8–11
Rousseau versus contemporaries' treatment of, 188–91
Saint-Preux overcomes, 151–52
scholarship on, 1–2
Social Man's susceptibility to, 58–59
unsatisfied, 226 n. 16

Arendt, Hannah, 6–7

authenticity
ethic of, 201
forgiveness, anger, and ethic of, 5–8
Rousseauvean, 205–6 n. 54

Bacon, Francis, 42–43, 103, 208 n. 19

Barkan, Elazar, 199

Barth, Karl, 17–18, 19, 204 n. 35

Blainville, Madame de, 125

Bloom, Allan, 3

identity constructed by, 108–9
and judgment of Rousseau, 107–8
Lacroix on, 217 n. 7
Madame d'Epinay halts public readings of,
209 n. 3
personalized and political forgiveness and
anger contrasted in, 104–6
Rousseau as victim and moral subject in,
109–10
secular objectivity in, 20
special consideration for Saint-Lambert and
d'Houdetot's relationship in, 120–22
transparency in, 110–11
conflict
ethical imperatives for expression,
acknowledgment, and resolution of, 11
and forgiveness in *Rousseau, Judge of Jean-
Jacques*, 44–45
influence of, on Rousseau and his writings,
14–15
resolution of, as theme in Rousseau's life
and works, 183
role of, in assessment of education, 159–61
conscience
awakening of, 93–94
comparison and, 210 n. 7
Confessions as confrontation of Rousseau's,
217 n. 7
and punishment in afterlife, 216–17 n. 3
and Rousseau's abandonment of his
children, 129–35
consensual nonconsensuality, 184, 185
Considerations on the Government of Poland
(Rousseau), 12, 61–65
Constant, Benjamin, 27, 193–95, 196, 197
Corinne (Staël), 192–93
Corneille, Pierre, 33–34, 190–91

de Man, Paul, 219 n. 23
Dent, Nicolas, 209 n. 10
depersonalized anger, 60–61, 84–86, 123, 139. *See
also* righteous indignation
d'Epinay, Madame
anger of, publicized within entourage, 125,
141
halts public readings of *Confessions*, 209 n. 3
Rousseau's reconciliation with, 106, 115–16
Rousseau's respect for friendship with,
137–38
Saint-Lambert brokers reconciliation with,
123–24
suspects affair between Rousseau and
Sophie, 113

Derrida, Jacques, 6–7, 198
Descartes, René, 35–36, 207 nn. 3–4
d'Etange, Baron, 156–58, 214 n. 14, 223 n. 15
de Warens, Madame, 220 n. 8
d'Houdetot, Count, 125
d'Houdetot, Sophie
and anger in intimate relationships, 122–26
hides letters exchanged with Rousseau,
221 n. 11
Rousseau blames, for scandal, 117–20
Rousseau's reconciliation with, 106, 112–17,
126–28
special consideration for Saint-Lambert and,
120–22
Dialogues (Rousseau). See *Rousseau, Judge of
Jean-Jacques* (Rousseau)
Diderot, Denis
Encyclopédie article of, on forgiveness, 39–42,
86–87
on rank and forgiveness, 144
Rousseau's break with, 124–25
Rousseau's reconciliation with, 106
Digeser, Peter E., 51, 225 n. 15
Dilthey, Wilhelm, 24–25
Di Palma, Marco, 30
discord, influence of, on Rousseau and his
writings, 14–15
Discourse on Inequality (Rousseau), 10, 13
Discourse on Political Economy, A (Rousseau),
65–66, 174–75, 215–16 n. 35
disdain, collective, 63–65, 67, 97
dividedness, of Sophie in *Émile and Sophie*,
161–62
divine forgiveness, Rousseau's rejection of, 15–17
due process
call for, in *Rousseau, Judge of Jean-Jacques*,
49–50, 78
Frenchman on, in *Rousseau, Judge of
Jean-Jacques*, 80
Hobbes on juridical pardon and, 50–51
private practice of, 98, 100
duty/duties
emergence of, 60
of Émile following separation from Sophie,
178–79
in intimate relationships, 116, 137–39
Rousseau's reconceptualization of, 21

Edouard
apologizes to Saint-Preux, 142–44
characteristics of, 222 nn. 5–7
friendship of, with Saint-Preux at fringes of
society, 145–46

——————————

Typeset by
BOOKCOMP

Printed and bound by
SHERIDAN BOOKS

Composed in
DANTE *and* ALTERNATE GOTHIC

Printed on
NATURES NATURAL

Bound in
ARRESTOX

————